Zimbabwe s Plunge

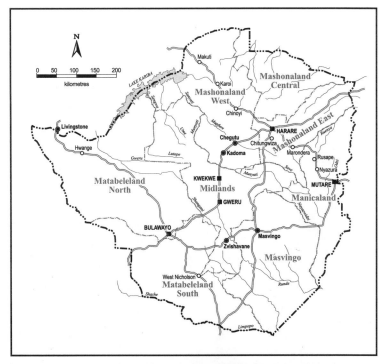

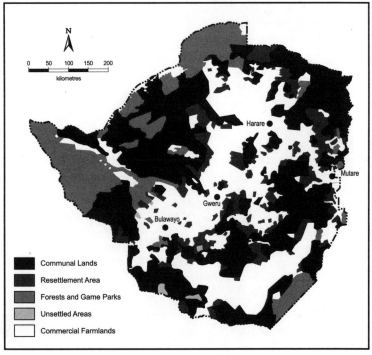

Zimbabwe's Plunge

Exhausted Nationalism, Neoliberalism and the Search for Social Justice

by

Patrick Bond

and

Masimba Manyanya

⊔ⁿ⊔ᵖ UNIVERSITY OF NATAL PRESS
PIETERMARITZBURG

THE MERLIN PRESS

Published by
University of Natal Press
Private Bag X01
Scottsville 3209
South Africa
E-mail: books@press.ac.za

Published in Europe by
The Merlin Press
P O Box 30705
London WC2E 8QD
www.merlinpress.co.uk

Distributed in Zimbabwe by
Weaver Press Ltd
P O Box A1922
Avondale
Harare
www.weaverpresszimbabwe.com

ISBN 1 86914 014 1 (University of Natal Press)
ISBN 0 85036 517 1 (The Merlin Press)

Cover design by Sumayya Essack, Dizzy Blue Dezign

Printed and bound by Natal Witness Commercial Printers, Pietermaritzburg

Contents

This book is dedicated to

Zimcodd

The Zimbabwe Coalition on Debt and Development is a non-profit economic-justice umbrella organisation founded in February 2000. Zimcodd's main objective is to promote participatory economic development processes in Zimbabwe. Zimcodd can be reached at zimcodd@africaonline.co.zw

Tables

Abbreviations

AFC	Agricultural Finance Corporation
ANC	African National Congress
BSAC	British South Africa Company
CA	Communal Area
Cosatu	Congress of South African Trade Unions
CZI	Confederation of Zimbabwe Industries
DRC	Democratic Republic of Congo
Esap	*Economic Structural Adjustment Programme*
Esarp	*Economic Stabilisation and Recovery Programme*
EU	European Union
GDP	Gross Domestic Product
HIPC	Highly Indebted Poor Countries
IMF	International Monetary Fund
LSCFs	Large Scale Commercial Farms
Map	*Millennium Africa Recovery Plan*
MDC	Movement for Democratic Change
Merp	*Millennium Economic Recovery Programme*
Nai	*New African Initiative*
Nam	Non-Aligned Movement
NCA	National Constitutional Assembly
Nedlac	National Economic Development and Labour Council
Nepad	*New Partnership for Africa's Development*
NGO	Non-Governmental Organisation
NRA	National Revenue Authority
OAU	Organisation of African Unity
PRSPs	Poverty Reduction Strategy Programmes
RA	Resettlement Area
SADC	Southern African Development Community
SAPs	Structural Adjustment Programmes
SSCFs	Small Scale Commercial Farms
TNCs	Transnational Corporations
UDI	Unilateral Declaration of Independence
UNDP	United Nations Development Program
US	United States

UZ	University of Zimbabwe
WB	World Bank
WTO	World Trade Organisation
Zanla	Zimbabwe African National Liberation Army
Zanu	Zimbabwe African National Union
Zapu	Zimbabwe African People's Union
ZCTU	Zimbabwe Congress of Trade Unions
Zesa	Zimbabwe Electricity Supply Authority
Zimcodd	The Zimbabwe Coalition on Debt and Development
ZSE	Zimbabwe Stock Exchange

Preface

Our intent to contribute more actively to political-economic analysis in Zimbabwe had its origins in the financial meltdown of 14 November 1997: 'Black Friday', when the currency fell from around Z$10 to below Z$30 to the US$ over four hours of trading time. The rapid response of the trade union movement a few days later inspired us, and signified the relationship between economics and politics that is at the core of our argument. On 'Red Tuesday', 9 December, Morgan Tsvangirai led the country's first post-independence national stayaway, sparking a process of political democratisation which included further mass strikes and protests during 1998, the National Working People's Convention in February 1999, the launch of the Movement for Democratic Change (MDC) in September 1999 and the vote against Mugabe's constitutional referendum in February 2000.

A sizeable share of our hope has since faded. In spite of the intervening parliamentary and presidential election campaigns, the subsequent months witnessed intense social turmoil, a massive increase in state repression, and severe economic deterioration – but to our regret there have been surprisingly few public debates over the linkages between financial and political phenomena, whether past, present or future. This is where we believe we are making some points in this book that anyone interested in progress for Zimbabwe must reckon with.

Back in late 1997, when Zimbabwe's current plunge began, the immediate catalyst, by all accounts, was President Robert Mugabe's decision to give each of the registered liberation war veterans a Z$50 000 pension payout plus Z$2 000 per month. The deal, aimed at quieting war vets' protest over the Mugabe regime's failure to meet even their basic employment and survival needs, was a 'budget buster'. At roughly the same time, Mugabe announced he would proceed with more active land redistribution.

International and local financiers pounded the Zimbabwe dollar, for reasons that ranged from punishing Mugabe, to urgently transferring their Zimbabwe dollars to hard currency, to making money from selling the Zimbabwe dollar through a common form of currency speculation ('shorting'). That currency crash was so severe – quite possibly, outside of wartime, the worst ever experienced in such a short time in modern history – that Reserve Bank governor Leonard Tsumba was faced with either seeing a complete drain of Zimbabwe's hard currency and oblivion for the dollar, or seizing the foreign currency accounts of corporations and wealthy individuals held in local banks.

The former course would have set repayment of Zimbabwe's foreign debt at a level that would entirely consume the national budget. As it was, Zimbabwe spent an historically unprecedented 38% of export earnings to service foreign debt in 1998, exceeded that year only by Brazil and Burundi. Added to foreign debt was the crushing impact of domestic indebtedness. Together, they grew larger and more destructive thanks to the tyranny of compound interest, whereby Zimbabwe found itself paying interest due on the interest on old debt that had been periodically rolled over. So arrived a period of nearly uninterrupted economic chaos. It became obvious to all careful observers that the problem of the public debt – both foreign and domestic – had become the most fundamental economic blockage to social progress.

There are still some who would deny this, and they include a few senior economists in the MDC, in whose interests it is to veil the debt problem as merely one of malgovernance and Mugabe's disregard for property rights. We are led to believe that the debt can be sorted out through a bit of rescheduling from foreign friends, including externalising the domestic debt, once the MDC takes power. Malgovernance is a core shortcoming of the ruling state elite, no doubt, but we want to be controversial by offering a more nuanced reading of what kinds of economic policies qualify as 'sound' and what don't, these days. In addition, we want to quickly rid this book of any collaboration in the extraordinary discourse of economists, for whom violation of property rights spells certain disaster when it means black peasants gain access to agricultural opportunities. An earlier version of land theft was celebrated by the same family of economists as 'modernisation', as 'Native Land Husbandry', and was closely correlated with strong economic growth when white Rhodesians forcibly displaced millions of black people over most of the twentieth century.

What most economists imply, simply, is that powerful people and institutions may loot the social, economic, environmental and cultural wealth of the many who are less powerful: whether in the historic form of rural land dispossession or the contemporary form of international odious debt repayment, or any number of other processes where class power plays a role. Yet this line of argument no longer intimidates people of conscience. The early twenty-first century demise of the 'Washington Consensus' brand of free-market fundamentalism is celebrated across the world, for this hegemonic ideology shaped economic policy parameters and options to the detriment of billions of people since the early 1980s, including most Zimbabweans.

Because of various economic catastrophes in all parts of the world since that time, especially since East Asia began its crisis a few months prior to Zimbabwe's in 1997, the free-market formula is being rejected. The October 2001 award of the Nobel Prize in economics to Joseph Stiglitz, who explicitly called for a 'Post-Washington Consensus' in early 1998 when he was the World Bank's chief economist, is just one reflection of Washington's legitimacy crisis.

Still, in Africa, and even Zimbabwe, there remains a great urgency in transcending 'neoliberalism', by which is meant fiscal austerity (especially through cuts in social spending), full cost-recovery and unaffordable user fees on even essential social services, liberalisation of trade and financial markets, high real interest rates, restructuring economies to emphasise export-orientation, mindless and often corrupt privatisation, deregulation and the like. To make this contention puts us in a tradition that includes Keynes – who tried to save capitalism from itself – and Marx. And while we criticise the damage wrought by neoliberal economists on Zimbabwe, we also firmly criticise Mugabe and his propagandists for absurd distortions of our critical tradition. For Mugabe has perfected, during many decades of demagoguery, the art of 'talk-Left, act-Right'.

We have heard Left rhetoric from Mugabe most vociferously when forceful popular challenges arise: the early 1960s resurgence of anti-colonial protest, the mid/late-1970s Left turn within the ranks of exiles and during the brief Zimbabwe People's Army experiment, the 1980 upsurge of worker confidence in the wake of liberation, the mid-1980s dissents from Matabeleland, the late 1980s student demonstrations against incipient neoliberalism, the 1996–1997 rural and war vet rebellions and the resurgence of protests by workers and genuine democrats since then. Acting-Right has been observed while Mugabe was in league with motley white tycoons (Rowland, Oppenheimer, O'Reilly, Cluff, Bredenkamp, and Rautenbach during the 1980s–1990s), white United States (US) government military advisors (early 1990s), and white economists from the World Bank and International Monetary Fund (beginning in 1981 but especially from 1990, until the falling out in 1998) – or simply acting in proto-fascist mode in between, and more so at the time of writing. We use the adjective 'white' advisedly, given Mugabe's often extreme racial nationalism.

It is, therefore, just as obvious that a political solution to Zimbabwe's crisis is urgently required, and that, given Mugabe's durability and the power of his cronies in the Zimbabwe African National Union (Zanu),[1] this will necessarily require a change of ruling party. At the time of the November 1997 meltdown, it was apparent to us that Zimbabwe was the potential site of an emergent 'post-nationalist' politics propelled by progressive currents. Fatigue associated with Zanu's corruption and mismanagement had finally reached break-point. But, as we asked soon thereafter, would such developments reflect a more general dynamic in the broader social struggle against the globalised, neoliberal form that international capitalism was then taking? Would Zimbabwe's opposition establish an ideology of social change based on thorough-going political democracy, economic justice, gender equity and environmental respect?

Since 1996, a fusillade of optimistic moments in the country's biggest cities – Harare, Bulawayo and Mutare – and in disparate rural sites of protest signalled the capacity of poor and working people to launch a mass democratic struggle against both the political dictatorship and its preferred neoliberal economic model. Paradoxically, Zanu had fallen far from popular grace, for this strategic southern African nation's 1980 independence was greeted as a major breakthrough against apartheid and imperialism. Yet save for some health and education programmes and patronage-based petit-bourgeoisification via the 1980s Africanisation and expansion of an already top-heavy colonial state apparatus, Zanu's subsequent record was one of entrenched inequality and political repression. Whether taking the form of unnecessary coercion during the 1970's *chimurenga* (liberation war), the mid-1980s *Gukurahundi* (state terror in Matabeleland), or early twenty-first century efforts to exterminate the MDC, the ruling party has 'many degrees in violence', as Zanu spokesperson Nathan Shamuyarira has commented.

The hopeful chronology from December 1997 to February 2000 – mentioned at the outset – included the embryos of a programme for more thorough-going economic democracy in February 1999. But progress was interrupted by two kinds of anti-democratic backlashes in early 2000: the sudden neoliberal turn taken by the MDC via its economic desk, and Mugabe's revival of a myth-heavy nationalism via promotion of land invasions alongside ridiculous assertions that the MDC threat was non-indigenous. Until then, the conjuncture appeared to be potentially – and uniquely for Africa – both post-nationalist and post-neoliberal. Mugabe, after all, had hunkered down in an extremely defensive mode, replete with the fierce tools of repression he inherited from white Rhodesia, supplemented during the early 1990s by US military co-operation and his own brand of opposition-bashing. Mugabe's radical rhetoric included regular accusations of 'counter-revolution' and even a late 1998 promise to resurrect 'socialism', repeated vociferously in October 2001. The oratory may have amused – but at this stage, no longer confused – the urban masses whom it was meant to intimidate.

Central to the critique of Mugabe, at that stage, was the fallout from the *Economic Structural Adjustment Programme (Esap)*. The programme was designed in 1990 in large part by the World Bank and International Monetary Fund (IMF), and aimed to quickly deregulate and indebt an economy seen as overprotected and inefficient. Economic downturn characterised most of the period since 1991, aside from 1996–1997, as all *Esap*'s targets for growth and development were missed by huge margins. In contrast to some commentators, we argue that Zanu broadly adhered to the programme, and that its failure was intrinsic to the model imposed on Zimbabwe by the internal/external neoliberal alliance led by the then finance minister, Bernard Chidzero. The failure of export-led growth and liberalisation was reflected in Zimbabwe's debut in the Swiss-based World Economic Forum's Global Competitiveness Report at 52nd out of 55 countries in mid-1997. Mugabe reversed course at that stage, zig-zagging back and forth into populist, interventionist economic mode in an attempt to fend off various challenges to his legitimacy and rule.

This book makes the straightforward case that a potent cocktail of dashed hopes – taking the interlocking forms of social desperation (since the early 1990s), ruling party political degeneracy (since the early 1980s) and a classical capitalist crisis (dating to the mid-1970s, but most severe since late 1997) – has finally evoked a new consciousness and new options for social resistance. Yet the progressive political project was evidently derailed during the run-up to, and aftermath of, the June 2000 parliamentary election. The hijacking of the labour movement's political party, the MDC, by a combination of white business (both Zimbabwean and international) and the urban black petit-bourgeoisie was largely the result of the party's financial needs and the lack – in quantity and quality – of strong shopstewards and union staff, or allied non-governmental organisations (NGOs), churchpeople, community activists, feminists, environmentalists and other progressives who could contest for positions in the new party and maintain its progressive orientation. The valiant left-wing intellectuals who did and still do struggle to make the MDC a site of social change beyond merely political musical chairs, deserve our admiration and gratitude, but we find them consistently on the losing end of policy debates.

We would still insist, however, that notwithstanding a false start by the MDC, it is still eminently feasible for genuinely democratic social forces in Zimbabwe to engage in social struggle that serves the interests of the majority and puts the deeper political-economic dilemmas, such as the debt, onto the table for debate. There are profound contradictions associated with Zanu's rule at the national level and either – depending upon the outcome of the 2002 election – its replacement or its urban augmentation by MDC neoliberalism. Those contradictions will culminate in a period of heightened social unrest rather than its resolution, and will inexorably provide progressive activists within organised labour, social movements, civic groups and the environmental community with far better prospects in coming years.

As a result, instead of the false choice of exhausted nationalism or looming neoliberalism, there exist excellent prospects for a sustained social-justice struggle. To understand why, requires us to consider prior episodes of political and economic change in Zimbabwe, as well as international social-change processes. In Chapter One, we provide an overview of core structural factors throughout Zimbabwe's history that parallel today's turmoil. Over a period of decades, the ruling elites' political choices during economic downturns prepared the terrain for important changes in social structure and accumulation strategies.

We may now be at a similar point, because the socio-economic distortions that have haunted Zimbabwean rulers these past two decades are coming to a head. A tired formula is now on offer to Zimbabweans in both the economic and political spheres: maintaining either economic policies which due to malgovernance are and will be ineffective, or extending the neoliberal disaster, as described in Chapter Two; and simultaneously, maintaining rule by a badly damaged nationalist party, or replacing it with a party whose political coalition cannot sustain the promised return to the neoliberal path, as described in Chapter Three. At a deeper level, the problem remains the nature of uneven capitalist development on the semi-periphery of the world economy during a period of international crisis, as we consider in Chapter Four. The solution entails Zimbabweans contesting global-scale capitalist dynamics, alongside a growing international anti-neoliberal, pro-democratic movement, as described in Chapter Five.

In each chapter, we consider first the broad subject matter at hand, and then consider aspects of the financial/political interface noted at the outset. The four appendices provide seminal contemporary excerpts on politics and economics from the exhausted nationalism of Zanu, the looming neoliberalism of the MDC economics desk, and the social-justice resolutions of the Working People's Convention and Jubilee Africa.

Here we must pause to again declare our own desire to see a national political transfer of power in Zimbabwe in 2002. But we have far greater hope for Zimbabwe than to see it turned over to the World Bank and IMF, as is hinted at by some members of the MDC. That hope comes from organisations and leaders we know will not sit still for another round of war on the living standards of the working class, as happened in Zambia when exhausted nationalism was replaced by neoliberalism. Since 1996, a measure of determination on the part of oppressed Zimbabweans has been restored, and with it, a louder rumble of grassroots activity.

To be sure, Zimbabwe demonstrates the multifaceted, often contradictory way in which political resistance to neoliberalism is now unfolding in many places. Sometimes the contradictions are muddied by the nature of the rhetoric and character of the regime, while sometimes they serve to unveil underlying power relations. But always, the country and people offer lessons and inspiration. Much of that comes from those who have directly influenced us over this difficult period. In addition to the thousands of social-change activists in Zimbabwe to whom this book is dedicated, we are grateful to intellectuals and professionals who worked directly with us on these issues,[2] who read and published our arguments in periodicals and books,[3] who fought with us in the *Zimbabwe Independent*[4] and who made helpful suggestions in the course of academic seminars.[5]

The book was put together over a period of several months in 2001, when we found opportunities in Harare, Mutare and Johannesburg to revisit and update arguments we have been advancing for several years.[6] These arguments interweave political and financial themes, so that even if we do not make any claim to a comprehensive survey of Zimbabwe's multifaceted contemporary plunge, we believe we share an obligation to try to specify correlations of capitalist crisis, rising (and then crashing) financial markets, environmental and social stress and political upheaval.

In trying to draw out these links, we received extremely helpful inputs from the main organisers and staff of the Zimbabwe Coalition on Debt and Development – Jonah Gokova, Davie Malungisa and Lydia Dhliwayo – and Yash Tandon of the Southern and Eastern African Trade Information and Negotiations Initiative. We were also kept well

xvii

informed by participants in several Zimcodd workshops held during 2001, including the June 'Seminar on Development Finance' and November 'Advanced Topics in Political Economy' course.[7] In Johannesburg, several groups of Wits University students gave useful feedback.[8] Donors were generous.[9] We are very grateful to our publishers, especially Glenn Cowley at the University of Natal Press and Murray McCartney at Weaver Press. Khutso Madubanya provided invaluable research assistance. Sally Hines, David Moore, Sara Rich Dorman and Moya Atkinson made many detailed suggestions for improving the manuscript.

Finally, we celebrate our families – Odette and Jan, and Bridget, Felix and Mary Ann – and their unending tolerance. And we honour the groups and individuals who support Zimcodd, which we see as part of the fast-growing international movement for social justice. This movement and in particular its African allies – such as the Africa Social Forum, Africa Trade Network, chapters of the Jubilee 2000 debt-cancellation movement, the Dakar 2000 gathering, the Southern African People's Solidarity Network, progressive trade unions, churches, women's and youth groups, environmentalists and other advocates of social change – are striving to roll back neoliberalism, replace the Washington Consensus with an 'African People's Consensus', and put human needs ahead of profits in the calculus of social organisation.

Notes

1. For purposes of simplicity, we ignore the Zimbabwe African People's Union (Ndonga), and refer to what is known as Zanu(PF) as Zanu.
2. For Manyanya, this book reflects work dating to the time of the initial discussions of neoliberal policy flaws within the government, through the Economic Justice platform in 1995 where critiques of *Esap* were honed, to various research papers and publications subsequently produced for the Zimbabwe Economics Society and Friedrich Ebert Stiftung dealing with the budget and financial policies, to the National Constitutional Assembly, to the August 2001 conference 'From Decline to Crisis' hosted by Transparency International Zimbabwe. Colleagues from the Ministry of Finance persevered through debates over *Esap* and Zimprest: Mutasa Dzinotizei, Phoebe Kufa, Judith Madzorera and Fudzai Pamacheche. Staff and friends of the Zimbabwe Council of Churches and Zimbabwe Congress of Trade Unions did the same: Lovemore Kadenge, Godfrey Kanyenze, Rene Loewenson, Deprose Muchena, Tawanda Mutasah and John van't Hoff. Bond adds thanks to Harare-based friends Tendai Biti, Opa Kapijimpanga, Loewenson, Allast Mwanza, Sam Moyo, Helga Patrikios, Brian Raftopoulos and Richard Saunders; and to Mutasah, Stanley Hove, Tandi Nkimane and Everjoice Win in the diaspora. And

Sara Rich Dorman kept us in tune with current events through her excellent media briefs.

3. Bond wrote articles on Zimbabwe from which material below is drawn, for *The African Communist* (Third Quarter, 2000); *Business Day* (27 June 2001 and 2 May 2000); *GreenLeft Weekly* (18 July 2001, 2 May and 24 March 2000, and 24 March 1999); *Indicator SA* (17, 3, 2000 and 16, 1, 1999); *International Viewpoint* (April 1999); *Red Pepper* (August and April 2000, April and May 1998); *Southern Africa Report* (Second Quarter 2000, May–June 1999); *Sunday Independent Reconstruct* (13 August 2000); *Sunday Tribune* (30 April 2000); *Z Magazine* (July–August 2001); *Zimbabwe Independent* (29 June and 8 December 2001); *Journal of Social Change and Development* (January 1999); and *ZNet* Commentary (24 June and 30 April, 2000). Longer contributions appeared as follows: 'Zimbabwe's Political Reawakening', *Monthly Review*, 50, 11, 1999; 'Economic Crisis in Zimbabwe: Outwards vs Inwards Development Strategy', *Labour, Capital and Society*, 2001; 'Radical Rhetoric and the Working Class during Zimbabwean Nationalism's Dying Days', in B. Raftopoulos and L. Sachikonye (eds) (2001), *Striking Back: The Labour Movement and the Post-Colonial State in Zimbabwe, 1980–2000*, Harare, Weaver Press, and in *Journal of World Systems Research*, 7, 2, March 2001; and (with Guy Mhone) 'Botswana and Zimbabwe', in M. Mansoob (ed) (2002), *Globalization, Marginalization and Development*, London, Routledge.

4. How could we not acknowledge the extremist pro-*Esap* contentions of Eric Bloch, in a polemic with Bond published in the *Zimbabwe Independent* (12 January, 26 January, 2 February, 23 March and 30 March 2001)? Davie Malungisa and Bond contributed to a debate in the same paper over the merits of foreign debt default (29 June, 6 July and 27 July 2001).

5. Bond thanks participants in seminars where earlier versions of chapters were presented during 1998–2001 (especially the hosts): the University of Natal, Durban Department of Political Studies seminar, 2001 (David Moore); the University of Cape Town Graduate School of Business Seminar on Globalisation, 2001 (Thomas Koelble); the Rand Afrikaans University Department of Sociology, Johannesburg, 2000 (Peter Alexander); the United Nations University's World Institute of Development Economics Research, Helsinki, 2000 (Mansoob Murshed); the University of Natal, Durban Economic History and Development Studies Department, 2000 (Bill Freund); the Wits University History Seminar, 2000 (Nicole Ulrich); an American University Development Studies seminar, Harare, 1999 (Erin McCandless); the Focus on the Global South Conference on Economic Sovereignty in a Globalized World at Chulalongkorn University, Bangkok, 1999 (Walden Bello and Nicola Bullard); and a York University Department of Political Science seminar, Toronto, 1998 (John Saul).

6. Details, context and expanded commentary can be found in Bond's PhD thesis and book, and in Manyanya's Zimcodd booklet, from which arguments, sources and quotes are revisited liberally below: Bond, P. (1992), 'Finance and Uneven Development in Zimbabwe', Johns Hopkins University Department of Geography and Environmental Engineering; and (1998), *Uneven Zimbabwe: A Study of Finance, Development and Underdevelopment*, Trenton, Africa World Press; and Manyanya, M. (2001), *The Politics of the Public Debt*, Harare, Zimcodd.

7. We thank the participants, including Kurauone Chihwayi, Blessing Chiripanhura,

Charles Dube, Rutendo Hadebe, Morgan Jeranyama, James Jowa, Opa Kapi-jimpanga, Naomi Kowo, Cainford Kunze, Joy Mabenge, Israel Mabhoo, Leadus Madzima, Sylvester Madzova, Erin McCandless, Muriel Mafico, Eunice Mafundikwa, Farai Makombe, Michael Mataure, Father Brian McGarry, Wilfred Mhanda, Grasian Mkodzongi, Deprose Muchena, O.J. Murakwani, Allan Mushonga, Memory Ncube, Dumisani Nkomo, Ezekiel Pajibo, Thembile Phute, Brian Sarare, Kudzaishe Sengurayi, Zvavamwe David Shambare, Jeffrey Takawira, Mary Tandon, Amos Tinarwo, Arnold Tsunga and Marlon Zakeyo. And we hope we have incorporated all their useful suggestions.

8. Manyanya taught the Graduate School of Public and Development Management masters course on Public and Development Finance, and Bond gave a Department of Political Studies third-year course on Politics and Society in Post-Colonial Zimbabwe.

9. Manyanya thanks Oxfam America and Diakonia Sweden for financing the Zimcodd debt research. The Ford Foundation graciously subsidised Zimbabwe distribution of this book.

CHAPTER ONE

A History of Uneven Development in Zimbabwe

1. Introduction

This chapter makes the case that ninety years of colonial development and underdevelopment in what was known as 'Southern Rhodesia' (1890s–1965) and 'Rhodesia' (1965–1979) were regularly interrupted by capitalist crises and intensified uneven development, around which debt bubbles rose and burst, and political change often ensued. The recent period reflects the durability of these processes, for in many respects, the same economic and political problems were replayed after 1980 but under a government ostensibly committed to socialism and with a far different social base than that of the white settlers. The patterns of uneven development remained relatively similar between settler-colonialism and independence. The residual economic stagnation and financial fallout together demonstrate how badly contemporary policy-makers have performed, and how once again, a political transition is badly needed – although as we argue in the following chapters, not necessarily one that leads to the reinvigoration of neoliberalism.

The historical objective here is to identify crucial moments when political-economic contradictions became insurmountable under the prevailing logic of uneven development. From there, we can assess the routes forward that appeared feasible under the circumstances. We identify these conjunctures as the late 1890s/early 1900s, late 1920s/early 1930s, late 1950s/early 1960s and the late 1970s/early 1980s. Politically, the periods were often characterised by social upheavals, fundamental shifts in development strategies, and even new ruling political parties. Macro-economic policy was often fundamental, as summarised in Table 1.

1

Within this chapter, Section 2 suggests that just before precipitous plunges in growth and profit rates, upsurges of speculative activity occurred, generating convulsive financial crises. Concrete examples of debt problems are provided in Section 3, for these key moments often unveil the political balance of forces quite sharply.

Table 1   Phases of inward/outward macro-economic policy: 1920s–present.

Period	Relevant policy	Economic conditions
1920s	Protection for local manufacturers.	Beginning of industrial development.
1930s–1940s	Relative isolation.	High growth and inward maturing of secondary industry.
1950s	Increasing financial and trade regulation.	Large inflows of foreign investment, but overproduction problems and unsustainable financial and trade relations.
1960s–1970s	Heightened financial/trade regulation coincident with sanctions.	Initial dramatic recovery, followed by a crisis of overproduction and civil war.
1980s	Gradual loosening of financial/ trade restrictions and strong export drive.	Enhancement of developmental state's human capital functions, yet uneven economic record.
1990s	Rapid liberalisation of finance and trade.	Dramatic volatility and vulnerability in many markets, de-industrialisation, underdevelopment.
1997–present	Uneven return to *dirigist* policies – e.g. exchange controls, a currency peg, luxury import tariffs (but followed by a regional free-trade agreement), foreign debt default, uncontrolled budgetary growth, negative real interest rates – under conditions of desperation and capital flight.	Deepening crisis across all sectors of the economy.

2.   A brief pre-independence political economy

Although it is beyond our scope (we write here about uneven *capitalist* development), far greater social stability characterised Zimbabwe prior to the settler-colonial epoch that began in 1890. Various tributary societies and states had prospered for centuries, including an empire whose 'Great Zimbabwe' fortress and city of an estimated 20 000 workers threw up artifacts suggesting trade as far afield as Islamic societies and even China. By the late nineteenth century the dispersed Shona peoples and, in the south-eastern part of what would become Zimbabwe, the strong Ndebele state had together established a distinctive petty commodity mode of production, in part through the influence of Portuguese merchants.[1]

Primitive settler accumulation

After the initial large-scale settler invasion – the 1890 Pioneer Column organised from South Africa – London financial capital flowed into Cecil Rhodes' British South Africa Company (BSAC), which had been granted occupation and governance rights by the Queen following a sham deal with a local African leader. Rhodes had missed the Witwatersrand gold rush in Johannesburg and was overeager to invest. Other exploration companies followed, anxious for a share of speculative land and mining profits.

The global context was important. Increasing geopolitical turbulence included the 1885 carve-up of the continent during the 'Scramble for Africa' at a Berlin negotiating table, which can be traced to what historian Ian Phimister cites as 'capitalism's uneven development during the last third of the nineteenth century, particularly the City of London's crucial role in mediating the development of a world economic system'.[2] Excess financial capital that could not find profitable outlets in London and Paris found its way to southern Africa.

Thanks to the inflow of overseas capital during the mid-1890s, the first indigenous uprisings (Ndebele *umvukela* and Shona *chimurenga*) were crushed by the white settlers. Through brutal means – land and cattle expropriation, various taxes, cattle-dipping and grazing fees, debt peonage, etc. – the colonists then began forcing African peasants off their land and into the mines, commercial farms and nascent factories. In large part, the systematic reproduction of the migrant workforce, especially during childhood, sickness and retirement, was carried out by unpaid rural women, who were often displaced from good farming areas to the arid, overcrowded 'Tribal Trust Lands' (subsequently relabelled 'Communal Areas').

Although labour shortages were thus solved, what was missing was gold, which was never discovered in the quantities that Rhodes expected. The racial basis for capitalist superexploitation was cemented when the new colony's financial bubble burst in 1898. In contrast to the dramatic deep-mining developments that characterised the Johannesburg gold complex during the 1890s, the Rhodesian route to riches was in reality a financial disaster.

Yet such large sunk investments had been made in land and telegraph development, that the speculative crash in turn required a shift towards a more permanent, inward-oriented economic approach. The colony was built up more steadily during the early twentieth century, with less reliance upon gold extraction and more upon the colony's extreme class, race and gender apartheid. Several tens of thousands of settlers were recruited, mainly from Britain and South Africa, to form an instant rural petit-bourgeoisie on the colony's best land, at the expense of the indigenous masses. The BSAC controlled the process, though it never turned a profit.

A crucial opportunity for the settlers to embark upon a decidedly 'national' economic policy occurred with transition to 'Self-Governing Status' chosen in a 1923 whites-only election, against an option to unite with South Africa which the BSAC favoured. Meanwhile, a tentative economic strategy based on substituting imported goods with local products began. By 1926, manufacturing contributed 13% of the colony's gross national product, as small firms engaged in subsidiary industries and production of rudimentary products for the local black consumer market.[3] But the economy remained extractive, as its mainly agricultural and mineral exports rose to £6.6 million in 1929.

Depression and prosperity
Just as had occurred during the prior world economic crisis (the 1870s–1890s), the Great Depression forced a shift in economic development whose implications were felt profoundly in southern Africa. Because of extreme international overinvestment and financial bubbling during the late 1920s, the early 1930s witnessed roughly a one-third contraction of economic activity. Foreign markets for the colony's goods disappeared, exports quickly fell by 50% and as a result, imports had to be slashed from £7 million in 1928 to £3.1 million in 1932. Overall, Southern Rhodesia registered a draconian 30% drop in net national income during 1931 as a result of its vulnerability to an earlier 'globalisation'.[4]

Thankfully for the white settlers, what we might today term 'deglobalisation' – i.e. a dramatic decline in the international flow of trade, finance and investment – was rapid and successful. In 1933, the young state came into its own after a whites-only election pitted lower-class settlers against local elites linked to the BSAC. The former included family farmers, low-level management, shopkeepers, artisans, some civil servants and even white workers: a bloc that would remain a formidable electoral coalition until 1980. An explicitly inward-oriented development trajectory got underway.

The manufacturing sector matured rapidly, thanks to the Depression era and wartime lull in international economic activity, which gave the infant local bourgeoisie space and incentive to grow. Formal apartheid-type social control was legislated in most areas of urban black residential life and at the workplace. Black trade unionism and early nationalist political initiatives were squashed. Although the colony's gold exports were an important safety net, it was through the turn inward, to meeting local, albeit racially-circumscribed needs, that economic recovery picked up rapidly.

Godfrey Huggins was elected leader, and shifted quickly from angry populist to managerialist in order to nurture relations with the colony's propertied elites. In the process, the state replaced the BSAC as the key economic actor. Huggins' strategies were varied. He embarked upon an aggressive public works programme geared largely to solving white unemployment. Parastatal industrial ventures, such as iron, steel and cotton spinning, were increasingly common. White farmers received hefty doses of state credit, subsidies and other supports. White miners were encouraged to operate small independent gold operations, as foreign companies' mineral rights were taken over. The railroad was nationalised. There were new anti-African labour laws and expanded race-based division and control of land. The result, in the wake of the 1929–1931 crash, was that output more than tripled over the next decade.[5]

Post-war boom, bust and racist reaction

Successful 'import-substitution industrialisation' policies made the colony increasingly self-reliant, and were amplified during and after the Second World War. Food processing soon accounted for a third of manufacturing, while sectors ranging from construction materials to low-quality consumables such as clothing and textiles for the domestic market grew rapidly. Indeed many small manufacturing enterprises initially aimed at African customers, whose wages grew to encompass a quarter of national income during the 1950s. On this basis, manu-facturing growth picked up spectacularly from 1944–1948, averaging 24.4% annually.[6]

Still, while profits were high, black workers' living conditions remained appalling. The construction of formal apartheid-style townships mainly formalised the slum arrangements.[7] Resistance was sporadic at first. After the foiled 1890s uprisings, early workplace revolts were put down at Wankie Colliery (1912) and Shamva Mine (1922 and 1927), and the first union drive, during the late 1920s and early 1930s, was crushed. But a 1945 railway worker strike was the prelude to a 1948 general strike. Although it was also repressed, the uprising generated leaders – like Joshua Nkomo – who were instrumental in the formation of the Southern Rhodesian Trade Union Congress in 1954 and Southern Rhodesian African National Congress three years later. However, the limited gains and weak position of these organisations meant that white capital and the settler-colonial bureaucracy would remain in control for many years to come.[8]

After the Second World War, with the economy still growing rapidly, both foreign direct investment and financial capital flowed into Southern Rhodesia. Multinational corporations nearly quadrupled the value of their holdings from 1948–1951, partly from fear of the new Nationalist Party rulers in South Africa, and in part looking forward to the colony's unity with its two northern neighbours in the Central African Federation.[9] A few temporary bottlenecks in materials and financing were overcome by huge loans from the World Bank and the big commercial banks of London, New York and Johannesburg.

But the repayment of foreign loans and profit repatriation to foreign investors soon became debilitating, as financial outflows reached 14% of Central African Federation income in 1956.[10] The regional economy overheated during the late 1950s due to excessive, capital-intensive investment and building speculation. Then it too rapidly cooled in the wake of local financial collapses and a copper market crash that wrecked the economy of neighbouring Northern Rhodesia (subsequently renamed Zambia in 1964). Unprecedented state intervention was required in Southern Rhodesia's financial system during the late 1950s and early 1960s, in turn preparing the ground for state-capitalist planning.[11]

Under conditions of economic contraction at home, fearing the forthcoming British decolonisation of Africa, and nervous about the African nationalist mobilisation then underway, the white electorate's fascist turn in 1962 saw the ascent of Ian Smith. After imposing much tougher exchange controls, the government responded to pressure for racial reform by declaring an illegal 'Unilateral Declaration of Independence' (UDI) in November 1965. Nationalist leaders were banned and jailed for ten years. International sanctions followed, but the state reacted with more rigorous central planning and strategic investments, and rapidly rejigged production towards an import-substituting industry.

Support came from South Africa and Portuguese-ruled Mozambique. The British notably failed to use military force to unseat the rebels, as 'kith and kin' in the army and navy signalled to the Labour government that Smith had their respect. No one objected much when Smith defaulted on Rhodesia's foreign debt, including loans that helped finance the massive Kariba Dam a few years earlier. Capital outflows were mostly prohibited. The result was one of the world's fastest growth rates – 9.5% annually – from 1966–1974. By all accounts, the success was again in part due to deglobalisation.

The rise and fall of UDI

The first, high-growth period of UDI depended most upon tightened exchange controls, which generated an economic hothouse effect and effectively prevented geographical capital flight.[12] Research by former Confederation of Zimbabwe Industries chief economist Roger Riddell showed that 'the major import-substitutions thrust occurred prior to UDI, with the major source of manufacturing growth in the UDI period being domestic demand expansion.'[13]

Rigorous exchange controls trapped local financial resources, profits of multinational corporations, and non-residents' bank deposits. Economist Duncan Clarke reported that by the late 1960s 'the controls worked, especially when combined with buoyant growth conditions in the economy associated to high net white immigration (and rising mortgage demand), rapid industrial development through diversification (and demand for hire purchase and leasing facilities), and expanded primary sector output (with demands for short- and medium-term financing).'[14]

But stagnation eventually set in, not only because of oft-cited (but unquantifiable) constraints such as civil war, drought, high oil prices and lack of foreign exchange. In addition, notwithstanding the state's efforts to balance investment in the appropriate sectors, UDI-era manufacturers placed exorbitant emphasis on luxury goods production for the domestic white market, rather than expanding into extensive low-cost basic consumer goods which might have helped generate increased buying power in the process and which would have had greater export potential into independent Africa.

The political-economic climate over-encouraged producers of certain capital goods, including steel, and ultimately widened the socio-economic and political divisions between whites and blacks. Overproduction, a dramatic increase in inventories and the refusal by Smith's regime to redistribute wealth together revealed the limitations of luxury-goods import-substitution industrialisation, as happened in so many other settings across the developing world.[15] Black workers – whose purchases accounted for more than half of turnover in furniture, clothing and footwear – still suffered terribly low wages. The peak settler population of 250 000 offered an insufficient luxury-goods consumer base to establish economies of scale in most manufacturing sectors. Even a quarter century later, these problems did not entirely work themselves out of an economy still characterised, in parts, by old machinery, excess capacity and monopolistic control of local markets.

Black oppression and political resistance

If, throughout Zimbabwe's history of settler-colonialism, white capital suffered from uneven development and periodic crisis tendencies, so too did black resistance. The nationalists relied upon a political alliance between black peasants, small commercial farmers, workers and the petit-bourgeoisie. Primarily strategic and tactical differences and uneven leadership prevented unity within the liberation movement in its early stages.

As noted, black workers rarely openly revolted, although there were many other more subtle modes of resistance prior to independence. During the 1960s and 1970s, leaders of emergent trade unions were detained and repressed by the Rhodesian security apparatus.[16]

The black petit-bourgeoisie was systematically stifled, usually through classical colonial racial constraints, restrictions on commercial activities and unworkable informal financial markets. By the early 1960s, black professional elites – lawyers, doctors, teachers and intellectuals – led both the Zimbabwe African People's Union (Zapu) and the breakaway Zimbabwe African National Union (Zanu). The latter split from Zapu in 1963 because of Nkomo's moderate strategy, and came to be dominated by Shona-speakers such as Ndabiningi Sithole and later Robert Mugabe, and hence gained an ethnic identity. After the bannings, neither saw an alternative to a radical turn and armed struggle, notwithstanding their leaders' incarceration. Within a decade, their peasant-based guerrilla war began having an impact. White fears mounted as Marxist-Leninist rhetoric drew nearer: Zanu was supported by China, Zapu by the USSR. The two 'Patriotic Front' liberation movements were countered by the Rhodesian army's intensified violence, which was in the main responsible for the war's 40 000 civilian deaths during the 1970s.[17]

The Rhodesians were destined to lose, notwithstanding Smith's claim as recently as 1976 that 'not in one thousand years' would black majority rule arrive. South African apartheid leader John Vorster withdrew explicit military support to Smith that year, in order to gain more room for his own regional co-option strategy. US secretary of state

Henry Kissinger attempted to slightly amend the region's geopolitics, and together with Vorster strongarmed Smith into agreeing to an untenable 'internal settlement' – called 'Zimbabwe-Rhodesia' – with the co-opted Bishop Abel Muzorewa in 1978.

Half the white population fled Rhodesia as the war dragged on. Economic depression cut economic output by 40% from 1976–1979. The Rhodesians finally surrendered at the 1979 Lancaster House peace talks in London, yet Zanu-Zapu's indecisive military victory, as well as nationalist infighting in the run-up to negotiations, left various kinds of residual economic and political power in white hands. White Rhodesians and the West were stunned at how much black voting support Mugabe garnered in the April 1980 election: 62%, with Zapu getting 24% and the collaborationist party of Muzorewa just 8%, on a turnout of 95%. Black voters were equally stunned, no doubt, at Mugabe's immediate willingness to compromise with white-owned capital in the name of racial reconciliation.

But even if Mugabe's regime had been more genuinely committed to overturning colonial power relations, for example through a democratic land redistribution process and economic development strategy based on the needs and capacities of the masses of people, there were several kinds of debt that he inherited. Amongst the most choking was the legacy of colonial development funded by foreign loans, and the durable capacity of the World Bank to set the agenda for post-colonial development.

3.   Who really owed what to whom? Legacies of pre-independence debt

The brutal history of uneven development over the 90 years of formal settler-colonial capitalism in Zimbabwe, 1890–1980, confirms that vast 'reparations' are owed the indigenous people. As just one example, the formal foreign debt that was passed on to Robert Mugabe at the time should have been repudiated.

More generally though, we will make a case in this and coming chapters that the power, the ideological orientation and the moral injustice associated with Zimbabwe's international financial interactions are untenable. The case rests in part upon the fact that black Zimbabwean taxpayers had to pay twice for colonial oppression via what has come to be termed 'Odious Debt': first when loans were taken out to oppress them, and second when the lenders demanded their money back. But moreover, the case against the international financial establishment is also against the *type* of development strategy – 'modernisation' –

promoted during colonialism, for the legacy includes not only the skews in society and economy that endured into the post-independence era, but the subsequent attempts to renew modernisation via a market-centred neoliberalism.

The early twenty-first century is a good time to raise these issues. Recent reimbursements to descendants of Jewish Holocaust victims whose wealth was pocketed by Swiss banks, and the September 2001 World Conference Against Racism in Durban, both opened up opportunities to question the merits of retaining profits made from such explicit racism as practised in Rhodesia. So too is there resonance with the contemporary Jubilee South Africa campaign to return apartheid profits made by Swiss and German banks, at the insistence of the Anglican archbishop of Cape Town, Njongonkulu Ndungane. It is, in this context, useful to consider a variety of foreign credits to the Rhodesian regime, including a detailed case study of the Kariba Dam and other World Bank projects and policies which evolved seamlessly from colonialism to the post-colonial era.[18]

Banking on colonialism

Once the Great Depression and the Second World War had ended, and the 1944 Bretton Woods agreement certified the US dollar as the world's main currency, international financial markets began to grow. The Southern Rhodesian colonial government issued £72 million in official debt on the London bond market during the 1950s, compared to £60 million on the local market, as total public debt soared from £27 million in 1946 to £137 million in 1954. Moreover, private corporations also sought credit from international markets, and borrowed an average of £23.5 million in net new foreign debt annually during the late 1950s.[19]

The World Bank lent US$140 million for projects during the 1950s and early 1960s, including the electrification of white areas, the Kariba Dam, the partial implementation of the intensely unpopular Land Husbandry Act and the expansion of Rhodesian Railways. A Bank official conducted a two-week visit to Southern Rhodesia in 1956. According to a local business newspaper report, 'The two note-books full of notes which he had made on the trip would be used both internally by the Bank, and as a source of information for use by Swiss, USA and other financial interests.'[20]

The modernisation logic of the Bank and the social control required by colonial rulers overlapped considerably, and in particular, the displacement of indigenous people appeared under both systems as a means of accelerating economic development. 'We do not want native peasants,' Garfield Todd told parliament: 'We want the bulk of them working in the mines and farms and in the European areas and we could absorb them and their families.'[21] According to analyst Cheryl Payer, the Bank-financed Native Land Husbandry Act, 'was designed in part to provide white industrialists with a captive labour force by denying migrant labour the right to return to land in the reserves . . . The registration of land to individual ownership destroys the security of traditional tenure forms, and African farmers were in general hostile to official attempts to change their tenure rights.'[22] Perhaps the most destructive single case of displacement was the submersion of the Tonga people's homeland during the late 1950s.

Damning Kariba

The Bank's biggest loan to Rhodesia's colonial authorities, Kariba, deserves special attention. The dam is the Zambezi River's largest, located between Zimbabwe and Zambia in a gorge occupied by 57 000 Tonga people for centuries until dam waters rose during the late 1950s. Begun in 1956, dam construction was complete by late 1959. The World Bank granted its largest single loan up to that point for the Kariba Dam, which when filled was the world's largest artificial body of water, with a volume four times greater than the then second biggest dam on earth. Kariba cost the Tonga most aspects of their traditional riverside domestic economy, and caused devastating disease and loss of livelihoods.[23]

The dam also raised crucial issues concerning power relations between colonialism and corporate interests, economic priorities, debt repayment under conditions of geopolitical stress, and the long-term relationship between hydro-power financing and electricity provision to Zimbabwe's citizenry, as discussed later. The main point behind building Kariba was to supply energy over 900 km of transmission lines to Northern Rhodesian copper mines and smelters owned nearly entirely by just two firms, Anglo American Corporation and Roan Selection Trust (in turn controlled by American Metal Climax, Inc.). Domination of politics in the Central African Federation by the two firms was observed by Colin Leys in his study, *European Politics in Southern Rhodesia*: 'Their role in the economy is in itself decisive and it is not too much to say that the meetings of their boards of directors can be as important for the inhabitants of the Federation as those of the Federal cabinet.'[24] According to Payer, 'The needs of these two companies seem to have been the main impetus behind the entire project.'[25] Prior to the Kariba hydro-electric project, the companies relied partly on inappropriate coking coal from the Hwange coalfields near Victoria Falls, and even resorted to burning local woodfuels for energy.

World Bank financial support for the dam's construction was crucial. After an assessment, the Bank estimated that 1 200 MW could be generated at peak capacity by the early 1970s, at a reasonable cost of just over £100 million (or US$0.33 per kiloWatt hour of energy). Financial rates of return justified the project, even if environmental and social aspects – or as we see below, economic opportunity costs – were not factored in adequately. But the Bank's initial phase cost estimate of £54 million was increased to nearly £80 million when a higher wall was chosen in 1956.

The corporate beneficiaries – Anglo American and Roan Selection Trust, with their allies British South Africa Company, Standard Chartered Bank and Barclays Bank – were approached by the Federation governor, Lord Malvern, to provide a substantial £28 million top-up loan for the project. Given that copper prices had soared, Malvern threatened that either the firms would have to grant the loan, or their windfall profits would be taxed. But the companies' loan diverted revenues that would have at least partially been captured for use in developing Zambia, which severely strained Federation relations. According to a team of researchers later mandated to assess the project by the World Commission on Dams:

> Lord Malvern's move 'stole' funds from the Zambian government which the latter was hoping to realise in a similar manner. In fact the idea to raise a loan from the copper mines was that of the Zambian Governor, Sir Arthur Benson, as he had earlier explained his plans to Lord Malvern. Zambia was seeking funding for a large rural development programme long discussed and promised to reverse the accelerated flow of rural people into the mining towns and along the line of rail.
>
> When Sir Arthur heard of Lord Malvern's coup, he tackled him, suggesting that Zimbabwe's tobacco farmers should be taxed more and that certain loan or bond systems be introduced by the Federal Government to raise the Kariba funds. He wanted the loans provided by the mines to fund the Zambian rural development scheme first, even if it meant that the kudos went to the Federal Government and not to the Zambian Government when the rural development scheme was implemented. (Sir Arthur was also a proponent of the benefits of Federation.) He warned Lord Malvern in a letter that the

'copper mine loans' for Kariba 'cannot fail to affect Zambia drastically from the financial, the economic and the political angles.'

Lord Malvern had solved a Federal problem but left a burning Zambian issue unattended and in tatters whilst rekindling the suspicions of the Federation and its bias with regard to finances and development. The two countries in the mid-1950s were capital hungry. Now one would go empty bellied and frustrated. Sir Arthur was correct, there were other ways of raising the funds that Zambia needed but it was to take time to swallow the large Kariba borrowings before extra finances became available. By then the copper prices had crashed and Zambia's golden days were over. Zambia has never managed to create a working countryside since that moment in her short history.[26]

Controversies over financial control and distribution of benefits from Kariba would hamper the dam and hydro-electric plant for many years to come. Even after Zambia temporarily nationalised the mining houses during the late 1960s at the cost of large foreign exchange contributions, and after Zimbabwe's independence in 1980, tensions periodically arose over cross-border energy utilisation and pricing, and over further development of the shared river's hydropower capacity.[27]

If the original priorities of the Kariba Dam's financial planners, including World Bank technical staff, were biased towards the narrow interests of multinational corporations – particularly as consumers of hydro-electric power to extract and smelt copper – this meant that establishing a sustained economic logic for large-scale infrastructure would not be easy. It may be impossible to determine whether Kariba was developmentally efficient (in comparison to the opportunity cost of the money invested), due to inadequate available data.[28] But it was clear that for economists of the period, a core problem was investment valuation, in light of the time-related rate of interest and repayment burden. Although it may seem an obscure factor, it is worthy of brief consideration, because the same issues inevitably apply to 'mega-project' financing everywhere.

The costs and benefits of large-scale credit

Evidence assembled by leading University of Rhodesia economists Pearson and Taylor in 1963 confirms that the Federation's infrastructure investments systematically underprioritised basic needs alternatives favoured by low-income people:

An inordinately high proportion has been invested in those assets whose income-producing potential is either intrinsically low, such as office buildings, or into types of investment whose income-producing potential cannot be realised until a very long time has elapsed. An example of this latter type is the Kariba hydro-electric scheme. It is open to question whether, in an underdeveloped country like the Federation, attention should be concentrated on those types of investment which can be expected to yield fairly quick returns, or upon those types of investment which are unlikely to prove to be real economic assets until some very considerable time in the future. There are, however, general economic reasons for assuming that people with low incomes – and this applies to the majority of the Federation's inhabitants – have almost immediate preferences; in other words, they will attach less importance to benefits which will accrue in the distant future. If this is true, there are considerable grounds for doubting whether much of the actual disposition of public investment resources which has taken place in the Federation over the last ten years reflects the time preferences of the majority of the consuming and producing population.[29]

Such criticism had also been recorded in a 1962 official expert committee report charged, amongst other responsibilities, with investigating development finance. The committee noted government's over-reliance on foreign loans from the World Bank, US Export-Import Bank and Commonwealth Development Corporation, including:

special problems in the negotiation and amortisation of such loans, which may make them an unsuitable vehicle for financing projects promising a return only in the distant future. In the case of such capital expenditures, the obligation of paying interest and the repayment of capital may become too burdensome, unless it can be arranged to borrow at low interest rates with capital repayments spread over a long period of time . . .[30]

Indeed, not only were returns on the investment greatly delayed for the majority of citizens – until 1980, when independence was finally granted, and indeed beyond, as shown below. Loan repayment also became a significant issue. Kariba represented not only the largest dam of its era, but also the largest ever default by a government on a World Bank project.

Rhodesian debt crisis

The initial mid-1950s boost to foreign reserves from the World Bank loan was appreciated by Federation authorities, but the subsequent repayment of the Kariba loan contributed sharply to the colony's balance of payments deficit. By the late 1950s, foreign financial flows – especially outflow of interest, dividends and profit repatriation – turned against the Federation. Impressive new foreign investments associated with access to Kariba power too quickly fostered a large net income drain, averaging 8.4% of total Gross Domestic Product (GDP), but reaching as high as 14% in 1956.[31]

By 1961, Southern Rhodesia's large debt to the World Bank, London bond holders, the US Export-Import Bank and Colonial (Commonwealth) Development Corporation aggravated foreign reserve shortages. The central bank was suddenly vulnerable to a controversial interest rate increase initiated by the London banks. A recession and minor financial crisis followed, which caused the closure of the majority of Southern Rhodesian building societies. The vicious cycle continued, and hence access to expensive, short-term international commercial bank loans became more important, simply to repay interest on old debt. Intensifying political turmoil, including the rise of white, right-wing populism, followed directly from the financial pressure and economic stress.

Tensions increased steadily. By mid-1965, the value of Rhodesian external government bonds dropped by 23%. In November, Smith declared UDI, effectively terminating Britain's power to gradually shift the colony towards neo-colonial black rule. When light financial sanctions were imposed by Britain, Rhodesia responded by defaulting on R$82.6 million in foreign debts (the Rhodesian dollar was approximately two-thirds the value of a British pound), including R$70 million of World Bank loans whose largest component was Kariba-related debt. Pro-Rhodesian economist John Handford commented:

> The Zambian Government, as guarantor of 50% of all Kariba loans, pays the necessary principal and interest repayments. The British Government, the government responsible for Rhodesia, has to reimburse the World Bank with the 50% not contributed by Rhodesia – amounting to several million pounds. The Rhodesian Exchange Control authorities, as part of their retaliation for the action taken by Britain against them, refused an application by the Central African Power Corporation to make the other half of its payments from its resources in Rhodesia. One of the loans that had

helped to build Kariba – that by the British Commonwealth Development Corporation – proved somewhat expensive, because the interest payable on it was linked to the price of money by being 1% higher than the British Bank Rate. Thus, when recurring financial crises in Britain led to raising of the Bank Rate, the cost of the loan also rose.[32]

Whereas British Prime Minister Harold Wilson claimed that 'the cumulative effects of the economic and financial sanctions will bring the rebellion to an end within a matter of weeks rather than months,' in reality, according to Elaine Windrich, Whitehall had acted too slowly, waiting three weeks after the UDI declaration to impose the sanctions: 'Criticism of the Government's delay ranged from the *Financial Times*, which pointed out that during the interval preceding the controls the Reserve Bank of Rhodesia had been buying up all the gold it could, to the *New Statesman*, which said that if the financial controls had been imposed with the UDI they might have toppled the Smith regime.'[33]

In this context, the financing for Kariba is significant not only in terms of its large relative volume, but with respect to geopolitics. The World Bank provided substantial hard-currency resources to the Rhodesian government for a project that would pay off for mining firms quickly, but over many decades for government. But with no future Bank loans in the offing, Smith saw no benefit to using scarce hard-currency reserves to repay the Kariba credit.

The Zambezi River soon became a battleground, as guerrillas of the Zimbabwe liberation movements crossed repeatedly. The road from Salisbury to the town of Kariba came under regular attack, and a Viscount plane travelling to the tourist resort was shot down by guerrillas. As for Zambia, the newly-independent government decided in 1969 to build its own power plant on the north bank of the Zambezi River. The river and Kariba Lake were further politicised because of poaching incursions, which required extensive policing during the 1980s.

In sum, not only did Kariba's financing initially support corporate interests through the provision of power, and colonial rule through the provision of hard currency. It was also a vital ingredient in the first successful decade of Rhodesia's vicious white backlash, once default on the debt – covered by Britain, with no punishment meted out to the Rhodesian Front regime – allowed a redirection of financial resources back into the siege economy.

Yet more loans for Rhodesia

But that regime could not withstand the combination of organic economic crisis and liberation war. Between 1971 and 1976, the budgets for defence rose by 600%, police by 300% and internal affairs by 400%. The budget deficit increased from 1.8% of GDP in 1976 to 13.5% in 1979.

UDI war expenditure was financed through loans and taxation. The Smith regime introduced a compulsory 12.5% levy on taxpayers and also acquired external loans. During the 1970s, loans were made available to the Rhodesian government in spite of United Nations-mandated financial sanctions. External loans during this period were secretive, and omitted from the Schedule of National Debt. What is known from official accounts is that in 1975, the UDI regime's foreign debts amounted to US$22.2 million. But the Smith regime hid a great deal, and by 1980 that figure had swollen to more than US$700 million by some accounts.

One reason was that Swiss and Austrian banks were involved in large-scale financial-sanctions busting, according to London *Sunday Times* investigations. For example, one US$63 million deal for steel-making equipment for the Rhodesian Iron and Steel Company included a US$29 million loan split between the Austrian equipment vendor (Voest), the Union Bank of Switzerland, the European-American Bank and the Austrian bank Girozentrale. The latter institution expressed nervousness because the UN secretary-general was Austrian Kurt Waldheim. A clause was even inserted to ensure immediate repayment of the loan in the event of 'political risk'. A South African 'dummy' corporation was established by the Rhodesians as the borrower, and a shell financier was set up in Zug, Switzerland 'to satisfy Swiss authorities'. But within eighteen months, a British banker living in Rhodesia slipped information to the *Sunday Times* and subsequently fled to Malawi. There, however, he was arrested, extradited to Salisbury and briefly jailed in 1974.[34]

Secrecy was crucial. However, by 1980 it was revealed that the Rhodesians had left to Robert Mugabe the following financial liabilities: multilateral debt of US$5.3 million, bilateral debt of US$97.9 million and private debt of US$593.9 million. More than US$65 million was required in debt servicing in 1980.[35] Could the first democratic government not have done more to question the Odious Debt inheritance?

Conclusion: Altering the political balance of forces?

In one case, that of the World Bank, the inheritance included not only the tens of millions of dollars that helped undergird settler-colonialism over a decade's time, or the US$5.3 million in outstanding Kariba debt, but political interference. Back in 1966, a top Bank official had served as a back-channel between British prime minister Wilson and Smith. Over time, the Bank's involvement in rebel Rhodesia became more direct. As Robert Mugabe put it:

> In the wake of the escalating war and the flight of so many European settlers, an African petit-bourgeoisie is being formed very rapidly as Africans move into white farms, suburban homes and even jobs. In 1974, with the help of the World Bank, local European businessmen launched a fund and a Foundation, called the Whitsun Foundation, to provide capital to the new black petit-bourgeoisie to buy property and to initiate a variety of economic studies. The national development plan proposed by the Foundation is a blueprint for neocolonialism that militates against the freedom of the future independent State of Zimbabwe to embark upon programmes for socialist transformation.[36]

That agenda was confirmed within the first months of World Bank and IMF post-independence involvement in Zimbabwe, as Bank missions came to the country to push loans and advise on policy. As we see below, these ranged across the entire spectrum of development, perhaps most notably land reform where instead of a fair system of redistribution, the Bank promoted status quo ownership relations mitigated by what turned out to be an unsustainable peasant credit scheme.

Without anything like a Truth and Reconciliation Commission to investigate such histories, the question of who really owed what to whom simply was not allowed to be asked. Instead, Zimbabwe was born in 1980, just as the neoliberal barrage against Third World economies began in earnest, led by the institution which already owed so much to black Zimbabweans: the World Bank. As we see in the next chapter, debt and economic policy advice from Washington were amongst the main causes for the 1990s crisis which by the twentieth century's close had left the currency in tatters, unemployment and inflation at record highs and per-capita GDP at levels lower than they had been three decades earlier.

Notes

1. Sibanda, A. (1985), 'Theoretical Problems in the Development of Capitalism in Zimbabwe: Towards a Critique of Arrighi', *Zimbabwe Journal of Economics*, 1, 2.
2. Phimister, I. (1992), 'Unscrambling the Scramble: Africa's Partition Reconsidered', Paper presented to the African Studies Institute, University of the Witwatersrand, Johannesburg, 17 August.
3. Wield, D. (1980), 'Technology and Zimbabwean Industry', in United Nations Conference on Trade and Development, *Zimbabwe: Towards a New Order: An Economic and Social Survey*, Working Papers, Geneva.
4. Frankel, S.H. (1938), *Capital Investment in Africa*, Oxford, Oxford University Press.
5. The economy grew from £9 million to £28 million in constant 1929 currency. Barber, W.J. (1961), *The Economy of British Central Africa*, London, Oxford University Press, pp. 103–104.
6. Phimister, I. (1988), *An Economic and Social History of Zimbabwe, 1890–1948: Class Struggle and Capital Accumulation*, London, Longman, p. 254; Sowelem, R. (1967), *Towards Financial Independence in a Developing Economy*, London, George Allen and Unwin, p. 18; Stoneman, C. (1981), 'The Economy', in C. Stoneman (ed), *Zimbabwe's Prospects*, London, Macmillan, p. 278.
7. Raftopoulos, B. and T. Yoshikuni (eds) (1999), *Sites of Struggle: Essays in Zimbabwe's Urban History*, Harare, Weaver Press.
8. See for example, Raftopoulos, B. and I. Phimister (eds) (1998), *Keep on Knocking: A History of the Labour Movement in Zimbabwe*, Harare, Baobab; and Gwisai, M. (2001), 'Revolutionaries, Resistance and Crisis in Zimbabwe', Unpublished manuscript, Harare.
9. Gann, L. and M. Gelfand (1964), *Huggins of Rhodesia*, London, Allen and Unwin, p. 212; Clarke, D. (1980), *Foreign Companies and International Investment in Zimbabwe*, Gweru, Mambo Press, pp. 15–38.
10. Pearson, D.S. and W.L. Taylor (1963), *Break-Up: Some Economic Consequences for the Rhodesias and Nyasaland*, Salisbury, The Phoenix Group, pp. 15–21.
11. There was a much tighter import quota regime for goods produced outside the sterling area; Bank Acts in 1956 and 1959; imposition of credit controls in 1952, 1956 and 1958; a ceiling on white immigration to 900 people (mainly Britons) per month; dampening of interest rate fluctuations in the late 1950s and early 1960s; and application of tighter currency and exchange controls in 1961 and 1963. Regulation of international financial and trade relations intensified dramatically when the far-Right Rhodesian Front won elections in 1962.
12. Seidman, A. (1986), *Money, Banking and Public Finance in Africa*, London, Zed Press, pp. 64–67.
13. Increased buying power within Rhodesia explains 61% of the manufacturing growth which occurred during the years 1964–1978, as compared to 30% attributable to import substitution industrialisation and 9% to export-based growth. Riddell, R. (1990), 'Zimbabwe', in R. Riddell (ed), *Manufacturing Africa*, London, Overseas Development Institute, pp. 341, 344.
14. Clarke, D. (1980), 'The Monetary, Banking and Financial System in Zimbabwe', in United Nations Conference on Trade and Development, *Zimbabwe: Towards a New Order: An Economic and Social Survey*, Working Papers, Geneva, Vol 1, p. 325.

15. Nixson, F. (1982), 'Import-Substitution Industrialization', in M. Fransman (ed), *Industry and Accumulation in Africa*, London, Heinemann.

16. Sachikonye, L. (1986), 'State, Capital and the Trade Unions', in I. Mandaza (ed), *Zimbabwe: The Political Economy of Transition, 1980–1986*, Dakar, Codesria.

17. Shamuyarira, N. (1965), *Crisis in Rhodesia*, New York, Transatlantic Arts.

18. The case for domestic financiers paying reparations to the Zimbabwean people for financing the colonial and especially UDI system is also strong. *Uneven Zimbabwe* demonstrates the variety of ways in which Salisbury bankers and investors did harm to the prospects for democracy and development in the country. However, for the purposes of addressing Zimbabwe's enormous contemporary foreign debt, the case for financial restitution – from Northern financiers to Zimbabweans – is much more urgent, and the history of foreign financial support for colonialism that much more onerous a burden for ordinary people to continue shouldering. Documentation on struggles against foreign bankers, to repay black South Africa for similar apartheid financing can be found at http://www.aidc.org.za

19. Advisory Committee (J. Phillips, J. Hammond, L.H. Samuels, and R.J.M. Swynnerton) (1962), *Report of the Advisory Committee: The Development of the Economic Resources of Southern Rhodesia with Particular Reference to the Role of African Agriculture*, Salisbury, Southern Rhodesia Ministry of Native Affairs, pp. 78–79.

20. *Property & Finance*, May 1956.

21. Cited in G. Arrighi (1973), 'The Political Economy of Rhodesia', in G. Arrighi and J. Saul, *Essays on the Political Economy of Africa*, New York, Monthly Review, p. 362.

22. Payer, C. (1982), *The World Bank*, New York, Monthly Review, pp. 239–240.

23. The original studies estimated that only 29 000 people would be displaced (approximately half the actual number), and that the cost of resettlement would be 0.7% of the project (also an underestimate). As an alternative to Kariba, a much smaller run-of-the-river dam on the Kafue River tributary of the Zambezi was also considered, and would have had the advantage of virtually no displacement of people. But since displacement was not factored in as an 'externality' to be paid for by society as a whole, this feature apparently played little or no role. International attention was, at the time, focused far more on the 'Noah's Ark' efforts of colonialists to rescue animals from islands caused by rising waters.

24. Leys, C. (1959), *European Politics in Southern Rhodesia*, Oxford, Oxford University Press, p. 111.

25. Payer, *The World Bank*, pp. 239, 251.

26. Reynolds, N., H. Masundire, D. Mwinga, R. Offord and B. Siamwiza (1999), 'Kariba Dam Case Study: Scoping Paper: Final Report', Submission to the World Commission on Dams, Johannesburg, August.

27. As the World Commission on Dams study notes:

> The mistrust generated by the Kafue/Kariba argument in the 1950s continued to influence relationships between Zambia and Zimbabwe over the years. This reached a climax when the two countries decided to reconstitute the Central African Power Corporation (CAPC) and almost to part company

in the common supply of electricity. At one stage the Zimbabwe government gave a unilateral instruction that all importation of electricity from Zambia was to cease . . . The reconstitution exercise which involved the distribution of the assets of the CAPC is still not complete as the resolution of the position regarding Kariba North Power Station remains outstanding. (Reynolds et al, 'Kariba Dam Study')

28. One indication is that the Kafue River project was rejected in spite of the fact that it would have taken just three years to build, and cost far less; the disadvantage was that Kariba had a longer-term lower average cost per unit of hydropower. The Northern Rhodesian authorities began work on Kafue two years after the Kariba project was floated to international financiers. Expansion and linkage of the copper fields to the nascent Belgian Congo electricity grid was also a practical alternative, and indeed allowed the financing and construction decisions associated with both Kariba and Kafue to be delayed a few years.

29. Pearson and Taylor, *Break-Up*, p. 9.

30. Advisory Committee, *Report*, p. 87.

31. Pearson and Taylor, *Break-Up*, pp. 15–21.

32. Handford, J. (1976), *Portrait of an Economy Under Sanctions, 1965–1975*, Salisbury, Mercury Press, p. 148.

33. Windrich, E. (1978), *Britain and the Politics of Rhodesian Independence*, London, Croom Helm, pp. 69–70.

34. *Sunday Times*, 14 April 1974; United Nations (1975), 'Special Report Concerning the Question of Southern Rhodesia on External Participation in the Expansion of the Rhodesian Iron and Steel Commission', United Nations Security Council, New York, Special Supplement Vol 3.

35. World Bank (1988), *World Debt Tables: External Debt to Developing Countries*, Vol II, Washington, p. 43.

36. Mugabe, R. (1979), Preface to 'Zimbabwe: Notes and Reflections on the Rhodesian Question', Mimeo, Maputo, Centre of African Studies, March, p. i.

CHAPTER TWO

Economic Constraints

1. Introduction

The last chapter posed two central questions that haunted Zimbabwe during the transition from colonialism to independence: should the economy become more or less dependent upon international trade and finance? And should the country's political leaders throw off debt shackles that were periodically attached by international financiers, including the Swiss and Austrian bankers during the 1970s and the World Bank during the fifteen years prior to UDI, as well as during the post-independence epoch when – as argued below – debt generated not development, but rather underdevelopment?

As for the first query, which is addressed in relation to the post-independence era throughout Section 2 of this chapter, evidence presented so far included the two pre-1980 periods of decisive deglobalisation – the 1930s and 1965–1974 – which were also the years of most robust economic activity in settler-colonial history. In contrast, the answer suggested by the World Bank in 1990, at the point Zanu adopted the *Economic Structural Adjustment Programme (Esap)*, was unambiguous:

> The overall model chosen to integrate the economy into the international markets . . . should aim at avoiding the appropriation of rents by suppliers of nontradables and workers. That is, they should maintain the real wage low, so that excess profits accrue to capital . . . In carrying out all these activities, a close alliance between government and private agents must be developed.[1]

That was Nicaraguan economist Manuel Hinds, writing in a publication which we found prominently displayed in the Bank's Harare office at the time. But was the answer so obvious? As we shall consider below, within a decade's time, the *Human Development Report* on Zimbabwe co-sponsored by the United Nations Development Program addressed the same issue forthrightly, and advocated the opposite: a return to inward orientation.[2] That is also the position we will argue below, and in the conclusion.

The second question, which is the subject of Section 3, is just as important and controversial. A leading official of the first Mugabe government, Finance Ministry chief economist Norman Reynolds, confirms that in 1980 there was an option for Rhodesian debt-default: 'The heavies – local and international bankers – came in and worked on Mugabe for a year and a half. That included lunches and dinners, and he finally relented and agreed not to default.'[3] At the point in 1980 when such a default would have been possible, what must be assessed is whether the costs outweighed the benefits. Costs would certainly have included some of the future loans and possibly substantial aid flows, and even potential restrictions on trade finance.

These costs were not predetermined, however. There was every moral justification to penalise lenders to Rhodesia, for their financing of the illegal racist regime. Benefits of default would have included not only more resources for Zimbabwe's post-independence development, but also a more decisive shifting of the terrain upon which state officials came to adopt Washington's economic strategy. Default would also have complied with the spirit of United Nations financial sanctions, and it is hard to imagine that the forces of imperialism would have stepped into the breach on behalf of commercial bankers and the World Bank.

Most importantly, perhaps, was the 'demonstration effect'. Had Mugabe embarked upon a high profile repudiation of Rhodesian-era debt, that might have deterred international bankers – especially the International Monetary Fund – from lending to South Africa during its 1980s crises, which kept apartheid in place for longer and with more durability than should have been the case. Progressive demands for financial sanctions against dictatorial regimes like that of Burma, would be taken much more seriously by bankers, if Mugabe and subsequently Nelson Mandela had enforced those sanctions with debt repudiation, once they assumed power.

Instead, Mugabe repaid the Rhodesian colonial debt, and, via a series of loans and policy papers made available during the early 1980s, his government surrendered so quickly before the World Bank and IMF that Ibbo Mandaza was led to comment in 1986: 'International finance capital has, since the Lancaster House Agreement, been the major factor in the internal and external policies of the state in Zimbabwe.'[4]

Thandike Mkandawire, subsequently head of the Geneva-based United Nations Research Institute for Social Development, confirmed: 'It seems the government was too anxious to establish its credentials with the financial world.'[5]

To comprehend the turn to export orientation and a high debt strategy, nearly from the very outset of independence, some further political background is required. Few have explained the Zimbabwe ruling elite more precisely than political scientist Rukudzo Murapa, who in 1977 predicted ruptures within the alliance between 'a politically ambitious petit-bourgeois leadership, a dependent and desperate proletariat and a brutally exploited and basically uninitiated peasantry'. As Murapa forecast:

> After national liberation, the petit-bourgeois leadership can abandon its alliance with the workers and peasants and emerge as the new ruling class by gaining certain concessions from both foreign and local capital and, in fact, forming a new alliance with these forces which they will need to stay in power. Of course, lip service commitment, *a la* Kenya, to the masses, will be made.[6]

Under the rubric of nationalism, Zimbabwe's state and ruling Zanu party became indistinguishable during the 1980s. A lower-middle class was quickly built through the bureaucracy and corruption and patronage systems emerged parallel to the growth of a *'comprador'* faction, i.e. a group of sell-outs – which came to identify more with Washington's logic than with popular needs.

There were also lamentable ethnic overtones. Shona dominance of the state included repression of the minority Ndebele people. The army's ruthless *Gukurahundi* containment of a brief armed uprising amongst apparently only a few dozen Ndebele-speaking people – 'Super Zapu', backed by apartheid-era Pretoria – included the massacre of an estimated 5 000 civilians during the mid-1980s.[7] Ethnic tensions simmered, but a 1987 unity pact between the two parties set the stage for a *de facto* one-party state which lasted until the 2000 parliamentary elections. Mugabe's early 1990s efforts to codify the one-party state in law were beaten back by not only human rights advocates and various small right-leaning political parties, but by international opinion, at a time Mugabe sought extended access to global financial markets.

Once Zapu was repressed and co-opted, the opposition consisted of two parties that could not attract more than a fifth of the electorate: the Zimbabwe Unity Movement in 1990 and Forum Party in 1995. Yet the legitimacy of the government was fading fast, as regular corruption scandals and growing hardship for urban residents began to breed discontent. In the countryside, the government provided new schools, clinics, seed and food packs during droughts, roads and a few water schemes. However, because of limited operating subsidies, these too began to decay and decline over time. School fees rose beyond rural affordability levels, clinics ran out of medicine, the rural agriculture support system faded especially when credit schemes failed, roads degenerated for lack of maintenance and borehole pumps often broke.

The contradictory process of bureaucratic petit-bourgeois class formation and the squeezing of fiscal resources, sometimes with help from unprincipled non-governmental organisations (NGOs), began to be evident by the late 1980s. Assisted by magazines like the Catholic social-justice magazine *Moto*, *Parade* (during the 1980s), *Horizon* (the most impressive periodical during the 1990s), *The Worker* and *Social Change and Development*, citizens began to view 'development' in a more critical light. Capable of shifting the blame, Mugabe remarked in 1989:

> There exists among the membership of . . . Zanu a minority, but very powerful bourgeois group which champions the cause of international finance and national private capital, whose interests thus stand opposed to the development and growth of a socialist and egalitarian society in Zimbabwe.[8]

That powerful group was led by finance minister Bernard Chidzero, who occasionally revealed his agenda (e.g. at a 1982 investment conference in New York):

> Does the government of Zimbabwe have something up its sleeves? We are socialists, are we encouraging you to come so that tomorrow we can grab you? If that's what you think, I can assure you that we have nothing up our sleeves, we are simple pragmatists . . . Let us not fight the battle on ideological grounds. Life is more serious than to be controlled by ideologies. Life is very down-to-earth, let us just look at the realities of life. And I believe that good businessmen enter into riskier areas than areas where we talk about ideologies without doing much about it.[9]

Mugabe had, early on, set an example for the 'bourgeois group', according to one leading US banker quoted in the early 1980s:

The management of the more sophisticated large companies, i.e. TA Holdings, Lonrho, and Anglo American, seem to be impressed by and satisfied with Mugabe's management and the increased level of understanding in government of commercial considerations . . . I feel it is a political pattern that Mugabe gives radical, anti-business speeches before government makes major pro-business decisions or announcements.[10]

A left-wing Zanu member of parliament, Lazarus Nzarayebani, confirmed in 1989:

The socialist agenda has been adjourned indefinitely. You don't talk about socialism in a party that is led by people who own large tracts of land and employ a lot of cheap labour. When the freedom fighters were fighting in the bush they were fighting not to disturb the system but to dismantle it. And what are we seeing now? Leaders are busy implementing those things which we were fighting against.[11]

International financial access was one part of the Faustian deal that Mugabe came to regret. Internally, the power of Zimbabwe's banks, controlled in part by London head offices, and their local business-oriented media allies grew enormously. Manufacturing industry was stagnating, as capital flows shifted into financial and speculative arenas, especially commercial real estate and the local stock market. By the late 1980s, Zimbabwe was overwhelmed by such phenomena as the rise of a new bureaucratic-financial *comprador* elite within and around the Finance Ministry, Reserve Bank and parastatal firms; unprecedented property and stock market speculation; an increasingly desperate search for external markets due to local stagnation; creeping but often definitive policy influence by IMF, World Bank and US AID missions; and very high levels of foreign debt followed by diminishing capacity to control the contours of the economy from the vantage-point of the nation-state.[12]

As discussed in more detail below, the early 1990s saw domestic financial markets imploding as international financial interests gained dominance in the local economy. As trade and financial restrictions were removed, Zimbabwe sank into a profound economic depression. Droughts in 1992 and 1995 exacerbated the situation. But more debilitating was Zimbabwe's sustained de-industrialisation and a crash in workers' real standard of living, which mainly reflected the half-baked and ill-phased character of neoliberal policy.

2. Export-led decline

Until the reversals beginning in 1997, the period since 1980 witnessed the relaxation – first gradual, then rapid after 1990 – of Zimbabwe's national economic regulatory apparatus. State economic management techniques that were established during the 1920s, enhanced during the 1950s and cemented during the 1965–1979 period of UDI were thrown away.

The success or failure of the liberalisation process is hotly debated, and the current turmoil in Zimbabwe rests to some extent upon tensions that were exacerbated particularly since the early 1990s adoption of structural adjustment: inequality, worsening unemployment, de-industrialisation, heightened shortages of basic needs ranging from land to housing to water to energy. The implications of failed outward orientation are important to contemplate, at a time of unprecedented social debate over the character of politics and economics in a potentially post-nationalist era.

Post-independence stagnation, 1980–1990

Economic decline and worsening unemployment associated with the 1975–1978 depression were not solved during the 1980s. The reasons for persistent lack of post-independence economic dynamism are complex, as they reflected in large part subjective issues such as white investor confidence (extremely negative until around 1984), an ongoing fall in the rate of corporate profit, and the failure by the Zanu government to substantially alter wealth and income distribution to improve the buying power of the masses. Some related to international economic factors, although Zimbabwe initially grew rapidly from 1980–1981, in the midst of the world's worst recession since the Great Depression.

Upon taking power, the new Zanu bureaucracy maintained the bulk of Rhodesian-era regulations over financial institutions and even added a few others. Short-term financial management measures were adopted: controls on interest rates, 'prescribed assets' (requiring some insurance and bank investments to be made in government securities), and restrictions on profit remittances and even payments to overseas pensions were occasionally necessary to stave off crisis. But these did not prevent the full-fledged deregulation of finance and establishment of high, positive real interest rates alongside trade liberalisation and price decontrol during the 1990s.

New institutions were created by the Finance Ministry and Reserve Bank to support financial, trade and local commercial liberalisation: the Zimbabwe Investment Centre in 1987, the Indigenous Business

Development Centre in 1990, and Zimtrade and the Venture Capital Company of Zimbabwe in 1991. Some were aimed at expanding financing to indigenous businesses as part of a general modernisation strategy of financial broadening and deepening. Small businesses were nearly completely ignored by commercial banks, and in 1989, the *Financial Times* reported that 97% of bank loans went to white-owned companies.[13]

Thus the state maintained an unsure hand on the reins of financial capital, ensuring that its only routes for speculative investment were at least local ones: the stock exchange and real estate. Meanwhile, most African countries suffered massive capital flight to offshore financial centres, so exchange controls at least served the purpose of locking finance into Zimbabwe through the 1980s. However, the main financial regulatory tools at the government's disposal did not address the underlying problems in the productive sector, or the excessive flows of money into speculation.

The deeper-rooted problems in the economy were not seriously addressed during the 1980s, and instead a temporary fix began to emerge through the expansion of financial markets. The underlying issue remained the excess productive capacity of the economy, in a context in which inequality prevented sufficiently high levels of consumption: i.e. what can be termed 'overaccumulation crisis'.[14] At the same time, the financial system was 'nicely protected and profitable', the World Bank confirmed, in part because 'the depth of the country's capital market places Zimbabwe ahead of many countries, including Chile, Korea, India, Singapore and Greece.'[15] With little further incentive to invest under existing circumstances, the late 1980s witnessed a dramatic rise of stock market and real estate speculation.

Although the Zanu government intervened in the financial markets, it largely corroborated rather than challenged the markets' dynamics. Prescribed assets were an important example of the temporary equilibrium established between financial control and speculation in the context of stagnation. Notwithstanding prescribed asset rates for institutional investors of up to 60%, 'it should be emphasised that there is little evidence of direct crowding out of the private business sector, owing to its weak demand for credit in this period,' the World Bank concluded of the 1980s.[16]

The linkages between financial and trade liberalisation are important, as is the evolution of international advice. Chidzero spelled these connections out as early as 1982, in a self-imposed promise of conditionality in a letter to the World Bank: 'We are convinced that we could appreciably increase the volume of our exports through liberalisation of credit facilities.'[17] The Bank soon heralded 'important policy directions – including an outward-looking, export-oriented industrial strategy'.[18]

By 1985, a joint World Bank and UN report on Zimbabwe noted possible 'success stories' in manufacturing exports, although no marketing studies were subsequently carried out.[19] A 1987 Bank report that was credited with winning over cabinet and bureaucratic support, suggested that 'it is highly difficult to predict which manufacturing subsectors will enjoy rapid growth, but there is sufficient evidence on the responsiveness of Zimbabwe's manufacturing sector to be optimistic on its export prospects . . . The European market is likely to be central to growth in manufactured exports.'[20] As business economist Roger Riddell presciently replied, 'Strikingly, the Bank fails to provide evidence to support such a bland conclusion.'[21]

Throughout most of the 1980s the majority of domestic manufacturers were definitely not oriented to global markets, in terms of which they would have required cutting-edge imported capital goods and advanced technology. On the contrary, white manufacturers had grown comfortable thanks to protection against international competition.[22] Moreover, in spite of continual complaints about foreign exchange shortages, manufacturers had access to a World Bank Manufacturing Rehabilitation Loan (1981), a Bank Manufacturing Export Loan (1983), and the Export Incentive Scheme, as well as enjoying the very generous depreciation allowances introduced at the trough of the late 1970s crisis, thus keeping fixed capital costs extremely low.

One strategy for increasing export revenues was periodic devaluation. The currency was allowed to fall in 1984–1985 by nearly 40%, accompanied by budget cuts and a reduction of the maize subsidy. The main beneficiaries were agricultural and minerals exporters, but the devaluations simply cheapened goods temporarily, rather than structurally improving Zimbabwe's export capacity. This would become evident as a result of debilitating changes to the Zimbabwean economy brought about during the structural adjustment era.

Structural adjustment and economic crisis, 1991–1997
The 1991 'Framework for Economic Reform' – better known as the *Economic Structural Adjustment Programme (Esap)* – was introduced by finance minister Bernard Chidzero and a very small group of technocrats. The key documents were prepared by the World Bank in 1987 and

then revised so that a majority of Mugabe's cabinet concurred.[23] The *Financial Gazette* named the key promoters as Chidzero, minister of industry and commerce Kumbirai Kangai and minister of state for finance, economic planning and development Tichaendepi Masaya.[24]

Chidzero and his team promised that by the end of 1995 there would be a 25% cut in the civil service, along with the demise of all labour restrictions, price controls, exchange controls, interest rate controls, investment regulations, and import restrictions, as well as many government subsidies. Privatisation of parastatals was practically the only major ingredient in the typical adjustment recipe that Zimbabwe declined, but even so, parastatal commercialisation was pursued with vigour. By 1995, 'rapid privatisation of the key parastatals' providing telecommunications, electricity, water and transportation had become a central World Bank demand.[25]

To what end? If government stuck with the medicine through 1995, Chidzero and the Bank promised that *Esap* would deliver the following remarkable benefits:

- Reaching 5% growth annually, the economy would have grown in excess of 4.3% for eight consecutive years (1988–1995) – in spite of the fact that the longest stretch of positive growth since 1973 had been just three years.
- The overall budget deficit would shrink to 5% of GDP.
- Although Zimbabwe's foreign debt would initially increase from US$2.4 billion in early 1991 to a projected US$4 billion in 1995, repaying the debt would become easier.
- The debt service ratio (repayments as a percentage of export earnings) – which peaked at 35% in 1987 and fell to 24% in 1990 – would drop further, to 18.5% by 1995, in spite of the addition of US$3.5 billion in new loans in the intervening years (while US$1.9 billion would be repaid).
- Private sector investment would rapidly overtake government investment, doubling from levels of the late 1980s.
- Total investment, which averaged less than 20% of GDP from 1985–1990, would reach 25% by 1993 and remain there.
- Inflation, running at 20% in early 1991, would be down to 10% by 1994.
- Relative to the rest of the economy, exports would grow by about one third from late 1980s levels; specifically, mining exports would increase from less than US$400 million in 1990 to more than US$500 million in 1994, manufacturing exports would double

from US$400 million in 1988 to US$800 million in 1995, and agricultural exports, which were in decline since 1988, would grow steadily through 1995.

- Except for 1991, Zimbabwe would have better terms of trade in its dealings with the world economy over the subsequent five years.
- New direct foreign investment would flood in (US$30 million a year from 1992–1995) notwithstanding the fact that such investment flooded out during the 1980s.

In reality, *Esap* failed miserably. GDP growth only reached 5% during one year (1994), and averaged just 1.2% from 1991–1995. Inflation averaged more than 30% during the period, and never dropped anywhere near the 10% goal. The budget deficit was more than 10% of GDP during the *Esap* era (with no prospect of getting down to the targeted 5% from a drought-related high of 13% in 1994/1995).[26] The core questions are firstly, did government stay the course with the treatment, and secondly, if so, was it the wrong medicine?

It is true that forces external to the logic of reforms – the 1992 and 1995 droughts and durable fiscal deficits in large part caused by heavy parastatals losses – all threw the model off track (yet the 1992–1993 and 1993–1994 rainy seasons were satisfactory). Conceptually, it is extremely difficult to control for the drought factor. However, the previous period of sustained economic crisis, from 1975–1978, was a time of extremely good rains, while the late 1960s and early 1970s period of booming growth witnessed years of severe drought, suggesting that weather is by no means the primary determinant of economic activity in Zimbabwe.

Nevertheless, the World Bank was impressed in 1995 that 'trade liberalisation proceeded without delays . . . [The] the foreign exchange control system has been largely dismantled. All current account transactions have been freed from exchange controls and import licensing and the exchange rate is now market-determined' (although 'anomalies remained in the tariff/tax structure').[27] The programme remained 'on course', commented Bank officials regularly, although *Financial Gazette* deputy editor Iden Wetherell complained in 1993 that their 'emollient statements over the past 18 months reflect the devotion of a faith unmoved by facts'.[28]

Likewise, leading businesspeople benefitted from luxury goods imports, declining real wages, their new-found ability to move money out of the country, and commercial deregulation. Business commentator Eric Bloch celebrated *Esap*'s 'dramatic advances' in 1995:

The extent that inflation has declined, the significant reductions in direct taxation, the liberalisation of trade and virtual elimination of import controls with a consequential elimination of most shortages, the immense relaxations of exchange controls, a somewhat more stable currency exchange rate environment, and the extent of new investment in the last two years are but a few indicators of the achievements of *Esap* to date.[29]

However, tampering with the complex system of protective tariffs, duties and quotas created several dilemmas that should have been foreseen. The 1991 Open Guaranteed Import License allowed speculative imports of luxury goods, raw materials and machinery. Once South Africa refused to renew its 1964–1992 Free Trade arrangement, Zimbabwe retaliated by taxing South African products at the border. The former comrades who ran Pretoria after 1994 were persuaded by local textile firms and trade unions not to renew Zimbabwe's favoured access. According to the Zimbabwe Congress of Trade Unions (ZCTU), 'tariffs on imported inputs were raised so that by 1995, tariffs on inputs were generally higher than those on finished products.'[30]

As a result, the trade deficit exploded during the early 1990s, and not only because, as Gibbon reports, the 'increase in imports was roughly double that anticipated'.[31] Exports also dropped from US$1.753 billion in 1990 to US$1.531 billion in 1992.[32] This was not purely due to agricultural failure – or the temporary rise in demand for formerly exported food products – in 1992; after all, manufactured exports had fallen from US$537 million in 1990 to US$434 million in 1991.[33] The demise of some export incentives was often blamed.

But the capacity to export was weak for several other reasons. Zimbabwe failed to qualify as a 'least-developed country' for trading purposes. Moreover, the ZCTU charged, trade liberalisation 'tended to turn manufacturers into traders . . . (as) firms have tended to stop manufacturing products locally, preferring to import them directly and then sell them to local consumers'.[34] Later, Zimbabwe also failed to receive export concessions under the US Africa Growth and Opportunity Act, due to its democratic deficit. (The benefits of the US law, however, were offset by structural adjustment conditionalities.)

Thus as shown in Table 2, the manufacturing sector's real (factor cost) contribution to GDP during the 1990s fell 18% from a peak of Z$4.530 billion in 1991 (in constant 1990 terms) to Z$3.724 billion in 1995, and did not subsequently recover much ground. The subsectors 'distribution, hotels and restaurants' became the largest contributor to GDP, rising 25%, from Z$3.267 billion in 1990 to Z$4.075 billion in

Table 2   Zimbabwe's Gross Domestic Product, 1990–1998 at factor cost (constant 1990 Z$, millions).

Industry of origin	1990	1991	1992	1993	1994	1995	1996	1997	1998
Agriculture	3 188	3 221	2 474	3 145	3 375	3 119	3 737	3 834	4 023
Mining/quarrying	845	841	823	805	892	936	913	895	899
Manufacturing	4 403	4 530	4 146	3 825	4 209	3 724	3 896	3 992	3 886
Electricity/water	543	512	501	443	486	477	469	473	447
Construction	615	619	645	633	635	483	541	633	661
Finance/insurance	1 336	1 338	1 373	1 578	1 673	1 723	1 794	1 848	1 865
Real estate	474	494	522	549	569	594	617	648	681
Distribution/hotels/restaurants	3 267	3 488	3 268	3 277	3 504	3 696	3 946	4 037	4 075
Transport/communication	1 185	1 230	1 334	1 273	1 383	1 706	2 043	2 062	2 062
Public administration	1 215	1 235	1 208	1 153	997	1 002	920	872	870
Education	1 269	1 286	1 290	1 307	1 325	1 357	1 495	1 612	1 712
Health	316	340	347	381	466	441	415	314	299
Domestic services	348	355	339	331	346	327	348	356	363
Other services	770	891	930	924	951	900	971	1 077	1 111
(–imputed banking charges)	–425	–448	–315	–412	–517	–402	–307	–288	–242
GDP (factor cost)	19 349	19 973	18 854	19 212	20 293	20 084	21 799	22 365	22 711

1998. Other increases were experienced in transport and communication (74%), real estate (44%), finance and insurance (40%), education (35%) and agriculture (26%).

But these did not balance the disappointing declines in volume outputs experienced in several manufacturing subsectors, as shown in Table 3. Total manufacturing output fell from an indexed peak of 143 (with 1980 = 100) in 1991 by 24% to 109 in 1999, as de-industrialisation ravaged the textiles (–64%), metals (–35%), transport equipment (–31%) and clothing (–28%) subsectors. The latter should have been a source of great expansion, particularly as further promises of enhanced market access to Europe and other Northern markets were made by *Esap's* promoters.

The core problem for many light manufacturers could be observed within months of *Esap's* launch, according to Peter Johnston of Saybrook clothes: 'The unemployed will probably not buy much of our products, whilst the few breadwinners will find it difficult to buy clothing for their dependents.'[36] Effective demand was lowered considerably across the economy. The ZCTU reported in 1996 that their average member was 38% poorer than in 1980 and 40% poorer than in 1990. The biggest losers in direct standards of living (average annual earnings) as a percentage of 1980 levels were civil servants (–65%), domestic workers (–62%), construction workers (–56%), teachers (–50%), and farm-workers (–48%). Least affected were miners (–20%) and manufacturing employees (–19%).

Dramatically lower wages did not translate into more jobs.[37] Unemployment remained rampant, with a tiny fraction of the 200 000 annual school-leavers able to find formal sector employment. Ironically, the Bank celebrated the fact that 'labour-intensive sectors, such as wood products and textiles, have benefitted from the sharp reduction in real wages, reinforcing the expansion of exports.'[38]

Workers and poor people faced an unprecedented financial crisis during the early 1990s. The 'social wage' fell sharply thanks largely to new cost recovery policies for health, education and many other social services, as well as the unprecedented interest rates on consumer credit. The trends generated by Zimbabwe's exemplary social policy during the first decade of independence – reducing infant mortality from 86 to 49 per 1 000 live births, raising the immunisation rate from 25% to 80% and life expectancy from 56 to 62 years, doubling primary school enrollment, etc. – witnessed ominous reversals. For example, primary school dropout rates soared during the 1990s, with girls particularly prone to suffer when school fee increases were imposed; and likewise, just as the HIV/Aids pandemic hit Zimbabwe, from 1990–1995, per

Table 3　Volume of manufacturing output, 1990–2000 (indexed, 1980=100).

Sector	(%)	1990	1991	1992	1993	1994	1995	1996	1997	1998	1999
Foodstuffs	13.5	144	147	150	123	130	142	128	135	133	137
Drink/tobacco	10.4	130	134	134	127	127	119	131	134	138	128
Textiles	10.1	217	226	177	192	206	81	80	80	83	77
Clothing/footwear	7.2	145	149	125	128	125	100	102	102	103	110
Wood/furniture	4.4	90	101	106	95	106	115	160	134	134	118
Paper/printing	6.1	137	144	143	150	169	156	153	153	149	101
Chemicals/products	12.5	159	159	138	129	149	134	137	156	140	121
Mineral products	3.7	161	170	158	130	170	156	182	177	176	161
Metals/products	28.8	111	114	101	82	92	88	89	94	85	78
Transport equipment	2.1	147	143	141	82	133	139	201	203	147	104
Other manufacturing groups	1.2	49	48	39	95	85	53	55	41	37	38
All manufacturing	100	139	143	130	119	131	113	117	121	115	106

Source for both Tables 2 and 3: *Central Statistical Office Quarterly Digest of Statistics.*

capita spending on healthcare fell by 20% in real terms.[39] 'Budget cutting appears to have been an end in itself,' even the World Bank conceded, leading to 'the widely reported brain drain of experienced teachers and health workers in the public sector, despite no official retrenchments in these areas'.[40]

The 1991–1997 period during which *Esap* was implemented can thus be considered a failure in many crucial respects, although, inexplicably, the World Bank 'Project Completion Report' for *Esap* gave the best possible final grade for the first stage of the programme: 'highly satisfactory'.[41] In contrast, popular opinion was reflected in 'IMF Riots', including 1993 bread riots which broke out in high-density suburbs of Harare and in the city centre in 1995. Public workers went on strike in 1996, and other private employees (including plantation workers) followed at an unprecedented rate in 1997. By the time that political opposition consolidated in 1998–1999, leading to a new, labour-led political party that nearly won the 2000 parliamentary elections, leading Zanu ministers had come to the conclusion that *Esap* was their most important policy error.

Still, the government was able to claim the following accomplishments during the period, in line with *Esap*'s 1991 commitments:

• 18 000 government jobs were abolished (with retrenchees numbering 7 000) and the civil service wage bill was reduced from 15.3% of GDP in 1990 to 11.3% in 1994.
• The foreign exchange control system was dismantled.
• Tariffs were lowered (except for some 'import-competing activities') to the 15–25% range (i.e. even below the World Trade Organisation requirement of 30%, which was only meant to take effect by the year 2005).
• There was extensive liberalisation of foreign investment regulations.
• Price controls were eliminated.
• Many local zoning and trading restrictions were abolished.
• Labour markets were largely deregulated (particularly regarding wage determination and employers' rights to hire and fire).[42]

If *Esap* was largely implemented, and if the implementation was unsatisfactory, the subsequent period suggests that the political costs and social instability generated by ineffectual international economic integration are substantial. Zimbabwean society followed the trade union lead and in late 1997 re-awakened from a deep post-independence slumber to demand socio-economic and political reform.

The unions had initially sent ambiguous signals. During the mid-1990s, nearly nine out every ten union members polled viewed *Esap* negatively. But, noted Sachikonye at the time, 'much of the workers' understanding and critique of *Esap* relates more to its effects rather than its rationale and objectives,' and hence when organised resistance did briefly emerge (such as a banned and ill-attended May Day 1992 anti-*Esap* demonstration), its 'amorphousness and porousness to state manipulation proved a weak basis for sustainability'.[43] Likewise, most ZCTU leaders and technical advisers also tended to seek solutions of a 'corporatist' nature – i.e. Big Labour + Big Government + Big Business – to their growing economic worries, as discussed in Chapter Three. The ZCTU leaders even began describing *Esap* as 'necessary but insufficient' in an attempt to find a common discourse with government.

But in late August 1997, the coming economic collapse was foretold by the crash of the massively overvalued Zimbabwe Stock Exchange, just prior to Mugabe's political zigzags and his rekindling of the ruling party's alliance with nationalist war vets and peasants. Indeed, the deep-seated collapse that continued through 2001 was not merely a function of the immediate September–November 1997 financial crisis. It reflected an apparently permanent ratcheting-down of industry, simultaneous with an upturn in inequality, which had its roots in the 1970s crisis, 1980s stagnation and 1990s austerity.

Economic collapse and policy reversion, 1997–2001

The precise moment that the Zimbabwe economy began its generalised plunge was probably the late morning of 14 November 1997, when over a four-hour period, the Zimbabwe dollar lost 74% of its value, as explained in the Preface. A quick Reserve Bank decision to defend the currency ultimately required the recapture of foreign exchange held in corporate foreign currency accounts. Although this restored a bit of the loss, the value of a Z$ fell from US$0.09 to US$0.025 over the course of a year. As a result, unprecedented inflation was imported – from levels below 15% in September 1997 to above 45% eighteen months later, with far higher price increases recorded for food – leading in January and October 1998 to urban riots over maize and fuel price hikes, respectively.

Interest rates were also pushed up by 6% in the course of November–December. The rate on government-issued Treasury Bills soared from a low of 16% in April 1997 to 26% by October and then 32% in December, and was raised again to 35% in August 1998. The stock market's industrial index, already quickly off by 9% from peak August

1997 levels, crashed by a total of 56% (in nominal terms, far more in real terms) over the course of the subsequent year. More than 30 000 jobs were lost through retrenchments during 1998.

Two political events in September–October 1997 attract the most blame from orthodox commentators, notwithstanding evidence of earlier rot. First, bucking strident advice and monetary arm-twisting from international financial institutions, Mugabe paid off a challenge to his legitimacy from more than 50 000 liberation war veterans by granting them Z$50 000 each plus a Z$2 000 per month pension. The ex-combatants were successful essentially because their 1997 demonstrations in Harare and intense harassment of Mugabe caused acute embarrassment. The World Bank immediately suspended balance of payments support.

There were doubts about the war vets' own legitimacy, given that their main leader, Chenjerai Hunzvi, sat out the struggle in Poland. The most powerful leftist guerrilla leader of the 1970s, Wilf Mhanda, condemned the mockery made of the *chimurenga* by opportunists parading as liberation leaders. After the payout, popular resentment materialised against the war vets when sales taxes – and indeed initially an income tax and petrol tax increase – were imposed to partially cover the costs.

Mugabe also suddenly announced that at long last government would begin implementing the Land Designation Act, and 1 500 mainly white-owned farms were identified for redistribution. Even though only partial compensation was promised – covering buildings and infrastructure, not inflated land value – again this raised the likelihood of fiscal convulsion. The damage to the commercial agricultural sector and related industries would be heightened by the fact (and past experience), as conceded by the agriculture minister in a subsequent radio broadcast, that the recipients of the farms would include wealthy politicians ahead of land-starved peasants. (This patronage route was important, at a time other state-based options for embourgeoisement were closing.)

Once again, Zanu elites were apparently not serious about thoroughgoing redistribution, which would require vastly greater resources, support structures and administrative staff than were budgeted and planned for, not to mention a shift in class power away from the emergent bureaucratic bourgeoisie and the residually potent white farming elite. The ambitious land designation exercise was not successfully brought to fruition via the Zimbabwean legal system: the courts, the World Bank and IMF, the British government and other donors, the private media, and other pressure groups sided with white farmers and together effectively vetoed any forced sales in 1998. Instead, a 'donor's conference' was held to work out a more gradual method of land transfer. It was only in 2000 that the land designation process took on substance, once war vets were mobilised by Hunzvi, with Mugabe's blessing, to invade more than 1 000 white-owned farms.

By that time, the first substantial opposition party threat to Zanu appeared from the trade union movement. In early 2000, the opposition registered a 55–45% victory in a referendum over a new constitution. It was widely seen as a proxy vote for Mugabe's legitimacy. As discussed in the next chapter, the Movement for Democratic Change (MDC) offered very mixed signals about its own economic strategy, emphasising a dramatic shift towards basic-needs provision on the one hand, but massive privatisation, deregulation and intensified World Bank and IMF intervention, on the other.

Mugabe and the Zanu government reacted to the threat – essentially from the political Left – by reviving its own dormant leftist rhetoric. Mugabe regularly claimed that he would 'restore' allegedly socialist policies. And indeed, there were some small hints of re-asserted Zimbabwean sovereignty in the face of financial meltdown, such as a mid-1998 price freeze on staple goods, a late 1998 tariff imposed on luxury imports, and several minor technical interventions to raise revenues, slow capital flight and deter share speculation. For example, 1990s exchange-control liberalisation had created such enormous abuse that new regulations on currency sales had to be imposed. Yet two days after a 5% capital gains tax was introduced on the stock market, a broker boycott forced a retraction, and a 2001 state threat to capture individual foreign currency accounts was retracted after threats from the wealthy. Indeed, the government was not, apparently, powerful enough to re-impose full exchange controls – which had been widely expected in the event a 1999 IMF bailout loan fell through, given the perilous state of hard currency reserves. Those reserves continued to dwindle, causing severe fuel and forex shortages from early 2000.

The Zimbabwe government found itself, as a result, under intense international economic pressure. Its 1998 'Zimprest' policy maintained many of *Esap*'s arguments, but also recognised the need for policy reversals in several areas. These included introduction of selective price controls, increased tariffs, import licensing on some goods, procrastination in meeting regional liberalisation targets, pegging of the exchange rate, suspension of foreign currency accounts, introduction of new export incentives and application of new levies on tobacco and consumer goods.

Although five major parastatals were privatised, a more rapid sell-off of state assets was postponed. The Value Added Tax, on the cards since the World Bank began pressing hard in 1996, was also delayed.

The IMF sent a high-level team to negotiate the disbursement of a US$53 million loan (which in turn would release another US$800 million from other lenders). There was a confused flurry in early 1999, when Mugabe sought funding elsewhere than the IMF.44 The IMF's Zimbabwe objectives were straightforward: reversal of both the luxury import tax and price controls on staple foods. According to Michael Nowak, the IMF official controlling a US$53 million loan tranche:

> There are two issues outstanding and these have stopped the IMF from making the standby credit available to the country. These issues are, one, we want the government to reduce the tariffs slapped on luxury goods last September, and secondly, we also want the government to give us a clear timetable as to when and how they will remove the price controls they have imposed on some goods.[45]

Later in 1999, the IMF agreed to increase the loan amount to US$200 million. But according to an IMF official, yet more conditions emerged, namely, access to classified Democratic Republic of Congo (DRC) war information and a commitment to pay new war expenditure from the existing budget: 'The Zimbabweans felt offended, shocked, but they all the same agreed to give us the information, we got all the clarification we wanted. They had no choice . . . We have had assurances [that] if there is budgetary overspending, there will be cuts in other budget sectors.'[46] A final deal arranged in August 1999 also compelled the Zimbabwe Reserve Bank to restore foreign currency accounts to local corporations. The deal soon fell apart, however, when Mugabe's government violated several provisions.

International economic integration made less and less sense to Mugabe, who was facing a national political-economic crisis more severe than any other challenge over the previous two decades. His policy reversals were incomplete and haphazard, and because of ongoing problems with government legitimacy (as well as widespread corruption and a reracialisation of political discourses), would not generate an environment conducive to economic revitalisation.

In short, export-led growth was revealed as a fantasy. As in most of Africa during the neoliberal epoch, exports increased but the economy declined. This was mainly due to the fact that as every country was encouraged to export more, the global prices of raw materials fell

**Table 4   Plunging export prices for Zimbabwe's raw materials
(1997–2001, measured in US$ and indexed, 1997=100).[47]**

Commodities	1997	1998	1999	2000	2001
Gold	100	96	95	93	90
Nickel	100	74	101	147	104
Asbestos	100	107	105	141	123
Black granite	100	100	115	105	100
Lithium	100	76	77	77	77
Tobacco	100	79	75	80	83
Cotton	100	72	59	66	55
Citrus	100	103	50	50	48
Flowers	100	92	100	90	88

dramatically during the 1980s–1990s. This trade treadmill generated more pressure for higher export volumes, which in turn led to faster decline. With few exceptions (nickel and asbestos), the problem became even more acute once the East Asian crisis began in 1997, as documented in Table 4.

As Belgian economist Eric Toussaint concludes:

> Since 1980, the value of a basket of sub-Saharan export products has been cut by about half relative to the value of imports from the North. Africa has reacted to this decline by increasing the overall volume of exports onto the world market. But this is not a solution, since prices for these export products have been dropping faster than those of imports from the North.[48]

Likewise, Zimbabwe's relations with international financial markets during the 1980s were very disappointing, once debt servicing became an acute strain. The next section considers the merits of Mugabe's decision in 1999 to halt repayments.

3.   Debt and default

Debt payments were not meant to spiral out of control, as they did within two decades of independence. In early 1983, finance minister Bernard Chidzero predicted Zimbabwe's ratio of debt payments to export earnings – which had soared from 4% at independence to 16% – would 'decline sharply until we estimate it will be about 4% within the next few years, depending on the world's economic position . . . Zimbabwean manufacturers would be in a position to capture the (export) market when the world economy reflated and recession receded.'[49] The World Bank concurred: 'The debt service ratios should begin to decline after 1984 even with large amounts of additional external borrowing.'[50] Large new foreign loans flowed into Zimbabwe. But even as the world economy began to pick up nicely, the predictions were found wanting. Debt servicing spiralled to an untenable 35% of export earnings by 1987.

Substantive rescheduling or debt relief were not under serious consideration. Reflecting its capacity to apply leverage, the IMF terminated a US$315 million line of credit due to a larger than expected fiscal deficit in 1984.[51] Subsequently, reports Colin Stoneman, 'the government took care to meet all debt obligations in full, without any rescheduling, and established a high (and rising) credit rating.'[52] Although the 1984 forex crisis had required Chidzero to restrict profit repatriation (from 50% to 25%) and maintain exchange controls, the World Bank noted in 1987 that with regard to external private debt, Zimbabwe had adopted a 'highly conservative policy' of full repayment.[53] Of US$420 million per annum in loans to Zimbabwe during the 1980s, more than 26% were made by commercial banks.[54]

The costs of the Bank's seal of approval included not only high interest repayments and a refusal to reschedule. There were also conditions on new loans by the Bank, which became Zimbabwe's single largest project lender with more than US$700 million in credits during the 1980s. The Bank initially provided loans 'confined largely to sectors where there was some agreement on policy and where some success was possible in the prevailing distorted macro-economic environment', as one report put it.[55] These included energy, railroads, agriculture, health and family planning, urban development, infrastructure and small business. But conditionality was imposed on many of the Bank loans which included: a 25% increase in interest rates for urban small businesses; an end to official support for agricultural co-operatives and tougher repayment conditions for peasant borrowers; and a veto of a proposed light commuter rail line for Harare's distant township Chitungwiza just as a crippling transport crisis threatened the township's future.[56]

Worse was still to come, for *Esap* was to require US$3.5 billion in new foreign loans over five years (as against existing external debt of US$2.5 billion during the late 1980s). But during the 1992/1993 fiscal year, interest payments on both foreign and domestic debt soared 15% more than projected due to exorbitant interest rates and dramatic (downward) exchange rate movements.[57] Still, Zimbabwe avoided rescheduling and default.

One of the main causes of untenable foreign debt was that with financial liberalisation, large domestic corporate borrowers (including banks) began seeking funding overseas. They had quickly discovered, in the process, that the nominal cost of overseas funds was as low as 7%, compared to in excess of 35% for domestic loans. The Zimbabwe Reserve Bank subsidised, on an immense scale, protection against currency devaluation on behalf of domestic banks' offshore borrowing (the subsidy essentially amounts to the difference between the seductively low 'nominal' interest rate on foreign loans and the 'real' rate at which the loans must be repaid, in hard currency, as the Zimbabwe dollar plunges in value). Reserve Bank losses in buying forward cover were Z$2 billion in 1991 alone, and were still estimated by the World Bank at Z$600 million in 1994.[58]

At the insistence of the IMF and World Bank, monetary policy was tightened in mid-1991. Some government interest rates soared from 27.5% to 44% in a single day, and the 90-day certificates of deposit rates rose from 32.5% to 40%. The stock market began a collapse that would reach 65% over a period of nine months. Banks imposed a wide-ranging credit squeeze.[59] Anticipated international financial support was not immediately forthcoming, and it was only in the middle of 1992 that most promises were finally kept.[60] The interest rate increases did not increase savings rates, which remained below 20% of GDP, given the desperate state in which most Zimbabweans found themselves at that stage.[61]

The high interest rates did, however, attract 'hot money' into Zimbabwe, which played havoc with the stock market. The inflows also required 'sterilisation' – preventing the foreign exchange from generating local inflation – through yet higher interest rates. As *Financial Times* correspondent Tony Hawkins concluded: 'The irony of the Zimbabwe case is that although liberalisation appears to be working in attracting capital inflows and the return of capital flight, it has been having a perverse effect on inflation and the exchange rate, leaving industrialists muttering gloomily about de-industrialisation.'[62]

The portfolio investment of the financiers also flowed out, usually in expensive bursts which then generated more pressure to borrow so as to sustain the capital account. After Zimbabwe's first decade of independence, outstanding foreign debt was US$3.247 billion; it reached US$4.372 billion by 2000, of which government accounted for 76%, public enterprises 18%, and the private sector 6%. At that stage, 90% of foreign debt was comprised of long-term debt. The main multilateral institutions – the World Bank, IMF and African Development Bank – had lent 53%, commercial institutions lent 31%, and bilateral creditors lent 16%.[63]

Repayment was often excruciating. The worst year was 1998, when Zimbabwe spent an historically-unprecedented 38% of export earnings on servicing foreign loans, exceeded that year only by Brazil and Burundi. Of US$4.92 billion in foreign debt at the beginning of the year, the World Bank alone was owed US$870 million. That year, US$980 million was repaid to foreign creditors, while foreign aid fell from its 1995 peak of US$310 million to just US$150 million. Although this was offset somewhat by US$390 million in new loans, exports were down to US$2.57 billion and Gross Domestic Product to US$5.91 billion. So, notwithstanding Zimbabwe's net payment of US$590 million, the debt was reduced only to US$4.72 billion.[64]

The foreign debt is unpayable

It soon became obvious that the debt was simply too large to repay. Finance minister Simba Makoni confirmed this basic fact in Durban at the southern Africa regional session of the World Economic Forum in June 2001: 'We are committed to fulfilling these obligations, but it's clear that our economy is in no state to generate sufficient funds to clear these arrears.'[65] If so, that should be the starting point for debt-cancellation negotiations.

But there are at least five other reasons why Zimbabwe's foreign debt should not be repaid. Firstly, one important basis for arguing that foreign loan repayment is unreasonable, especially to the Bretton Woods Institutions, was the role of South Africa's apartheid-era destabilisation activities. As a result, Zimbabwe's defence budget was increased dramatically during the 1980s, particularly to contend with the threat to Mozambique's Beira Corridor by Pretoria-backed Renamo rebels. As part of its programme to destabilise and weaken regional economies in its wars against advancing black rule, South Africa used economic and military strength to cause trade route diversions towards the use of its ports and harbours, and then contrived freight delays on those same routes. Pretoria's economic destabilisation activities substantially added to Zimbabwe's acute cash-flow and balance of payments problems, forcing the government to borrow in order to finance persistent deficits. According to a study conducted for Jubilee South Africa, apartheid-caused debt for Zimbabwe amounted to US$400 million, while the total economic cost was estimated at US$10 billion.[66]

Meanwhile, the Bretton Woods Institutions lent South Africa more than US$2 billion during the apartheid era, ranging from IMF balance of payment loans in the wake of the Soweto uprising and gold price collapse in 1981, to World Bank loans that funded white South Africans' access to electricity (while black people were denied) and railroad expansion during the 1950s and 1960s, and the construction of a new bulk water supply system linking Lesotho to Johannesburg, as recently as the late 1980s.[67] The Bank and IMF were repaid handsomely for their various apartheid-strengthening loans. The institutions should be made responsible both for paying reparations to black South Africans, and for compensating the region for the massive apartheid-destabilisation costs, which forced so many Frontline States to borrow excessively.

Secondly, it can be reasonably argued that the foreign debt has already been paid, in the form of the excessive squeeze on Zimbabwe's trading and debt repayment capacity. Terms of trade worsened dramatically over the past quarter century. Rapidly falling prices of Zimbabwean exports since the 1997 onset of the East Asian crisis are only the most recent evidence, as shown in Table 4. Moreover, massive amounts of social surplus have already been spent servicing foreign debt, as noted above. Because of the tyranny of compound interest, new debt is continually required to service past debt.

Thirdly, the conditions associated with new IMF and World Bank credits are excessively painful to the most vulnerable Zimbabweans. There were, for example, three main conditions attached to US$200 million in IMF loans promised in 1999, as recorded above. Mugabe was ordered to immediately reverse the only redistributive policies he had adopted in a long time, namely (a) a ban on holding foreign exchange accounts in local banks (which immediately halted the easiest form of capital flight by the country's elites); (b) a 100% customs tax on imported luxury goods; and (c) price controls on staple foods in the wake of several urban riots. Meanwhile, tellingly, the IMF permitted Mugabe to continue the DRC war at a crucial negotiating stage in mid-1999, but on condition that 'there will be cuts in other budget sectors'.[68] In other words, the IMF gave permission to penalise health, education and other badly-defended sectors on behalf of Mugabe's military adventures and business cronies.

Fourthly, there is one reason *not* to default, namely *punishment*, that can be partially discounted. It is possible to withhold foreign debt repayments and live to tell the tale. Over the last two centuries, more than one third of all countries have simultaneously experienced debt crises on four occasions, every fifty years. Those countries defaulted on foreign debts during the 1820s, 1870s and 1930s, and then recovered.

The same would have happened over the past two decades, when once again more than a third of all countries could not service their debts. Unfortunately, because they were not permitted to default by the IMF and World Bank, the desperate countries instead 'rescheduled' their debts, which meant borrowing more money to service old debt, and lowering their citizens' standard of living to squeeze out untenable debt servicing payments each year.

Has Zimbabwe been punished for failing to make most foreign debt payments since 1999? The government's arrears exceeded US$1.25 billion at year-end 2001, according to finance minister Makoni's 2002 budget statement. Some asked, what use is it to pay, for even if the arrears were cleared, the IMF's Stanley Fischer had already told Makoni at the 2001 Durban conference that no new loans would be forthcoming until the government fulfilled new conditions, including getting war vets off commercial farms they had occupied since early 2000. Zanu's political agenda prior to the 2002 presidential election prohibited interference with the farm occupations, thus maintaining the disincentive to repay foreign debt.

Yet to almost everyone's surprise, Zimbabwe was able to get away with the *de facto* default.[69] While no new credit flowed in, neither did the US Marines or other hostile military forces aiming to collect collateral, as had been the practice a century earlier against defaulting countries in Latin America.

Thus the question arose: in the wake of having effectively defaulted on foreign debt and subsequently facing chronic foreign exchange shortages, what further material punishment could the world economy impose on Zimbabwe? Aid was withdrawn by most donors, or redirected to civil society. Trade sanctions proposed by United States senator Jesse Helms would in any case not bite much harder, unless South Africa took up Tsvangirai's January 2002 call for fuel, electricity and transport cuts, as discussed in Chapter Four. So-called 'smart sanctions' approved within the Zimbabwe Democracy and Economic Recovery Act by the US Congress in late 2001 promoted asset seizure and made US travel impossible for Mugabe and key government leaders accused of undemocratic behaviour.

Fifthly, the foreign debt could and should have been addressed more forthrightly as a matter of joint liability. Lenders – especially from Washington – must share the blame for structural adjustment and other failed loans and loan procedures. As noted above, in 1995, the Bank had judged Mugabe's turn to neoliberalism as 'highly satisfactory' (the highest possible ranking). Most macro-economic, sector and financial objectives were 'substantially' achieved (again, the highest mark), said an official Bank evaluation. In reality, the formerly well-balanced economy became de-industrialised and massively indebted. The social wage collapsed as budget cuts bit deep. Gender, race and class inequity soared. And Zimbabwe became much more vulnerable to international shocks.

Over the period 1990–1995, gross domestic product measured by the World Bank in US$ terms fell by a fifth, from US$8.50 billion to US$6.80 billion, as foreign debt soared 55%, from US$3.25 billion to US$5.05 billion. It is true that in 1992 and 1995, droughts reduced Zimbabwe's GDP and human development index. Even so, the World Bank has come to admit – through the Structural Adjustment Participatory Review Initiative – that it misjudged the ability of Zimbabwe's economy to take advantage of liberalisation.[70]

Moreover, not only did conditions on loans throughout the post-independence period lower the standard of living of ordinary Zimbabweans. The foreign credits also created space for degeneracy by elites, who used the hard currency to import inappropriate luxury goods and unsustainable machinery, to be repaid by the future generations. Imports soared: TVs and VCRs by 45% (after adjusting for inflation) from year-end 1990 to 1995; passenger cars by 258% and yachts and pleasure boats by 243%.

Moreover, foreign lenders should also have been aware of the implications of overloading the Zimbabwe economy with debt. The State Loans and Guarantees Act empowers the finance minister to borrow funds to finance budget deficits, *within the government's capacity to repay*. The powers include guarantee for debts taken out by statutory corporations or local authorities, or granted by the Reserve Bank of Zimbabwe. The Act stipulates that external debt servicing shall not exceed 20% (for medium-term loans) and 15% (for long-term loans) of export proceeds. Furthermore, parliament must, in terms of the Act, ratify all loan agreements that the government enters into. Loan agreements are also to be implemented after due consideration by parliament.[71] For more than 40% of loan agreements we have studied, parliamentary approval was only sought *after* the agreement was already in implementation.

Indeed, a recent report by the Comptroller and Auditor General on Zimbabwe's public debt indicates that there are serious shortcomings in the loan management system. For example, inadequate record keeping, absence of monitoring systems and co-ordination and bureaucratic delays in government ministries have all led to the failure to recover loans or meet aid agencies' contractual requirements. Inadequate co-ordination among key institutions has also led to delays and non-disbursement of external loans.[72]

Should Zimbabwe's citizens continue to be liable for foreign debt granted by the Bretton Woods Institutions under such conditions? What blame do the Bank, IMF and African Development Bank – Zimbabwe's three main lenders – share for the failure of *Esap* and the rapid buildup of debt during the early 1990s? And going further back, what proportion of the US$3.25 billion in debt taken on during the 1980s, plus billions of dollars more in repayments on debts incurred during that decade and inherited from Rhodesia, can genuinely be considered legitimate? How many loans were truly necessary, how much hard currency supplied by foreign financiers was diverted for non-essential imports, and how many loans funded projects that were genuinely successful?

Such questions can only be answered through a comprehensive audit of debt. A 'debt tribunal' – as was held by Brazilian civil society groups during 2000 – is probably required to generate broader social understanding and consensus about how to handle the unrepayable debt.

An even more detailed consideration of debt and 'development' lending is required to answer another question: what responsibility do Zimbabwe's masses have for repaying loans that went to projects as diverse as microfinance and electricity lending? Whereas it is obvious that the Zimbabwean state took on too much debt and the structural adjustment and other projects associated with the debt did not pay off, similar findings emerge from these two particular local-level cases, which show the futility of 'solving' underdevelopment with more Washington-sourced loans.

Peasants fight finance

Part of Zimbabwe's foreign debt was contracted from the World Bank allegedly to support peasants. Historical background may be useful, because the post-independence era was not the first effort to draw peasants into the market – nor the first time that such a crude approach was rewarded with market failure.

During Zimbabwe's colonial era, an earlier generation of loan programmes for small-scale black farmers – invariably men – expanded as an integral element of the white Rhodesian regime's rural pacification strategy. 'At the risk of being criticised for seemingly over-playing the theme of credit,' recommended the government's Advisory Committee on Economic Resources in 1962, 'we must once again state how much importance we place upon the provision of adequate, soundly administered credit for the stimulation of both the petty and the somewhat more expansive activities of the rural producer.'[73]

But conditions were suboptimal. Rural problems reflected not only the looting of land, cattle and labour during the initial decades of colonial settlement. Environmental problems emerged due to overcrowding. Formal laws and regulations – especially the Land Apportionment Act of 1930 – cemented the injustice of settler-colonialism.[74]

Still, the colonial regime introduced various kinds of pacification and modernisation strategies to divide-and-rule the rural masses. During the late 1940s, a credit scheme began for some of the relatively better-off black farmers, who formed the African Farmers' Union. In 1959, these farmers adopted a conference resolution in favour of boycotting a 10% tax on their produce on the grounds it was discriminatory. Their appeal went unheeded, so they responded by lowering loan repayment levels significantly.[75]

By the early 1960s, new contradictions in the rural pacification strategy emerged just as the availability of government credit increased dramatically, corresponding to the 1962 Advisory Committee report. The black farmers required major changes in basic production and marketing conditions. Without these, credit could not solve debilitating problems of racial disparity in access to good land, state resources and agricultural markets. Arrears and defaults by both black farmers and rural traders increased dramatically, to more than 10 000 by 1964.[76] 'Co-operative officers spent an increasing proportion of their time as debt collectors to the detriment of their other co-operative functions,' according to the Whitsun Foundation, the World Bank-linked liberal business lobby that strongly promoted small farm credit:

> A number of organisations had offered facilities without adequate supervision or knowledge of peasant farming conditions and experienced severe losses, resulting in either their closure or the withdrawal of their credit schemes . . . Loans would appear to have been issued fairly liberally and without adequate recovery plans . . . The poor level of repayments almost brought the demise of the co-operative movement as it became heavily indebted to the Agricultural Loan Fund.[77]

Would independence change matters? Ironically, within a decade, in spite of rather more legitimate government-sourced finance, the result was an even higher, not lower, rate of small farmer default. At that stage, Zimbabwean agriculture was roughly stratified as follows: 4 800 Large Scale Commercial Farms (LSCFs) (controlled mainly by white farmers and farm corporations); 8 500 black Small Scale Commercial Farms (SSCFs); 57 000 Resettlement Area (RA) farms; and approximately one million Communal Area (CA) peasant households, of which 10% produced 90% of all CA maize output. (The latter three are considered 'small farmers'.) From 1980–2000, an estimated 70 000 households moved from CA areas to RA farms.

For most peasants, the promise of land redistribution was never kept, until in 2000 the land invasions and fast-track resettlement began at the point at which it appeared Zanu would lose power. Earlier, government officials and cronies were well served by purchase of large-scale white farms, and co-operative farms were disempowered by both the government and World Bank.[78]

Indeed, the 1993 Land Designation Act was 'shelved', as member of parliament Lazarus Nzarayebani complained in late 1994, because it was 'not in conformity with the World Bank and IMF'.[79] Instead of thorough-going land reform, Washington's strategy for the Zimbabwean countryside was to expand credit dramatically during the early 1980s. Financiers included the parastatal Agricultural Finance Corporation (AFC) and its partners in the World Bank and foreign aid agencies, and local commercial banks with long histories of serving white farmers.[80]

Loan volumes to black farmers soared after independence. Given the influence of the Whitsun Foundation, the institutions and processes established during the colonial era were retained intact, and mainly just expanded. CA farmers received six times more loans (worth ten times more) from 1979/1980 to 1980/1981, and RA and SSCF farmers also witnessed dramatic increases in credit flows. The state's loan system catalysed renewed interest in black agricultural credit supplied by traders, tobacco auction floors and chemical and pesticide manufacturers. Yet as the World Bank recorded in 1982, 'In almost all cases they suffered heavy losses, primarily due to lack of management and this led to severe curtailment or abandonment of credit facilities' by the firms.[81]

The Bank responded with a US$30.4 million credit that the AFC used to finance 27 000 CA farmers and 4 000 SSCFs. Existing AFC operations were by and large endorsed, and within a few years of independence, 60% of the AFC's 'moderately conservative' and 'generally competent' staff (in the Bank's words) were making loans to small farmers. The Bank approved the AFC 'stop-order' system whereby marketing boards would first deduct loan repayments before paying peasants for their harvest. Loan conditionality imposed by the Bank compelled the AFC to raise interest rates. Nevertheless, thanks to the flood of money, the AFC raised its lending volume by 133% to CA and RA farmers in 1985.[82]

Women struggled under even more onerous conditions, for their first formal access to credit only came after the 1982 passage of The Age of Majority Act. The AFC's existing gender bias was exacerbated by high female illiteracy and patriarchal barriers to acquiring the AFC marketing board card (a prerequisite for credit). Women accounted for only 30% of borrowers, far smaller than their proportion of heads of farm households. Specific World Bank programmes were aimed at increasing women's access, but the context remained one of modernisation theory and increasing rural desperation.

How did Zimbabwe's AFC programme fare over time? Arrears on short-term loans were 33% in 1983 (short-term loans outnumbered long-term loans by ten-to-one). The ambitious expansion programme was simply not geared to the existing realities facing small farmers: unpredictable markets for small farmer products; barriers and bottlenecks in input provision, product marketing and distribution, transport and communications; drought; and other non-economic factors.[83] Still, the flow of credit continued rising until 1988, when the AFC lent to 18% of all CA farmers (a total of 94 000). But this impressive rate fell to 13% (50 000) the following year, and by 1991 was down to 5%.[84] SSCFs followed similar trends, and RA farmers witnessed a decline in AFC loans from 20 000 to 5 000 from 1984 to 1989.

Affordability was one factor in the waning of credit for peasants. A typical lender's overhead and collection costs represent 15–22% of the amount of a small loan, including incorporation of a 4% default rate. In Zimbabwe, the AFC cost was 24% due to very high administration costs (11%), with bad debt pegged at 4% – far lower than ultimately transpired. Yet to small farmers, even standard AFC loans that were the equivalent of a few hundred US dollars represented enormous burdens when, according to one agriculture ministry survey in 1989, the average net crop profit per hour of labour was just US$0.15.[85]

Under such conditions, debt easily became a slippery slope to financial ruin. The World Bank, however, continued to focus on crop production based on credit, notwithstanding the problem that the AFC scheme was capable of tapping into the small farmers' income stream only via the marketing boards' stop-order system. But stop-order repayment became relatively easy for peasants to evade thanks to an emerging informal market or to using non-defaulting friends or relatives for the purpose of marketing produce through official channels.

By 1987, the AFC's bad debts rose to more than 60% of total AFC costs, because of droughts; an 18-month breakdown of the AFC's computer system; the erosion of the stop-order system; and the biased deployment of AFC officers in Harare instead of in the field. Citing these reasons, one World Bank report neglected to note that to be found behind each reason (aside from the brief drought) was the Bank's own procedural approval and conditionality on the original 1982 loan.[86] The Bank proceeded to grant another loan: US$36.3 million over 20 years. Instead of arresting the soaring arrears rate, the new loan and improved procedures had the opposite effect. By 1990, the proportion of borrowers in arrears reached 80% of CA farmers, 68% of SSCF farmers and 77% of RA farmers.[87]

How did these flawed loan programmes appear from the bottom up? According to a *Sunday Times* journalist in 1992, 'A number of resettled farmers are fleeing the resettlement areas with their AFC debts unpaid. They accuse the AFC of exploitation through what they alleged to be its exorbitant interest charges and unreasonable conditions.'[88] In a detailed Midlands case study, Michael Drinkwater observed that 'the increase in credit use means farmers have to market more to stay solvent . . . at the household level it is commonly debts not profits that are on the rise.'[89]

The World Bank pushed the AFC to grab collateral, including meagre farm utensils seized by the police during the early 1990s. Front-page newspaper warnings with photographs of recovered wheelbarrows, hoes and shovels had no apparent effect on the small farmers. As the AFC credit was then withdrawn, fertiliser companies suffered and began to extend their own credits.

Even though it had failed to truly confront the growing arrears problem either practically or intellectually, the World Bank continued lending to the Zimbabwe government, but with the proviso that the AFC shift its resources back to large-scale commercial farmers. Small farm defaulters initially did not resist this shift. Then, as drought became widespread in 1992, small farmers began demanding rollover of existing AFC debt. Under pressure, the AFC approved such forbearance, but this was quickly reversed due to insufficient funds.[90]

The AFC had retreated rapidly from small loans, but it never shook the bad debt problem. AFC chief executive Taka Mutunhu conceded that of a 1993 AFC budget approaching Z$300 million, losses due to small farmer defaults would require Z$45 million in provisions, but even that was not adequate and by early 1994 the AFC was facing an additional Z$11 million deficit for small farm credit. It was only by halting the hated stop-order method of loan recovery in 1994 that the AFC began to increase recoveries.[91]

What conclusion did the World Bank draw from this and other wretched experiences promoting the neoliberal-modernisation version of rural finance? One Bank economist, Sababathy Thillairajah, conceded in 1993 that 'those co-operative rural credit and banking operations in the villages [of Africa] with the least direct financial input from donor agencies did best . . . [My advice to colleagues is] leave the people alone. When someone comes and asks you for money, the best favour you can give them is to say no.' His advice was, however, rejected.[92]

After all, microcredit programmes – particularly those designated for women farmers – remain convenient as a means for the Bank and like-minded agencies to deflect criticism that they are not reaching the poorest of the poor with market-oriented strategies. In 1995, the Bank introduced a US$200 million line of credit aimed at poor women, just prior to the UN gender conference in Beijing. To criticisms that this was just the latest fad, Bank gender expert Minh Chau Nguyen replied, 'Fashion comes and fashion goes but I don't think it is a fashionable area. Investing in women, particularly in credit for micro-enterprises, is a very effective way for reducing poverty.'[93]

But is agricultural credit – sourced from hard-currency World Bank loans, lent under neoliberal conditionality, and recycled through bureaucratic state agencies in local currency – the most useful input for African peasants, especially women? The monetisation of the masses of rural Zimbabwe certainly failed, repeatedly, because the context of a rural economic structure profoundly biased in favour of large-scale farming could not be changed through microcredit. Instead, finance made small farmers more dependent, and exposed their vulnerabilities to a variety of hostile forces: the vagaries of state interference (including pricing policies influenced by large capitalist interests and bureaucratic manoeuvres), speculative financial markets, foul weather, and external attempts to alter the chosen configuration of land, environment, cultural norms, material inputs, crop choices, etc.

Not only peasants, but policy-makers and international development financiers discovered the hard way that deep-rooted contradictions in Zimbabwe's agricultural system – including uneven input supplies, chronic excess production, and unpredictable state-controlled marketing and distribution rules faced by small farm producers – could not be resolved merely by expanding access to finance. That did not, however, stop more than a few honest practitioners (like Thillairajah) from propagating the myth that to solve rural underdevelopment, peasant credit is vital. The same problems in South Africa, in the wake of 1998–1999 interest rate increases which devastated the microlending industry, did not prevent the dogma that instead of the redistribution of income, the unemployed masses and poor rural women simply required better access to credit.

Perhaps humility in the granting of rural microcredit would require an even greater shock, namely, a repayment crisis at the world's most lauded scheme, the Grameen Bank of Bangladesh. 'To many, Grameen proves that capitalism can work for the poor as well as the rich,' according to the *Wall Street Journal,* as the bank 'helped inspire an estimated 7 000 so-called microlenders with 25 million poor clients worldwide'. Yet the world's leading newspaper of the rich had to concede in late 2001 that a fifth of the bank's loans were more than a year past-due: 'Grameen would be showing steep losses if the bank followed the accounting practices recommended by institutions that help finance microlenders through low-interest loans and private investments.' New competitors, adverse weather conditions and a backlash by borrowers left Grameen to justify rescheduling loans that were unpaid over as much as two years instead of writing them down, leaving the entire world microcredit industry 'alarmed'. Not even extreme pressure techniques – such as removing tin roofs from delinquent women's houses – improved repayment rates in the most crucial areas, where Grameen had earlier won its global reputation.[94]

Even if the 1990s fad for microfinance was in reality mainly hype and hucksterism, the more general question must continually be posed: can capitalism actually work for the masses, on the world's periphery, especially through introduction of a pressure-ridden credit system that relies on little more than women's mutual aid by way of a palliative? The Zimbabwean rural credit system promoted by the Rhodesian government, the Whitsun Foundation, the post-independence AFC, the World Bank, and other such agencies was simply not, the evidence strongly suggests, a product greatly appreciated by Zimbabwe's small farmers. Their response was to default, notwithstanding the fact that this made it impossible for the borrower to ever access credit again.

Most importantly, perhaps, a macropolitical lesson emerges from this case: by refusing to countenance serious land reform, and by instead promoting willing-buyer, willing-seller deals plus microcredit based on residual-colonial rural relations of production and reproduction, the World Bank and its local allies ensured that the land problem would not be resolved. It was only a matter of time before the contradictions in the countryside would make themselves felt in the society as a whole.

Kariba and electricity pricing

Another case from which to debate whether liability for bad 'development' debt should go to the lender, is the Kariba hydro-electric dam, whose costs continued to be evident over a period of more than half a century. It is illustrative not only because the World Bank's largest loan to date overwhelmingly benefitted corporate capital at the expense of the entire society, which began repayment on the loan prior to Smith's 1965 default. In addition, after independence, the Bank's policy influence ensured that the *povo* (the masses) would never benefit from the dam's generation of hydro-electricity.

In Chapter One, we considered the Kariba Dam as an example of colonial-era power relations, indebtedness and eco-social destruction. Notwithstanding the costs involved, after 1980, there were grand hopes that Kariba's hydro-electric power would help light up rural Zimbabwe. In 1980, only 14% of Zimbabwe's households – virtually none in rural areas – had access to electricity, in spite of a 9% annual national growth of electricity consumption during the 1970s.

At independence, hydro-electricity generation was still responsible for nearly 30% of the national grid's supply. Kariba was perhaps better known as a major tourism complex, whose high-quality accommodation and recreational facilities were and still are enjoyed by a tiny minority of extremely wealthy Zimbabweans. But merely from the standpoint of energy supply, the distributional problems associated with Kariba hydro-electricity deserve comment. The case also illustrates the power of the Bank to commodify, commercialise and ultimately privatise what should really be considered a basic need: household electricity.

Within the national grid supply, pricing of Kariba hydro-electricity was micromanaged by the World Bank following a joint study with the United Nations Development Program (UNDP) in 1982 and a Bank energy sector loan in 1984. The Zimbabwe government, assisted by the German government, also independently attempted to get a rural electrification scheme going in 1985. But in 1987, still only 20% of households were electrified, and there has been no subsequent progress. Given the high price increases of the late 1990s, the percentage of Zimbabweans who use electricity is assumed to have decreased. (In contrast, a rapid 1990s electrification programme in South Africa raised the household access rate from below 20% to above 65%.)

The failure of the country's 1980–1990s electrification programme is one of the country's most worrisome development challenges. In addition to the obvious economic merits and increased productivity that comes from having electricity, there are crucial gender, public health and environmental benefits. Women would be the primary beneficiaries of expanding electricity to rural households, given the enormous time they spend in gathering fuelwood, and the hazards of non-electrical energy sources. Other benefits of electrification include abatement of respiratory diseases that activate HIV/Aids opportunistic infections, prevention of paraffin burns and noxious fumes, halting deforestation caused by the need for fuelwood, and improving the environmental conditions in high-density areas that would otherwise rely on coal or wood for heating and cooking.

Even though the Kariba Dam had been paid off by this stage, the World Bank remained a crucial player, because it could impose new, market-oriented conditionalities on electricity pricing. Unfortunately, the Bank persistently refused to take the positive eco-socio-economic 'externalities' fully into account when pricing electricity, so the benefits of electrification never reached those who could not afford market-related rates.

As a result, in 1982, the Bank and UNDP argued that Zimbabweans' 'income levels will not rise sufficiently to encourage fuel substitution by the African population'. Therefore, instead, 'an extensive reforestation program is urgently needed.' These conclusions were based on the assumption that 'rational energy pricing policies' would replace the slightly subsidised rate structure then in operation. The Bank and UNDP went even further to downplay positive benefits from electricity, by revising the 'income elasticity demand for energy' downwards by 33%. This allowed them to downgrade the merits of providing retail electricity to the masses.[95]

Had such policies not been adopted, there would have been ample room for growth in the energy sector through residential electrification, with resulting economic multiplier effects in electrical machinery and appliances, as well as enhanced productivity of the society. But such an outcome relied upon a strong political commitment to electrification that would extend services beyond market determinations of affordability. That commitment was never shown, and so a US$105 million Bank energy sector loan in 1982 – mainly to expand the Hwange thermal plant – was conditional upon, amongst other changes, a dramatic 60%

increase in retail prices and the prohibition of new debt-financed investment until the Zimbabwe Electricity Supply Authority's (Zesa's) debt/equity ratio fell below 60/40.[96]

In 1987, the Bank granted a US$44.4 million loan for refurbishing the Kariba facilities. It too was conditional on 'economic pricing for energy products'. But 'economic pricing' was based on an 18% profit rate, as recommended by accountants Coopers and Lybrand. The existing 'estimated opportunity cost of capital' was, at the time, just 5%, so the 18% rate was another artificial deterrent to rolling out the electricity grid to poor people.[97] Because such extreme measures were taken to avoid cross-subsidisation to sub-economic consumers, the Bank could claim that it 'made a strong impact on strengthening the organisation of the power subsector and its financial situation'.[98]

The Bank then vetoed a proposed expansion of the Kariba South hydro-electric plant in 1989. According to the *Financial Gazette*, 'The World Bank is understood to be considering the withholding of all future loans for Zimbabwe's electric power projects because the Zimbabwe Government, against expert advice, has decided to proceed with the Z$300 million Kariba South Extension scheme.'[99]

By 1991, frustrated Zesa researchers complained publicly that the Bank's conditionality had resulted in an

> apparent inability of the Bank to carry out timely reviews and decisions on Zesa's investment programmes . . . It is also a requirement for Zesa to finance 40% of its capital investments from internally generated funds, which is an extremely onerous condition as it imposes high tariffs on consumers, with negative consequences on the economy . . . *The World Bank's influence and policies in the electricity sector are therefore inconsistent with the Bank's supposed support for the country's economic structural adjustment programme.'* (original emphasis)[100]

During the early 1990s, when *Esap* was in full swing, Zesa was 'permitted to adjust consumer tariffs to cover specific cost categories agreed with the Bank' thanks to a conditionality on the second tranche of the Bank's *Esap* loan, and as a result, 'large tariff increases [were] effected.'[101] One result of the Bank's pressure to raise prices was that by 1996, Zesa was only providing electricity to 21% of the population. Promises continued; within a decade electricity would reach half the population and within four decades all Zimbabweans would have power. This would depend in part upon a proposed dam and 1 600 megaWatt hydropower station planned for the Batoka Gorge, to be financed by the Bank, in the process destroying Africa's greatest whitewater river run, directly below Victoria Falls.[102]

Zambia opposed that dam on the grounds that one of its functions is to supply water to Bulawayo. If Batoka Gorge proceeds, once again, as with Kariba, geopolitics will play an important role in the ultimate process of dam financing. And as with Kariba, the pricing of electricity will, following a series of above-inflation Zesa tariff increases, run the risk of actually lowering the coverage of Zimbabwean households using electricity. In sum, the case of Kariba hydro-electricity raises the more general issue of why the Zimbabwean citizenry should be required to pay for foreign debt which did not meet social needs.

Conclusion: Lessons of neoliberalism?

The foreign debt treadmill and balance of payments crisis that resulted from loans such as Kariba and subsequent energy debts were amplified by Esap, which pushed foreign debt as a percent of GDP from 8.4% to 21.8% from 1991–1996. The problem was mirrored in the meteoric rise of domestic debt. A series of policy options, including those practised by Mugabe's government and those proposed by the MDC, are considered in Chapter Five. But some general conclusions can also be drawn from this excessively brief survey of post-independence economics and international financing, and from the previous chapter's review of pre-independence processes.

Most importantly, international economic integration prior to 1980 entailed severe imbalances, while on the other hand at least two decade-long periods of inward-oriented capital accumulation (1932–1941 and 1965–1974) were the years of both fastest GDP growth and most coherent economic linkages. In both cases, the economy prospered under circumstances that included the adoption of brutally racist state policies, but as argued below, this feature was not *responsible* for economic growth, but rather *impaired* sustainable economic development by undermining prospects for mass consumption.

The skewed inheritance meant that, from the 1980s, the overall structure of Zimbabwe's economy and society left it ill-suited for rapid liberalisation and international economic integration, given that these were accompanied by extremely high real interest rates, a dramatic upsurge in inflation and devastating cuts in social spending. Although Mugabe often confused matters by using rhetoric that was extremely hostile to the Washington financial institutions, three orthodox finance ministers (Bernard Chidzero, Ariston Chambati and Herbert Murerwa) and two Reserve Bank governors (Kenneth Moyana and Leonard Tsumba) followed a fiscally-conservative, deregulatory agenda until late 1997. As Deloitte Touche had concluded even before the adoption of *Esap*: 'A close analysis of post-independence Zimbabwe reveals a pragmatic and indeed conservative government policy as far as monetary and financial strategies are concerned.'[103]

The results of orthodox policies, especially the trade/financial liberalisation and conditionality associated with *Esap*, included an amplification of existing high levels of inequality. As a direct result of funding cuts and cost-recovery policies, exacerbated by the HIV/Aids pandemic, Zimbabwe's brief 1980s rise in literacy and health indicators was dramatically reversed. In contrast, the stock market reached extraordinary peaks in mid-1991 and mid-1997, but these were followed by crashes of more than 50% within a few months along with massive hikes in interest rates. More steadily, manufacturing sector output crashed from peak 1991 levels, and the standard of living of the average Zimbabwean worker was devastated. Comparing other indices of pre-*Esap* and *Esap*-era economic activity, total formal-sector jobs (including agricultural) rose from just under a million at independence to 1.244 million in 1991 and then remained flat. Urban employment (not commercial farmwork) rose from 454 000 in early 1980 to 620 000 in 1991 before falling back to 590 000 by year-end 1995. Average annual earnings (after inflation) rose a half-percent each year from 1980–1990, but fell by more than 10% annually from 1991–1995. Between 1980 and 1990, the Zimbabwe dollar lost 70% of its value against the US dollar; between 1991 and 1995 (half as long a period), it lost 67%. Inflation averaged 13.4% from 1980–1990, and 27.6% from 1991–1995.[104]

In sum, international economic integration, excessive foreign debts and their offspring in the form of *Esap* together had a pernicious impact on Zimbabwe. This appears true both historically and especially in recent years. We come to the conclusion that whatever the many other flaws of Robert Mugabe and Zanu, the first post-independence government was driven into a cul-de-sac by the forces of neoliberalism, both local and global. Political degeneration was the next logical process, once it became evident around 1997 that *Esap* was incapable of lifting Zimbabwe from chronic dependency, and had indeed greatly exacerbated underdevelopment.

Economic constraints to the country's democratisation remained formidable. And as a result, it would be up to the nascent social, labour and related movements of the post-*Esap* era – not the government, the political opposition or organised business – to change Zimbabwe's history, via an inward-oriented, low-debt, economic development strategy. It is the multifaceted political challenge, especially in relation to the balance of forces within the two main parties, to which we turn next.

Notes

1. Hinds, M. (1990), *Outwards vs. Inwards Development Strategy*, Washington, World Bank, pp. 15–17.

2. United Nations Development Programme, Poverty Reduction Forum and Institute for Development Studies (2000), *Zimbabwe: Human Development Report 1999*, Harare.

3. Interviews, July 1987, November 2001.

4. Mandaza, I. (1986), 'The Post-White Settler Colonial Situation', in I. Mandaza (ed), *Zimbabwe: The Political Economy of Transition, 1980–86*, Dakar, Codesria, p. 53.

5. Mkandawire, T. (1984), ' "Home-Made" (?) Austerity Measures: The Case of Zimbabwe', Paper presented at seminar on Austerity Policies in Africa: Under IMF Control, Dakar, Senegal, 19–21 June, p. 43.

6. Murapa, R. (1977), 'Geography, Race, Class and Power in Rhodesia', Working Paper, Council for the Development of Economic and Social Research in Africa, presented at the Conference on the Special Problems of Landlocked and Least Developed Countries in Africa, University of Zambia, Lusaka, 27–31 July, p. 28.

7. There are many sources, of which the most recent and balanced is Alexander, J., J. McGregor and T. Ranger (2000), *Violence and Memory: One Hundred Years in the 'Dark Forests' of Matabeleland*, Oxford, James Currey, Chapters Eight and Nine.

8. Mugabe, R.G. (1989), 'The Unity Accord: Its Promise for the Future', in C. Banana (ed), *Turmoil and Tenacity: Zimbabwe 1890–1990*, Harare, College Press, p. 358.

9. African-American Institute/American Bar Association Conference (1982), 'Investment in Zimbabwe', Conference Proceedings, New York, 26 March, p. 4. For a brief unofficial biography of Chidzero, see Bond, *Uneven Zimbabwe*, Chapter Seven.

10. Cited in Hanlon, J. (1988), 'Destabilisation and the Battle to Reduce Dependence', in C. Stoneman (ed), *Zimbabwe's Prospects*, London, Macmillan.

11. *Sunday Mail*, 10 December 1989.

12. For details, see Bond, *Uneven Zimbabwe*, Chapters Seven–Twelve.

13. *Financial Times*, 21 August 1989.

14. Bond's book *Uneven Zimbabwe* demonstrates how massive over-investment occurred during the early 1970s. There was a limited absorption capacity for final products and production inputs by both the captive, small (white) luxury-consumer class and by (white-owned) manufacturing firms which were producing on ever-shorter runs. The vast, unmet socio-economic requirements

of the masses of (black) workers and peasants were downplayed in state economic planning. While Rhodesian UDI was initially a great economic success due mainly to the financial 'hothouse' factor described in Chapter One, it was the classical capitalist tendency to over-accumulate capital, driven by over-investment, that led to such a dramatic decline from 1975–1978. Zimbabwe's post-independence economy never subsequently recovered.

15. World Bank (1989), 'Zimbabwe: Private Investment and Government Policy', Southern Africa Department, Washington, pp. 23, 56.
16. World Bank, 'Zimbabwe: Private Investment and Government Policy', p. 23.
17. World Bank (1982), 'Report and Recommendation of the President of the IDA to the Executive Directors on a Proposed Credit in an Amount Equivalent to US$1.2 million to the Government of Zimbabwe for a Petroleum Fuels Supply Technical Assistance Project', Energy Division, Eastern Africa Regional Office, Washington, Annex IX, p. 39.
18. World Bank (1983), 'Report and Recommendation of the President of the International Bank for Reconstruction and Development to the Executive Directors on a Proposed Loan in an Amount Equivalent to US$70.6 million to the Republic of Zimbabwe for a Proposed Manufacturing Export Promotion Project', Eastern Africa Projects Department, Washington, p. 13.
19. Sunday Mail, 6 October 1985.
20. World Bank (1987), 'Zimbabwe: A Strategy for Sustained Growth', Southern Africa Department, Africa Region, Washington, p. 70.
21. Riddell, R. (1990), Manufacturing Africa, London, Overseas Development Institute, p. 382.
22. Riddell, R. (1983), 'A Critique of "Zimbabwe: Government Policy and the Manufacturing Sector: A Study Prepared for the Ministry of Industry and Energy Development, April 1983, Submitted by Dr. Doris J. Jansen"', Unpublished paper, Confederation of Zimbabwe Industries, Harare, July.
23. World Bank, 'Zimbabwe: A Strategy for Sustained Growth'. For interpretations, see Cliffe, L. (1991), 'Were they Pushed or did they Jump: Zimbabwe and the World Bank', Southern Africa Report, March; Dashwood, H. (1996), 'The Relevance of Class to the Evolution of Zimbabwe's Development Strategy, 1980–1991', Journal of Southern African Studies, 22, 1.
24. Financial Gazette, 5 September 1991.
25. World Bank (1995), 'Project Completion Report: Zimbabwe: Structural Adjustment Program', Country Operations Division, Southern Africa Department, Washington, p. 35.
26. Zimbabwe Economic Review, September 1995.
27. World Bank, 'Project Completion Report: Zimbabwe: Structural Adjustment Program', p. 7.
28. Wetherell, I. (1993), 'Good Governance: Separating the Reality and the Rhetoric', Financial Gazette, 9 June.
29. Financial Gazette, 5 January 1995.
30. Zimbabwe Congress of Trade Unions (1996), Beyond Esap, Harare, p. 3.
31. Gibbon, P. (1995), Introduction in P. Gibbon (ed), Structural Adjustment and the Working Poor in Zimbabwe, Uppsala, Nordiska Afrikainstitutet, p. 13.
32. World Bank, 'Project Completion Report: Zimbabwe: Structural Adjustment Program', p. 163.

33. ZCTU, *Beyond Esap*, p. 52.
34. ZCTU, *Beyond Esap*, p. 49.
35. Source for both Tables 2 and 3: Central Statistical Office *Quarterly Digest of Statistics*.
36. *Financial Gazette*, 28 November 1991.
37. ZCTU, *Beyond Esap*, p. 68.
38. World Bank (1995), 'Zimbabwe: Achieving Shared Growth', Southern Africa Department, Washington, Vol II, p. 3.
39. UNDP/PRF/IDS, Zimbabwe: Human Development Report 1999, pp. 33, 36.
40. World Bank (1995), 'Zimbabwe: Performance Audit Report', Southern Africa Department, Washington, p. 9.
41. World Bank, 'Project Completion Report: Zimbabwe: Structural Adjustment Program', p. 23.
42. World Bank, 'Zimbabwe: Performance Audit Report', p. 20.
43. Sachikonye, L. (1995), 'From Equity and Participation to Structural Adjustment: State and Social Forces in Zimbabwe', in D. Moore and G. Schmitz (eds), *Debating Development Discourses: Institutional and Popular Perspectives*, London, Macmillan and New York, St Martin's Press.
44. *Wall Street Journal*, 12 April 1999.
45. *Financial Gazette*, 12 March 1999.
46. Agence France Press, 20 July 1999.
47. Units vary but are consistent across commodity. Source: Government of Zimbabwe (2001), 'Budget Statement 2002', Presented to Parliament by Minister of Finance and Economic Development Simba Makoni, Harare, 1 November, p. 31.
48. Toussaint, E. (2001), 'Debt in SubSaharan Africa on the Eve of the Third Millennium', Unpublished paper, Committee for the Abolition of Third World Debt, Brussels.
49. *Herald*, 22 February 1983.
50. World Bank (1982), 'Zimbabwe: Issues and Options in the Energy Sector', Report of the Joint UNDP/World Bank Energy Sector Assessment Program, Washington, p. 3.
51. *Herald*, 23 August 1984.
52. Stoneman, C. (1990), 'The Impending Failure of Structural Adjustment: Lessons from Zimbabwe', Paper presented to the Canadian Association of African Studies, Dalhousie University, 11 May, p. 2.
53. World Bank, 'Zimbabwe: A Strategy for Sustained Growth', pp. 20–22.
54. Surprisingly, however, Zimbabwe was rated only 'C' quality by Euromoney debt evaluators in 1987. Hughes, J. (1987), *Sovereign Risk*, London, Euromoney Publications.
55. World Bank, 'Zimbabwe: Performance Audit Report', p. 16.
56. Maliyami, S. (1990), 'The World Bank Trap', *Moto*, 84.
57. World Bank, 'Project Completion Report: Zimbabwe: Structural Adjustment Program', p. 35.
58. World Bank, 'Project Completion Report: Zimbabwe: Structural Adjustment Program', p. 21.
59. *Financial Gazette*, 31 October 1991.

60. Gibbon, Introduction, p. 14.
61. Muzulu, J. (1993), 'Exchange Rate Depreciation and Structural Adjustment: The Case of the Manufacturing Sector in Zimbabwe, 1980–91', Doctoral dissertation, University of Sussex.
62. *Financial Gazette*, 28 June 1995.
63. Ministry of Finance, Budget Statements.
64. World Bank (2000), *Global Debt Tables, 2000*, Washington.
65. *Financial Gazette*, 14 June 2001.
66. http://www.aidc.org.za
67. The latter entailed the Bank opening a secret London trust fund which the ANC accused of being a 'financial sanctions-busting' exercise. For more details, see Bond, P. (2001), *Against Global Apartheid: South Africa meets the World Bank, IMF and International Finance*, Cape Town, University of Cape Town Press, Chapter Three.
68. Agence France Press, 20 July 1999.
69. Instead of repaying foreign debt, the government captured 40% of foreign exchange earned by tobacco and other exports to pay for fuel and electricity, which were sold to the National Oil Company of Zimbabwe and the Zimbabwe Electricity Supply Authority at the low, fixed exchange rate. Virtually all other imports were priced at the parallel rate, which was sometimes seven times as high as the official rate during 2001.
70. http://www.sapri.org/
71. The Audit and Exchequer Act governs public expenditures, and sections 26 and 27 indicate that the executive arm of government retains powers, in the form of special warrants, to direct the minister of finance and economic development to withdraw from the Consolidated Revenue Fund, even in advance of appropriation by parliament. In this case, the reasons for overriding parliament and other stipulated procedures may simply be stated as funds required for meeting expenditures that the president considers, among other factors, to be important 'in terms of the public interest'. The interpretation of 'public interest' is, however, subject to controversy, especially when this is not an output of participatory processes.
72. Comptroller and Auditor General (2000), 'Report on the Management of the Public Debt: Disbursement and Recovery of Loans and Donor Funds', Ministry of Finance, Economic Planning and Development, Government of Zimbabwe, Harare.
73. Advisory Committee, *Report*, p. 54.
74. Palmer, R. (1977), *Land and Racial Domination in Rhodesia*, London, Heinemann.
75. Yudelman, M. (1964), *Africans on the Land*, Cambridge, Harvard University Press, p. 158; Cheater, A. (1984), *Idioms of Accumulation*, Gweru, Mambo Press, p. 167.
76. Sowelem, R.A. (1967), *Towards Financial Independence in a Developing Economy*, London, George Allen and Unwin, p. 193; Whitsun Foundation (1980), 'Peasant Sector Credit Plan for Zimbabwe', Project 3.04(2), Salisbury, Whitsun Foundation, p. 39.
77. Whitsun Foundation, 'Peasant Sector Credit Plan for Zimbabwe', pp. 29, 36.
78. Bond, *Uneven Zimbabwe*, Chapter Ten.

79. *Financial Gazette*, 9 February 1995.
80. Later, during the late 1990s, the AFC was relaunched as Agribank.
81. World Bank (1982), 'Zimbabwe: Small Farm Credit Project', Staff Appraisal Report, Eastern Africa Projects Department, Washington, p. 7.
82. World Bank, 'Zimbabwe: Small Farm Credit Project', pp. 42, 43.
83. World Bank (1991), 'Zimbabwe: Agriculture Sector Memorandum', Southern Africa Department, Agricultural Operations Division, Washington, Vol II, pp. 176, 187.
84. In comparison, Asian and Latin American small farmers average 15% access to formal credit.
85. World Bank, 'Zimbabwe: Agriculture Sector Memorandum', Vol III, pp. 130–145.
86. Kydd, J.G. (1990), 'Rural Financial Intermediation', Background document for Agriculture Division, Southern Africa Department, Washington, World Bank, p. 106.
87. Kydd, 'Rural Financial Intermediation', pp. 101–104.
88. Mwale, M. (1992), 'Resettlement Programme: An Economic Policy of a Political Gamble?', *Sunday Times*, 19 January, p. 9.
89. Drinkwater, M.J. (1991), *The State and Agrarian Change in Zimbabwe*, London, Macmillan, p. 89.
90. *Financial Gazette*, 24 June 1993.
91. *Financial Gazette*, 8 and 15 July 1993.
92. *Financial Gazette*, 20 May 1993.
93. *African Agenda*, October 1995.
94. *Wall Street Journal*, 27 November 2001.
95. World Bank, 'Zimbabwe: Issues and Options in the Energy Sector'; and World Bank (1982), 'Zimbabwe: Power Project', Energy Division, Eastern Africa Regional Office, Washington, Report 3884-ZIM, 16 November.
96. World Bank, 'Zimbabwe: Power Project', pp. 33, 40–41.
97. World Bank (1987), 'Zimbabwe: Power II Project', Industry and Energy Operations, Southern Africa Department, Washington.
98. World Bank, 'Zimbabwe: Power II Project', p. 39.
99. *Financial Gazette*, 19 May 1989.
100. *Energy and Communications*, March 1991, p. 10. The research unit of Zesa that produced the anti-Bank statement was not expressing universally-held views. It subsequently emerged that top Zesa managers were apparently engaged in corruption through the Bank financing process. In mid-1992 internal Zesa documents (written by the deputy general manager) alleged that 'some funds from the World Bank intended for the rehabilitation of the Hwange power station had been deposited into a secret account in London.' (*Financial Gazette*, 13 August 1992.)
101. World Bank, 'Project Completion Report: Zimbabwe: Structural Adjustment Program', p. 27.
102. *Financial Gazette*, 25 January 1996.
103. Deloitte and Touche (1990), 'Doing Business in Zimbabwe', Harare, Deloitte Haskins and Sells, p. 5.
104. Central Statistical Office, *Quarterly Digest of Statistics*.

CHAPTER THREE

Political Constraints

1. Introduction

In a seeming reversal of the early 1960s 'winds of change' remarked upon by British premier Macmillan while liquidating the formal British empire, the surface-level appearance of multiparty opposition in Zimbabwe at the turn of the millennium was of African nationalism in rapid retreat. A young, fresh, democratic, and pro-Western gale was gathering to blow away Zimbabwe's old-fashioned, proto-Stalinist 'socialist' rulers. President Robert Mugabe's reaction to the new opposition's dramatic rise in popularity, after all, occasioned a renewed round of bashing a few thousand white farmers, British imperialists and the IMF.

As portrayed by the mainstream media, Zanu, and nationalism more generally, were in their dying days. The MDC, featuring ostensibly market-oriented politicians including modern trade unionists, would inevitably sort out state mismanagement, end the ruling party's notorious corruption, respect property rights, and revoke the government's incompetent left-wing economic policies.

That broadly remains the impression that the mainstream international media project of Zimbabwe, with the addition of an omnipresent, sometimes implicit sometimes explicit query: 'Is Mugabe nutters?'[1] This latter point has to be dismissed straightaway, given evidence since at least early 2000 of:

- Mugabe's brilliant, machiavellian management of state repression;
- the coherence of his resurrected nationalist rhetoric;
- his staged tirades against white people;
- the vitriol of the attacks he continues to wage against opponents, notwithstanding the death of three controversial lieutenants;
- his capture of a once-hostile judiciary through intimidation; and
- the strong possibility of his winning re-election in what is without doubt going to be an unfree, unfair national vote scheduled for March 2002.

Opponents often remark, under their breath, that only the 'Abacha option' – death in office, like Nigeria's recent tyrant – will save Zimbabwe from its ongoing ruin. Yet each time he suffers a physical accident, publicly grieves the death of close colleagues, or is rumoured to be undergoing emergency hospital treatment (invariably abroad), the president returns, seemingly with more zest than ever.

Beyond what some consider to be the harsh reality of Mugabe's personal longevity, political interpretations of Zimbabwe are terribly muddy. We must depart quickly from that caricature media perspective, to understand why Zanu is not by any means the 'socialist' social force in Zimbabwe, and why the MDC will certainly be challenged by grassroots and shopfloor activists to revisit its economic strategy, which is inconsistent with either democracy or change.

Separating the truth from the myth-making in Zanu's repertoire is important, for the contestation of political rhetoric and reality remains profound. The potential for violence and terror in such a process was already witnessed before the June 2000 parliamentary elections, when more than three dozen murders were amongst 5 000 recorded incidents of state-sanctioned intimidation.

At surface level, sites of legitimacy crises by late 2001 included a massive fiscal deficit that had worsened dramatically in 2000 as Mugabe's election-patronage strategy unfolded. The country was periodically hampered by foreign exchange shortages, with the normal six months of import cover reduced to a few days' worth. After supplies were meant to have been ensured through Libya, it transpired that a day's strike on the railroads in November 2001 could revive the despair-inducing petrol queues. Both city and countryside are vexed by periodic fuel scarcity that began in late 1999, with no end in sight. The army remained overcommitted in an endless stalemate between hopeless war and brittle peace, with more than 10 000 troops deployed faraway in the DRC (although several thousand were being recalled to vote in the March 2002 election). Zimbabweans mourned lost family and friends in the midst of the HIV/Aids pandemic, with more than one in five adults HIV-positive. The economy suffered unprecedented price inflation (higher than 100% by late 2001), as business failures and unemployment soared. Income inequality had risen during the 1990s to amongst the world's worst levels, especially with respect to control of good farming land. The country's 12 million people are restless and often furious, as demonstrated in periodic urban riots.

However, these symptoms are rarely explored in relation to the underlying character of the struggle, confused as it is by ideological fudging. The 2000 election did not clarify much, with Zanu taking 48% of 2.5 million votes, against 46% for the opposition MDC, a difference of just 70 000. Zanu thus gained 62 of 120 contested seats, with an additional 30 appointed directly by Mugabe according to an outmoded, unpopular constitution.[2]

A few months earlier, in February, a national referendum on a new constitution – 55–45% against government proposals – had revealed an impressive mobilisation of MDC supporters and an apathetic turnout from peasants who normally champion the ruling Zanu party. If the referendum and parliamentary election were widely interpreted as 'yellow cards' (soccer referee warning) for Mugabe, the MDC hoped to use its 'red card' (eviction) emblem in the 2002 presidential election, under the leadership of the charismatic ex-trade unionist, Morgan Tsvangirai. But the MDC scored own-goals repeatedly as well, particularly when the two most debilitating yet crucial financial/logistical forces within – big business and the urban petit-bourgeoisie – engaged in undemocratic programmatic work and internecine conflict, respectively.

These issues we take up below: Section 2 is devoted to consideration of Zanu's decay, and Section 3 puts MDC neoliberalism under a microscope. But here we might flag the logic of our argument as follows:

• The rhetoric of nationalism – attempting to disguise the exhaustion of a capital accumulation cycle – itself becomes delegitimised.
• Yet in this context, as a new working-class ideology struggles to emerge but cannot (certainly not when the financial levers of opposition party-building are held by business interests and the practical logistics are controlled by an overconfident urban petit-bourgeoisie), there is a residual power associated with left-sounding discourses within nationalist rhetoric.
• Then, even though the word and idea of 'socialism' can mean little – indeed has only negative connotations – under the weight of such systemic distortion, the blatant neoliberalism of the opposition must be disguised by its own 'social democracy' rhetoric as the ruling party, too, continues talking-Left, acting-Right.

This convoluted, interlocking combination of factors is the source of Zimbabwe's terrible contemporary confusion. While resolving the confusion through intensified social struggle remins vitally important, as we discuss in Chapter Five, that struggle is more likely in the short term to be prosecuted *against* the *povo* by international, regional and domestic capitalist classes. Later, we more precisely identify external problems such as IMF policy dictates and South African subimperialism. Our fear is that these will be accommodated either happily by the MDC or unhappily by Zanu, even if Mugabe implements the 'necessary' stabilisation measures, apparently kicking and screaming. The fundamental problem remains the weakness of the contending forces: Zanu because of the atrophied yet violent nature of its nationalist ideology; the MDC because of the neoliberal capture of its core programme.

2.   Exhausted nationalism

Perhaps Frantz Fanon most eloquently took the measure of decadent African nationalism four decades ago, when he wrote of 'The Pitfalls of National Consciousness' in *The Wretched of the Earth*. Zanu was not yet around, but it was as if the Martinique-born, Paris-educated, Algerian-aligned psychologist had Mugabe and Jonathan Moyo in mind when he warned that

> very often simple souls, who moreover belong to the newly born bourgeoisie, never stop repeating that in an underdeveloped country the direction of affairs by a strong authority, in other words a dictatorship, is a necessity. With this in view the party is given the task of supervising the masses. The party plays understudy to the administration and the police, and controls the masses, not in order to make sure that they really participate in the business of governing the nation, but in order to remind them constantly that the government expects from them obedience and discipline . . .
>
> The progressive transformation of the party into an information service is the indication that the government holds itself more and more on the defensive. The incoherent mass of the people is seen as a blind force that must be continually held in check either by mystification or by the fear inspired by the police force. The party acts as a barometer and as an information service.[3]

A political party dominated by what Mugabe himself in 1989 termed the 'very powerful bourgeois group which champions the cause of international finance and national private capital', is necessarily doomed to internalise the contradictions that Africa faces in its relations with international finance and national private capital. Under such conditions, Fanon forecast the end is very near for those who are having a good time in Africa. Their government will not be able to prolong its own existence indefinitely. A bourgeoisie that provides nationalism alone as food for the masses fails in its mission and gets caught up in a whole series of mishaps. But if nationalism is not made explicit, if it is not enriched and deepened by a very rapid transformation into a consciousness of social and political needs, in other words into humanism, it leads up a blind alley. The bourgeois leaders of underdeveloped countries imprison national consciousness in sterile formalism.[4]

At what point did Zimbabwe's ruling party begin its final degeneration? Sterile formalism was a problem identified periodically in pre-independence Zanu/Zapu politics.[5] But to consider, first, the post-independence electoral terrain, Zanu defeated Zapu initially (1980) through a combination of its mass popular fighting reputation and superb grassroots coverage – and capacity to intimidate non-believers – in three-quarters of the country's core constituencies during the liberation war. The next national vote was won through increasing brutality which destroyed Zapu (1985). The same fate met the renegade Zimbabwe Unity Movement (1990) and petit-bourgeois Forum Party (1995), although by then, coercion was augmented by Zanu's overwhelming party-patronage machine power and dominance of political discourse, as well as by ever more sophisticated electoral trickery.

But voter apathy became endemic. From more than 90% participation during the 1980s the voting public slumped to less than 50% of those eligible to vote during the 1990s. The build-up of tension in society finally filtered into Zanu's ranks around 1998. Confidence in Mugabe's leadership plummeted, in part because the fourth-term leader simply refused to anoint a successor. By the time of the April 1998 gathering of the Zanu Youth League, air force leader Josiah Tungamirai told Mugabe, 'Your excellency, the party is in crisis and only a fool can say otherwise.'[6] A key Masvingo provincial leader, Dzikamai Mavhaire, openly revolted at the same time, receiving temporary procedural support for his critique by Zanu's parliamentary leader.

Interlocking legitimacy crises, 1998–2000
The plunging economy made political crisis management all the more difficult. After the November 1997 currency crash, again in August 1998 Zimbabwe was subjected to intensive speculation. Raiding of

foreign reserves cut another 60% off the Zimbabwe dollar's value over an eight-week period. On-again, off-again funding lines from the IMF contributed to official sentiments of virtually unprecedented nervousness.

Reacting to these and many other challenges, Mugabe repeatedly overstretched, centralising all possible power and putting loyalty above all other political values and talents. In August 1998, he formally gazetted a regulation that named most industrial activities as 'essential services', hence rendering strikes illegal. Though he backed down from this unconstitutional position as political outrage rapidly materialised, a few months later he imposed another dubious ban on strikes that the Zimbabwe Congress of Trade Unions took to the courts.

In September, without consulting even his politburo, much less parliament – again unconstitutionally, and with virtually no popular or business support – Mugabe sent thousands of army troops to the Democratic Republic of the Congo in defense of discredited leader Laurent Kabila, who had come under attack by Rwandan- and Ugandan-backed rebels, in turn backed by the US State Department. Dozens returned in body bags amid reports of Zimbabwean troop participation in the Congolese army's blatant violations of human rights.

Zimbabwe's intervention was seen as a crucial, if temporary, crutch to Kabila's rule, particularly during 1998 when Kabila refused to meet the rebels for peace talks. But once the military networks were in place, Mugabe's rationale for the intervention, joined by the Angolan and Namibian armies but rebuffed by South Africa, was widely understood to include an economic incentive for ruling-party interests and related entrepreneur allies.[7] When a January 1999 IMF mission probed the war costs, Mugabe announced that Kabila's government and Angola were compensating Zimbabwe, requiring no extra budgetary spending. Just one of a myriad of war lies, it transpired that approximately US$1 million a day was going into the DRC. The United Nations later accused Harare elites – generals, politicians and business middlemen – of systematically looting the wretched DRC, given the role of businessman Billy Rautenbach in exploiting mines alongside semi-official Zimbabwean companies that enjoyed military patronage.[8]

Amidst these events, other rancorous political background noise rose inexorably. Ongoing and increasingly vociferous demands came from an indigenous business lobby still shut out of white-controlled markets and financial institutions. Land-starved peasants and farmworkers invaded a few white-owned commercial farms during 1997–1998, egged on by the uproar over the land designation exercise, although they were regularly cleared off by authorities. University students, inspired by their Indonesian counterparts in February 1998, also took to the streets, prematurely predicting a Suharto-type endgame for Mugabe.[9] Widespread popular alienation from government intensified with:

- each new revelation of political and civil service corruption (e.g. rigged official tenders such as the construction of an opulent new Harare airport);
- shady and incongruous international investment partnerships (especially with Malaysian firms);
- ubiquitous conspicuous consumption by political elites (e.g. continuing import of luxury German cars); and
- repeated instances of socio-cultural delegitimisation (e.g. of the devout Catholic Mugabe who sired two children out of wedlock during the 1980s, or of former president Canaan Banana, who when accused of sodomising and raping members of his security staff and soccer team – Mugabe evidently having covered matters up during Banana's early 1980s tenure in the then-ceremonial presidential post – temporarily fled the country in disgrace in late 1998, before his prosecution and time in jail).

In one emblematic scandal, a vocal black-empowerment entrepreneur with close ties to Mugabe, Roger Boka, brought down his own large merchant bank (Unibank) and a massive debt-laden tobacco processing-based empire when in the wake of the 1997–1998 interest rate hikes he faced bankruptcy. Resorting to selling hundreds of millions of dollars worth of counterfeit bonds he claimed were issued by the state-owned Cold Storage Commission, Boka eventually skipped the country. Until the very end of Boka's antics, Mugabe searched for a taxpayer bale-out mechanism.

With Zimbabwe at its most politicised level in two decades, occasional but quite vicious police clampdowns did not deter public dissent. Responding to rumbling discontent, Mugabe imposed a mid-1998 set of price controls on staple goods (corn meal, milk, bread and flour), but within a few months there was more rioting. The opposition press continued to harangue government, mainly from a liberal business perspective, but popular monthly magazines also carried left-populist sentiments. A gay rights movement surfaced, notwithstanding Mugabe's energetic, internationally-renowned homophobia and the oppressive conservatism of Zimbabwe's white/ black petit-bourgeois and black traditional societies. A small Trotskyist

group of the 'International Socialist' tendency was sufficiently aggressive to attract Zanu's condemnation, eventually becoming the
(very frustrated) left-wing conscience of the official opposition party.
The 1980s atrocities against Ndebele peasants were constructively
publicised by human rights groups. There continued to be inklings of
electoral challenges in the emergence of independent, mainly petit-
bourgeois candidates who in late 1998 founded a minor oppositional
party around ex-Zanu firebrand Margaret Dongo, who had won a
parliamentary by-election in Harare South after Zanu was found
guilty of cheating. Perhaps most notably, a widely-supported human-
rights campaign was launched to amend the country's constitution;
by mid-1999 the National Constitutional Assembly forced Mugabe
to attempt his own constitutional rewrite.

In sum, a cross-class alliance composed of organised labour, the
constrained petit-bourgeoisie, church-based critics, students, some
sympathetic business liberals and various other activists emerged around
issues of accountability and abuse of public funds, fuelling a growing
sentiment that after two decades in power, Zanu could quite possibly
be voted down in the 2000 parliamentary election. It did not look good
for Mugabe, especially as the masses became increasingly politicised,
something that Zanu elites had attempted to quell through 'de-
velopmentalist' rhetoric during the 1980s. Repression only worked
sporadically, in forms as diverse as labour minister John Nkomo's
repeated divide-and-rule attempts against the ZCTU, and annual
running battles at the University of Zimbabwe. Mugabe's best chance
to confront potential Left opposition during the late 1990s was probably
the turn to a mock corporatism.

The idea that Big Government, Big Business and Big Labour could
establish a consensus for governing Zimbabwe while Zanu implemented
neoliberalism was, surprisingly, attractive to the ZCTU leaders, as
discussed below. Yet by early 1999, ZCTU general secretary Tsvangirai
himself felt sufficiently confident to condemn government's national
Economic Summit as a 'circus', for it was evidently a public relations
exercise. His labour troops came out repeatedly in protest, winning
partial concessions on the hated retail taxes, although not on a 65%
gasoline price hike which had doubled commuter transport prices
overnight, or more general reforms.

Under the circumstances, it is easy to see why Zimbabwe's nationalist
project was exhausted in 2000, a phenomenon widely understood
throughout society at the point its rule reached two decades in duration.
One sign, early that year, was the electorate's rejection of a constitutional

referendum promoted heavily by the Zanu government. In desperation, Mugabe resurrected Zanu's most militant, often virulent strain of nationalist demagoguery, attempting as time ran out to simultaneously 'solve' the long-standing land distribution problem, terrorise supporters of the opposition, and pass the buck for his own failings to the country's small white population, foreign countries (especially Britain and the US), imperialism in general and the IMF in particular.

In short, during this period, Mugabe's leadership of Zanu was threatened but remained airtight, even during the worst of the crisis that began in 1997. He occasionally raised hopes, including within the branch of Zanu that correctly saw him as a popular liability, by hinting that he would not stand again. But in early 2001 he announced he would run for a fifth term as leader. There was no obvious successor in the wings of his fractious party, given that a December 2000 Zanu congress rid the leadership of at least one potential successor, the Harvard-trained neoliberal lawyer Eddison Zvobgo, thanks to Mugabe-authorised purges. Former minister of justice Emmerson Mnangagwa, who in the 2000 election lost his constituency seat to the MDC, was brought back by Mugabe to become speaker of parliament, and was usually mentioned as a logical heir. So too was Zanu chairperson John Nkomo, from the Ndebele ethnic minority, probably preventing him ever becoming national leader. An additional candidate, Simba Makoni, a much younger technocrat-politician was named finance minister in July 2000. But when Mugabe announced his return to socialism in October 2001 he also pointedly referred to cabinet ministers who he believed were unreliable: Makoni did not have to be named for the signal to be crystal clear.

Ironically, the most influential advisor to Mugabe during the most rapid decay of Zanu nationalism was Jonathan Moyo, a former liberal political scientist educated at the University of Southern California. During the 1990s, Moyo directed the Ford Foundation in Kenya but turned to hardline nationalist discourses in 1999. Mugabe showed his tenacity by hiring him as election spokesperson for June 2000, and then as information minister, after Moyo had performed miserably as Constitutional Commission spokesperson in 1999. Charges were laid against him for theft of funds at previous workplaces in Nairobi and Johannesburg, after the urban intelligentsia made the 'Sheraton professor' the butt of their jokes, and after Zanu leaders reportedly rebelled at Moyo's implausible U-turn: from being the most consistent liberal critic of Mugabe in *Financial Gazette* columns during his stint as a University of Zimbabwe politics lecturer, to becoming his closest confidant within seven years.

In response to the crises, the president's rhetoric became white hot. Shifts in political winds allowed Mugabe to posture Left, so as to merge critiques of white Zimbabweans, ex-Rhodesians, the 'gay mafia' of Tony Blair, European Union diplomats, the US right-wing, neoliberals, Ugandans and Rwandans fighting his troops in the DRC, and virtually all of civil society within Zimbabwe. With Moyo beside him, Mugabe weathered the loss during 2001 of war veterans leader Hitler Hunzvi, gender/youth/employment minister Border Gezi, and defense minister Moven Mahachi, within weeks of each other due, reportedly, to Aids and two auto accidents respectively.

Most ominously, Zanu's electoral techniques appeared as potentially effective in March 2002 as they were in June 2000: applying fierce intimidation – including murder, torture and kidnapping – to thwart opposition votes here; shaving the tally from MDC strongholds by disallowing voter registration there; refusing access to election observers here; deploying police in a biased way there; getting rural headmen to disqualify or intimidate pro-MDC voters here; refusing youth the vote there; distorting political perceptions through the state-owned media (especially radio) here; prohibiting alternative radio and arresting private journalists there; detaining the opposition leader here; gerrymandering voting districts there; submitting bogus votes by overseas troops here; preventing votes by exiled Zimbabweans there.

It was occasionally suggested that Mugabe sought to retain office until the last minute, dispensing patronage and probably terror in equal measure, hoping to assure some kind of amnesty for crimes in which he could face prosecution – whether associated with corruption or his role in the murder of civilians in Matabeleland. MDC leader Tsvangirai publicly offered such an amnesty in early 2000, when it appeared his party would win the parliament convincingly; Mugabe turned instead to a campaign of intimidation and squeaked through that poll with a bare majority of contested seats.

Land and politics [10]
But apparently something much more profound was at stake in the president's heart and mind: the 'dignity' of having resolved the most embarrassing vestige of colonialism, land hunger. Certainly, the land occupations beginning in February 2000 can be read as a direct response to the referendum humiliation, and as political codewording for revenge against white farmers on the one hand, and emotive delivery vehicle and vote-catcher on the other. But for several decades, the most emotive issue in Mugabe's discourse has been rural land. With it comes

the violation of property rights, which by all objective considerations is required to resolve the problem, given the failure of willing-seller/ willing-buyer policy, plus failed credit schemes over the prior two decades. Did Mugabe, here if only here, potentially break the talk-Left, act-Right mould?

If the answer is yes, a paramilitary-style force would be required. In 1997, he restored the prominence of the War Veterans' Association, after a long period of neglect. The vets, in turn, became Mugabe's shock troops after the February 2000 referendum defeat, invading more than 1 500 white-owned farms, and allowing Mugabe to resurrect, yet again, the claim that only Zanu can resolve Zimbabwe's land inequality. With that claim, albeit contradicted by two decades of land-reform failure, came something else: a *memory* of an anti-colonial struggle that only Zanu can invoke, and an image of a time when the party was in fact a Maoist-type 'fish within the sea' of the rural masses.[11]

Even if there are numerous complex structural relationships and extraordinarily diverse politics at play in the countryside, the essential problem is simple: land hunger for millions of peasants and small farmers (relegated to the country's worst soils and driest regions), alongside vast unutilised arable land on more than 4 000 white-owned commercial farms. The land question entails many factors: durable colonial/neocolonial relations and deep-rooted white racism; a bad deal struck by the liberation movements with the outgoing Rhodesian regime at the 1979 Lancaster House power-transfer agreement; subsequently a failed market-oriented land reform (and microcredit) programme overly reliant upon World Bank money and advice; widespread ruling-party corruption in the land acquisition process; bureaucratic bungling; worsening international commodity market conditions; rising costs of agricultural inputs; devastating cycles of speculative credit and land prices; and growing inequality associated with the disastrous 1990s structural adjustment programme, whose scanty rural benefits were overwhelmingly concentrated amongst white commercial farmers exporting tobacco and agri-exotica: crocodiles, ostriches, horticulture and the like.

The gender and generational dimensions of the land question remain extremely important due to residual aspects of colonial-capitalist labour-power reproduction. Consistent with classic systems of 'articulations of modes of production,' many functions – child-rearing, medical care for sick workers and old-age care, without adequate state support – were traditionally farmed out to rural women instead of being intern-alised within the capitalist labour markets. Such internalisation would ideally, under a humane capitalism, occur through adequate state-provided schooling, worker healthcare plans and pensions (whether public or private), none of which were universally available to black Zimbabweans.

Although over time, a net positive remittance of wages flowed from urban workers to rural kin, and although there were some post-independence improvements in rural social welfare provision, nevertheless the rural-urban subsidy provided by African women emerged again during the 1990s via transfers of maize and other staple foods to kin in towns and cities, transfer of children back to rural areas where school fees were lower, and the return home of workers sick with Aids. The simple reason was that urban-rural wage remittances declined dramatically due to structural adjustment, as women not only continued labour-power reproduction but also took on the additional burden of being super-exploited providers of safety-nets for a manifestly failing Zimbabwean capitalism. Research has shown this was the lot of women the world over under neoliberalism.[12]

Likewise, environmental pressures associated with land hunger are terribly important. They include not just traditional concerns over woodlot deforestation, soil erosion, watershed siltation and land exhaustion. Additional household environmental problems emerged under economic stress, such as excessive use of wood and paraffin indoors due to lack of electricity in even urban areas (with attendant public health problems), poor quality sources of water and sanitation, and worsening vulnerability to drought and flood. The latter problems became acute during the 1990s and into the twenty-first century.

A central if sometimes unstated presumption in the most rigorous left-nationalist discourse, such as that of Zimbabwe's premier land scholar, Sam Moyo, is that these kinds of very durable problems cannot be resolved by mere judicious state intervention, whether via the 1980s World Bank credit plan explored in Chapter Two (in lieu of adequate land reform), or the state land acquisition process proposed during the 1990s but only haltingly implemented. Post-colonial history in Zimbabwe and similar settings demonstrates that states, ruling parties, bureaucrats, rich farmers and local power-brokers can and do together resist radical change in rural land, property and social relations. Thus the war vets' invasion of white-owned commercial farms has been promoted by varied Zimbabwean left-nationalists and their allies abroad (including some South African communists, pan-Africanists, land-rights activists and other radicals).[13]

More than 1 000 white-owned farms continued to be occupied by
settlers in the months after the June 2000 election, with ongoing
invasions in the northern and eastern-central parts of the country
through 2001. But given resource shortages of fertilisers, pesticides,
marketing support and credit, the sustainability of resettlement
operations was rapidly thrown into question. The lack of support partly
reflected empty state coffers. Indeed, the Zanu government had originally
pledged to compensate white farmowners for their built improvements
(buildings, irrigation and related works), but not underlying land
values.

However, as land occupations continued and the fiscal deficit rose,
that prospect also faded, and the option of Britain coming in to re-
imburse white farmers for resettled land, as Zanu had demanded, was
vetoed by Tony Blair on the specious grounds, as his aid minister Claire
Short unconvincingly explained, that the New Labour Party was not
the coloniser of Zimbabwe, just as her own roots were in colonised
Ireland. A September 2001 deal worked out in Abuja to provide British
and other donor funds for land purchase and resettlement was derailed
from the start, as it was apparently only a sop signed by Zimbabwe
foreign minister Stan Mudenge to try to help Mugabe survive a
forthcoming Commonwealth Heads of Government meeting. In any
case, no compensation was ever discussed for the tens of thousands of
(black) farmworkers displaced in the process, notwithstanding proposals
to that effect by MDC MP Munyaradzi Gwisai. Xenophobic reactions
from both officials and many ordinary Zimbabweans emerged when it
was pointed out that people of Malawian and Mozambican descent –
many resident on Zimbabwe commercial farms for generations – would
be displaced in their tens of thousands.[14]

However, even if unevenly implemented and characterised by
continually broken promises to all parties, the occupations and official
resettlement exercise had one durable result which would, it appeared,
assure some degree of land redistribution: white farmers, five of whom
were killed while contesting the war vets during 2000 followed by
several others in subsequent violence, were sobered by the attacks and
softened their resistance to land reform. Many dozens gave up their
land to emigrate. The more rational of permanently-settled white
farmers conceded that they had not turned over sufficient land to the
government for resettlement at independence, protected as they were
by the willing-seller clause in the transition settlement agreed to at
London's Lancaster House. Indeed, in many parts of the country, white
farmers professed a willingness to help parcel out chunks of land they

were not using, often estimated in excess of 20% of their holdings. Sometimes they even persuaded selected neighbours who mismanaged their plantations to turn them over for resettlement.

The state, however, already possessed vast quantities of land once owned by white farmers which it did not have the capacity to redistribute. Resettlement on the best land was regularly delegitimised by blatant cronyism and corruption. Another dilemma was the prolific use of good farmland for tobacco, Zimbabwe's main source of foreign currency. When some war vets began tearing up tobacco plants to plant the staple maize crop, they were quickly dissuaded by officials.

The land invasions, assaults and cases of rural intimidation occurring prior to the June 2000 election and also during subsequent parliamentary by-elections and local government votes, also reflected long-simmering personal grievances that, in this tumultuous political context, re-appeared with a vengeance. In addition, argued Wilf Mhanda, a former leader of the Zimbabwe African National Liberation Army (Zanla) – subsequently a progressive dissident with the 'Liberators' Platform' group – only approximately 2 000 of the roughly 50 000 war vets were involved in the farm occupations. Most other occupiers emerged from the huge pool of impoverished urban survivors, and were issued plastic war-veteran credentials at Zanu headquarters in Harare.[15] There are significant numbers of women occupiers, but just prior to the parliamentary elections they issued a statement expressing dissatisfaction at the control of occupied land and the need for women-headed households to be given at least a quarter of the plots that will subsequently be carved up.

Winning hearts and minds?
Here the MDC's urban popular and proletarian base proved incapable of widening into the countryside, and especially winning the older generation's support. For the 2000 and 2002 elections, the MDC promised only the establishment of an ill-defined commission to assess who owns what land, how much compensation should be paid for redistribution, and who should be resettled. The overarching MDC rhetoric on land included three points: (a) condemnation of Mugabe and the war vets for opportunism and their use of land as a populist distraction from Zanu misrule; (b) concern over the implications of the occupations for farmworkers; and (c) the need to restore the perception of strong property rights so as to provide potential investors with confidence in the rule of law. When shortly after the election, Gwisai told his urban working-class constituency of the need for radical land reform, Tsvangirai promptly and publicly disciplined the maverick.

Tellingly, the way that a leading MDC farmer-advocate (writing under the name of Martin Ngwenya) eloquently explained the legal situation just prior to the December 2001 Supreme Court ruling in favour of the government's fast-track resettlement programme, against white commercial farmers, was devoid of any reference to social justice:

All you need to judge the legal position of the government is to ask what would the decision be of the International Court of Justice in the Hague if they were asked to judge the legality of the farmers' case. Just list a few of the fundamental strengths of the farmers' position:

(1) They are bona fide citizens of the country.

(2) They are genuine investors holding legal freehold rights to the land they use.

(3) They are protected by international agreements covering investments of this nature.

(4) Over 80% have made their investments since 1980 when this government came to power.

(5) The majority of them have purchased their properties with a legal certificate of 'no interest' issued by the Ministry of Agriculture on behalf of the government.

(6) They owe creditors money against which their land is the main form of collateral.

(7) The government already controls 80% of all land in Zimbabwe including over 55% of the 'most productive' farm land and has yet to use productively the majority of the four million hectares purchased from commercial farmers since 1980 using foreign funds donated for this purpose.

(8) They have no plans for the proper settlement of these illegally acquired farms or for the subsequent support of the new farmers.

(9) No selection is being applied to the new settlers and they are not being obliged to accept liability for the assets they are illegally taking over from the current owners.

(10) No satisfactory forms of compensation have been agreed or even the method by which such compensation will be established and paid.[16]

In this context, the ruling party could claim a certain degree of success through championing crude, race-based, macho rhetoric linked to the electoral-campaign claim 'the land is the economy, the economy is the

land.' But it was reminiscent less of an inspired nationalist revival and
more of the last kicks of a dying horse. The newly-appointed minister of
gender, youth development and employment creation, Border Gezi,
announced in mid-2000, for example, 'If you want to work for the
government you should be prepared to support Zanu.'[17] Matabeleland
North governor Obert Mpofu appealed to the public, 'If you see a
government car carrying an MDC supporter or a civil servant eating or
drinking with an MDC member in a car, confiscate the keys and hand
them over to the authorities.'[18] Party loyalty was paramount, as vice
president Simon Muzenda told a rural rally just prior to the 2000
election: 'Even if we put a baboon in Chivi, if you are Zanu you vote for
that baboon.'[19] Meanwhile, race relations deteriorated, as reflected in a
not atypical comment of a Zanu member of parliament, Isaac MacKenzie,
in the wake of his party's February 2000 referendum defeat:

> Let me assure you whites here, that once you support MDC, Zanu
> is not going to treat you as business people, but as politicians. Then
> if you are treated as politicians, it is like signing your own death
> warrants. The political storm will not spare you. Let you be informed
> that our reserve force, the war veterans, will be set on you.[20]

As the main war veterans leader, Hunzvi, confirmed a few weeks before
the parliamentary election, 'Like in any revolution, the path is always
bloody, and that is to be expected, and hence no one should raise
eyebrows over the deaths of four white farmers . . . God told us to grab
the farms: from them we shall get something to eat.'[21] As for Mugabe's
perspective on the farm occupations, 'This is a clear peaceful demonstration and there is no problem with that.'[22]

In response to this vulgar, intimidating version of politics, a seemingly
westernised 'good governance' discourse arose. True, Tsvangirai was
once drawn into the spirit of battle, as the MDC celebrated its first
anniversary in September 2000: 'What we want to tell Mugabe today is
that please go peacefully. If you don't want to go we will remove you
violently.' Explaining this remark as a slip-of-tongue, Tsvangirai had,
more to the point, threatened 'mass action' – ordinarily interpreted as
non-violent civil disobedience – against the government.[23] Occasional
militancy aside, the MDC reaction to the Zanu leaders' race-conscious,
patriarchal, anti-imperialist nationalism, was to talk of a civilised
democracy backed by 'the international community'.

To consider one crucial example of discursive differentiation, around
the omnipresent issue of international financial pressure, Zanu leaders

continued talking-Left while the MDC talked-Right. Asked whether Zimbabwe needed a financial lifeline from the IMF and World Bank, Tsvangirai replied ambiguously, 'I still hate the World Bank and IMF, but I hate them like I hate my doctor,' and explained the need for a pragmatic not ideological posture:

> They have put us into a serious debt trap. We may have to negotiate with the IMF to get out of that. What is important, down the line, is for Zimbabwe to work itself out of the IMF and World Bank's grip. In the short term, we have to distinguish between financial support that serves Mugabe, versus that which serves the country.

Was it, thus, fair to assert – as did Jonathan Moyo – that Tsvangirai had become a 'sell-out', given the MDC's retreat from progressive positions on land and international financial dependency? Was there already, in short, a politically fatal penetration of the MDC by neoliberal values and personalities?

3. Looming neoliberalism

The phrases structural adjustment, neoliberalism and the Washington Consensus are not used here as swearwords, but are rather used to signify a certain philosophy that has roots in nineteenth-century *laissez faire* political and economic theory but which really only came of age in the late 1970s. At that stage, as Susan George has eloquently shown, a profound ideological and material project that had been prepared over several decades became hegemonic.[24] The neoliberal recipe, cooked up by economists such as Hayek and Friedman, was first served on a high-profile platter by Pinochet, Reagan, Thatcher and Kohl. It included the standard items found in *Esap*, as discussed in Chapter Two: the demise of state-mandated labour restrictions, price controls, exchange controls, interest rate controls, investment regulations, import restrictions, government subsidies, a great many civil service jobs and the very existence of state-owned enterprises, which were meant to be privatised.

In Zimbabwe, not everything on the menu was eaten over the first five years. But as documented above, the World Bank was a 'highly satisfied' customer, especially given the reputation that the local chefs had for populism, corruption and sounding off about racial and geopolitical inequality at the great globalisation table. Zanu's 2000 parliamentary electoral manifesto bragged that 'one of the rewards of economic liberalisation has been the privatisation of parastatals to give our people an opportunity to take indigenous ownership in the economy while also reducing public expenditure and promoting the efficiency of operations and effectiveness of service delivery.' Five companies' assets were partially sold up to that date under the direction of Cephas Msipa, minister of state in the president's office: Dairy Marketing, the Cotton Company, Commercial Bank of Zimbabwe (formerly the corrupt, bankrupt Bank of Credit and Commerce International), Zimbabwe Reinsurance Corporation and the Rainbow Tourism Group.[25]

Yet if neoliberalism was to become the Zanu elites' staple diet during the 1990s, it was obvious to the main politicians by 1997 or so that food poisoning was imminent. To illustrate, the Zimbabwe National Students Union and its affiliates at Bulawayo Polytechnic, Harare Institute of Technology, Kwekwe, Masvingo Technical and the University of Zimbabwe (UZ) began mass protests in mid-2000 over outsourcing of catering. Thanks in part to creative politicisation by the International Socialist Organisation of Zimbabwe, the very word privatisation came to signify, not 'indigenous ownership in the economy', but instead, a corrupt vehicle for Zanu cronies. Commented University of Zimbabwe student leader Tinashe Chimedza: 'As UZ students, we have experienced privatisation. It is a monster which banishes students to a state of perpetual poverty and is a monumental failure. Students have resorted to unorthodox means like sodomy and prostitution to raise money for their basic food.'[26]

Whether Zanu's earlier offerings were welfarist in nature – education and health programmes, especially – or took the form of patronage and civil-service jobs, the party could at least claim to be raising living standards during the 1980s. In contrast, Esap was soon translated as 'Eternal Suffering for African People'. What that meant, at the crucial mid-1990s political conjuncture, was that interlocking civil-society forces were becoming as dissatisfied with the status quo, as committed neoliberals were satiated. Politicians worried about ever-weakening legitimacy on the part of the state and ruling party. The more enlightened sections of the business elite also realised, gradually but inexorably, that a liberalised Zimbabwean economy was not sustainable. So it may have appeared reasonable for the trade union opposition to try to resist neoliberalism in a most confusing way: by begging for a seat at the table.

Labour's corporatist gambit

A key reason for the ZCTU to turn towards a harmonious vision of Big Government, Big Business and Big Labour was the 'Nedlac' (National Economic Development and Labour Council) model adopted by the Congress of South African Trade Unions in 1994 to hash out major debates with its 'social partners' over public policy. But perhaps of even greater importance to the ZCTU leaders was the recent memory of failed resistance to neoliberalism. The late 1980s 'hooligan generation' at the University of Zimbabwe began that process by demonstrating against early manifestations of *Esap*, including politicians' corruption and a multinational corporate red carpet laid out by Mugabe in 1989.[27] When Tsvangirai supported them, he ended up in jail for two weeks. After anti-*Esap* labour-student demonstrations were repressed from 1990–1992, the only other outlets for socio-economic stress were the self-destructive 'IMF Riots' by unorganised young people (which occurred in Harare in 1993 and 1995) and a dramatic rise in petty crime and domestic violence.

The lost years were unfortunate, because there had initially appeared good prospects for militant anti-neoliberal resistance. The early 1990s witnessed the emergence of a deep-rooted *urban* political alienation from nationalist discourse, and the rapid maturing of political consciousness. Organised labour had a potentially crucial role.

The ZCTU had managed, under Tsvangirai's leadership (1988–2000), to break out of the paternalist grip in which Zanu had held the federation since its 1981 founding.[28] During the 1980s, union strategies, tactics and politics were controlled from the ruling party. By 1991, Tsvangirai identified neoliberalism as one of the most important issues – along with corruption – dividing the Zimbabwe government from the masses. He correctly predicted a difficult period ahead, at a time when mainstream commentary was universally optimistic:

> What we are looking for in Zimbabwe is a democratic space. Because what is going to be sacrificed in this programme [*Esap*] is democracy. When people go to the streets, complaining about these things, the state will be forced to use power to quell these riots, and in fact one of the ironies is that we are arming our own people – the police and the army – to turn against our people . . . At the end of the day we become the marginalised group, because the government has put itself in a position so that it cannot take a stand against the IMF. The only way to defend against international capital marginalising further the indigenous businessman, the worker, the peasant, is to have all these groups together.[29]

Yet the ZCTU was not well-placed to take advantage of the opening, and instead devolved from an anti-imperialist critique of externally-imposed structural adjustment (1990–1994), to a desire for corporatist technical solutions (1994–1997) to a broad-based front-building strategy aimed at dislodging the authoritarian Zanu regime (1997–present).[30] The erratic nature of ZCTU politics can probably best be explained by the movement's initial political marginalisation, for the Zanu government's divide-and-conquer strategy was enhanced by residual nationalist loyalties in several key union affiliates. Together, these seriously threatened the ZCTU's very existence, after an initial anti-*Esap* union protest on May Day, 1992 was met with repression. As the ZCTU retreated into an aspirant-corporatist mode, even Tsvangirai sought an accommodation with neoliberalism.

To this end the ZCTU's important 1996 *Beyond Esap* policy advocacy document was penned by a diverse group of technical associates, including progressive economists from Britain and Malawi, and one noticeable Harare merchant banker. Blinkered by the desire to remain relevant to reforming *Esap* in potential tripartite settings, *Beyond Esap* in fact repeated many of the Mugabe regime's worst conceptual errors and policy recommendations. As Tsvangirai himself wrote in the foreword: 'While acknowledging that SAPs (Structural Adjustment Programmes) are necessary, the study shows that they are insufficient in fostering development.' A more realistic assessment would have been the affirmation that *Esap* was *un*necessary and that it fostered *under*development in Zimbabwe.

Beyond Esap's neoliberal policy suggestions included (1) avoiding 'subsidisation of nonproductive uses'; (2) means-testing 'welfare and relief funds'; (3) 'trimming the public sector'; (4) 'repeal[ing] any regulations . . . that discriminate against non-formal sector activities or small-scale firms'; (5) 'hav[ing] the peasant captured by the market'; and (6) 'close government collaboration with private business' on industrial policy. *Beyond Esap* also suggested that 'financial resource mobilisation' should include 'government selling off its assets using the proceeds to reduce the stock of debt' and 'encourag[ing] people to save by providing incentives that would encourage them to invest in shares quoted on the Zimbabwe Stock Exchange'. The document also made a fatal concession for future ZCTU strategies, namely that 'there can be no return to pre-*Esap* policies, partly because of the stranglehold that foreign creditors have on policy through the substantial debt that has accumulated, paradoxically, because of the failure of the policy.'[31]

The basis for such concessionary language was a consistent, mainly fruitless attempt to establish a broad 'social contract' that would, as Tsvangirai put it in a typical mid-1990s remark, 'involve the three parties reaching a consensus where workers agree to restrain wage demands on the one hand and employers agree to control price increases for commodities, invest surpluses to create more jobs and train workers on the other. For Government, you would expect them to cut spending.'[32]

Post-nationalism, post-neoliberalism?

Corporatism on the semi-periphery of world capitalism is never as easy as Tsvangirai seemed to suggest, especially under conditions of falling commodity prices, worsening terms of trade more generally, high debt repayments, and slower world growth during the last quarter-century of the 1900s. Class struggle was inevitably the route workers would take, instead of what some have termed the 'class snuggle' favoured by Tsvangirai.[33] As Zimbabwe's economic crisis deepened during the 1990s, autonomous, shopfloor-based actions outran the ability of union bureaucrats to control or direct the membership. The mid-1990s corporatist strategy mistakenly pursued by the ZCTU leaders quickly became irrelevant.

Notwithstanding a terribly weak legacy of union organising under the malevolently paternalistic post-independence ministry of labour, the ambitions of the better-mobilised unions were by no means snuffed. In 1994 industrial action was revived by postal and telecommunications workers, Air Zimbabwe engineers (on strike four days), bank employees (six days), construction workers (four days), and physicians (which led to the firing of all junior doctors from the public health service). Then, as two years of economic rebound followed the 1991–1995 downturn, workers tested their muscles *en masse*.

With inflation still above 20% and public sector wage offers in the low single digits, unprecedented civil service militancy emerged, signalling the great gap between rulers and subjects. For nearly a fortnight in mid-1996, a strike of more than two thirds of the civil service (160 000 workers) paralysed government. Daily demonstrations in downtown Harare attracted the support of trade union leadership, who had grappled unsuccessfully for several years to incorporate the civil servants' organisation into the trade union movement. The ZCTU president Gibson Sibanda and general secretary Tsvangirai threatened a general strike in solidarity with the civil service, and public sector workers refused to compromise on wage demands and protection for strike leaders.

Just back from a honeymoon after a lavish wedding to his (40-years younger) secretary, Mugabe revealed to journalists his lack of comprehension of civil service grievances. With even tougher pressure by workers, the government quickly folded to worker demands. Following this example, in mid-1997, 100 000 private sector workers were involved in strike action, even extending to poorly-organised agricultural plantations, and again real wage increases were finally won.

These labour victories meant that when the series of economic catastrophes began in late 1997, the ZCTU easily stepped in to assume national oppositional leadership.[34] Well-organised general strikes and demonstrations in December 1997 and March and November 1998 won nearly universal worker support, and were punctuated by a minor rebellion within the ruling party at a December 1997 conference and, via a few leading renegades, throughout 1998. In the township communities, days of rioting over food and gasoline price hikes left several people dead at the hands of the police in both January and October 1998. Emblematic of the growing conflict, Tsvangirai was himself badly beaten by Zanu-supporting thugs – apparently war veterans, who soon became something of a paramilitary force for Mugabe – after the first national strike. A few months later the second most important ZCTU office, in Bulawayo, was razed by arsonists.

Thus by 1998, in the wake of an unprecedented year-long wave of worker militancy (including previously docile public sector employees and even atomised plantation workers) and two successful national mass strikes against Mugabe's policies, Tsvangirai had changed direction again, this time apparently back to the Left. Instead of joining a National Economic Consultative Forum in January 1999, as expected, he led a ZCTU walkout on the grounds that Mugabe's government could not be trusted. A few weeks later, Tsvangirai convened a broad-based National Working People's Convention (a significant name), which cited not only good-governance concerns, but also

> the inability of the economy to address the basic needs of the majority of Zimbabweans; the severe decline in incomes, employment, health, food security and well being of people; the unfair burden borne by working women and persistence of gender discrimination in practice; the decline, and in some cases collapse of public services; the lack of progress in resolving land hunger and rural investment needs; the weak growth in industry and marginalisation of the vast majority of the nation's entrepreneurs . . .

In contrast, the Convention resolved that

> national policies should prioritise the mobilisation and organisation of resources to meet people's basic needs for food security, shelter, clean water, health and education; the equitable distribution of

resources such as land, skills, capital and technology for production and industrialisation strategies that are based on building and using the capabilities of the people for production . . . The country should aim to reduce its dependency on foreign loans and the loss of sovereignty that this brings . . . The right to a minimum standard of health inputs (food, water, shelter) and health care must be defined and entrenched in the constitution, guaranteed and funded on an equitable basis by the state through its mobilisation of national resources . . . The Convention thus resolved to take these issues to the people across the country, to mobilise them towards the working people's agenda, and to implement a vigorous and democratic political movement for change.[35]

Tsvangirai also chaired the National Constitutional Assembly process that in 1998–1999 garnered sufficient popular support to force Mugabe to set up his own constitution-rewriting commission. And in a telling move, he explicitly – if unsuccessfully – informed the IMF that any further funding to the Zanu government in August 1999 would be firmly opposed. Finally, when in mid-1999, the ZCTU leaders Tsvangirai and Sibanda announced the formation of the 'labour-backed' MDC, a founding manifesto balanced its overall good governance orientation with quite expansive socio-economic visions.[36]

Interestingly, at the MDC's launch in September 1999, Sibanda attempted to undermine Zanu's claim to nationalist memory by describing the new democratic struggle as another *chimurenga* war, in the same spirit as the 1890s insurrection against the initial white-settler invasion, and the 1960s–1970s guerrilla war against Rhodesian colonialism:

> Our struggle in Zimbabwe has always been a struggle for the dignity and sovereignty of the people. We, the workers and peasants have always been in the leadership of that struggle, In our first *chimurenga/umvukela*, workers fought against massive exploitation in the mines, farms and industry, and peasants against the expropriation of their land. The nationalist and liberation movement that led the second *chimurenga/umvukela* was born from and built on the struggles of workers and peasants. But after twenty years of Independence, we now have a ruling nationalist elite that has exploited this long history towards its own ends, betraying the people's struggles. Is this the country that we fought for and rejoiced in 1980?[37]

A few months later, Tsvangirai provided more clarity about the potentially post-nationalist, post-neoliberal MDC project:

> In many ways, we are moving from the nationalist paradigm to politics grounded in civic society and social movements. It's like the role and influence that in South Africa, the labour movement and civil society organisations had over the African National Congress in the early 1990s. MDC politics are not nationalist inspired, because they focus more on empowerment and participation of the people. Zanu's nationalist thinking has always been top-down, centralised, always trapped in a timewarp. Nationalism was an end in itself instead of a means to an end. One of Zanu's constant claims is that everyone in Zimbabwe owes the nationalist movement our freedom. It's therefore also become a nationalism based on patronage and cronyism.[38]

For Tsvangirai, a logical discourse was 'social democracy':

> We are social democrats. The MDC can never be pure, ideologically, because of our broad orientation. Besides, social democracy is a half-way house, a spaghetti mix. In our case, the main characteristic is that we are driven by working class interests, with the poor having more space to play a role than they do now. But one of the components is an element of participation by business, which is just not able to develop under present conditions.

In slightly more concrete terms, the implications involve a strong commitment to meeting basic needs:

> Development must be genuine, defined by people themselves. We know that export-led growth is not a panacea. And we place a high priority on meeting basic needs. How could we not, with 75% of the population living below poverty? So our development strategy will highlight land, health, education and the like.

Concerns were already being expressed at that stage, that with such a multi-class project, the MDC would end up like the Movement for Multiparty Democracy in Zambia. There, trade unionist Frederick Chiluba won the 1991 election against veteran nationalist Kenneth Kaunda with a multiclass alliance, and quickly applied neoliberal economic policy with even worse results than his predecessor. Tsvangirai remarked:

I think Chiluba did not come on board with any ideology at all. But the main lesson there is that if the workers are not careful, they may give up their initiative over the party. That means that even though we need to build coalitions, the structure of MDC has to be, and is, participatory, with far more control from the base than normal parties.

Tsvangirai thus made a profound triple promise that in retrospect appears to have been broken in all ways. Did he mean that MDC leaders *were* committed to a progressive, not corporatist ideology? Would workers retain their initiative? Would the MDC be genuinely controlled from the base? When the question was posed regularly enough in the *Worker* newspaper, and when a candidate hostile to the MDC – Isidore Zindoga – appeared on the verge of winning the job of ZCTU secretary in February 2001, Tsvangirai returned to a ZCTU congress to plead his case.

And what of the other major class-actor on Zimbabwe's early twenty-first century political stage, the urban petit-bourgeoisie? The 1990s demise of the Forum Party and late 1990s experience of vicious internecine battle between petit-bourgeois intellectuals had given hope to some progressives that the MDC could emerge fully-matured as a workers' party. The February 1999 National Working People's Convention was a good start for a more pro-proletarian, pro-poor politics. During the 1999 party-forming process and 2000 election campaign, it was the ZCTU's resources, offices, networks, personnel and legitimacy that permitted both a successful 'No' referendum vote, and the contestation of all 120 parliamentary constituencies by the nine-month old MDC.

But not only did the urban petit-bourgeois intelligentsia – especially lawyers! – take control of the party during 2000 in logistical terms, hence softening the class-conscious character of the MDC programme and recommending against mass action during the crucial late-2000 moment of turmoil when 'ungovernability' could have advanced the democratic cause just as had happened fifteen years earlier in South Africa. In addition, the petit-bourgeoisie brought to the MDC an astounding capacity for infighting.

Such conflict was always the Achilles Heel of Zimbabwean party politics, dating to the 1950s–1960s struggles within the early nationalist movement, the mid-1970s murder of Zanu's leader Herbert Chitepo – apparently by 'Mugabe's thugs' according to Chitepo's widow Victoria – and the various personality squabbles and ethnic/regional divisions of the post-independence era. The MDC would be no different. Within two years of its founding, five members of the national executive were suspended for a vendetta which had turned debilitatingly violent: official MDC spokesperson and MP for Kuwadzana, Learnmore Jongwe; security chief and MP for St Mary's, Job Sikhala; MP for Zengeza and national executive member, Tafadzwa Musekiwa; shadow minister for finance and MP for Hatfield, Tapiwa Mashakada; and Chitungwiza provincial chairman Alex Musundire. In one nighttime attack that Sikhala blamed on Mashakada's youth followers, his two-year old daughter was badly injured.

The same tendency surfaced in the National Constitutional Assembly (NCA), which during 2001 was a scene of fisticuffs over leadership. But even so, the more fundamental debates over political-economy were neglected in this impressive network led by urban professionals. For example, it is unkind – but necessary – to point out the plagiarism to which the NCA succumbed, in copying South Africa's *Constitution* for its own *Working Draft*.[39]

These kinds of problems are probably, at the end of the day, minor details. But do they signify a problem with what Fanon termed the 'national middle class', in its internecine turns inward, and its turn outward, to the neoliberal West, for inspiration? Fanon's critique of exhausted nationalism is powerful, but to the extent that the urban petit-bourgeoisie gravitated to supporting the MDC, another warning emerges from *The Wretched of the Earth*:

> The national middle class discovers its historic mission: that of intermediary. Seen through its eyes, its mission has nothing to do with transforming the nation; it consists, prosaically, of being the transmission line between the nation and a capitalism, rampant though camouflaged, which today puts on the mask of neo-colonialism. The national bourgeoisie will be quite content with the role of the Western bourgeoisie's business agent, and it will play its part without any complexes in a most dignified manner. But this same lucrative role, this cheap-Jack's function, this meanness of outlook and this absence of all ambition symbolise the incapability of the middle class to fulfill its historic role of bourgeoisie. Here, the dynamic, pioneer aspect, the characteristics of the inventor and of the discoverer of new worlds which are found in all national bourgeoisies are lamentably absent. In the colonial countries, the spirit of indulgence is dominant at the core of the bourgeoisie; and this is because the national bourgeoisie identifies itself with the Western bourgeoisie, from whom it has learnt its lessons.[40]

And what of a 'settler-bourgeoisie', somewhere in between? Here, perhaps, the late 1990s promise of a post-nationalist, post-neoliberal politics was most spectacularly broken. In February 2000, a leading official of the Confederation of Zimbabwe Industries (CZI) was appointed economic secretary of the MDC. This was the decisive signal that Tsvangirai and his core leadership allies aimed to ally with big business – at the expense of programmatic, ideological integrity.

The MDC's crossroad

At first blush, it is a simple problem of *compradorism*. Eddie G. Cross comes from a faction of capital that has long supported the introduction of structural adjustment, and which applauded Mugabe for turning to free-market policies during the 1990s. Even after *Esap's* miserable record, Cross remarked to the press in May 1999, 'We in industry believe that the only way to make a significant impact is to comply fully with the IMF conditions.'[41] Although in mid-2000, Cross was told to take a backseat role because his public statements were controversial, he re-emerged repeatedly as the central figure pulling the MDC to the Right, mediating between the opposition party and both its local (white) business and commercial-farming funders, and its regional/ international business and political supporters.

The transcript of a speech Cross gave to a packed house at Harare's Book Café in March 2000 is one of the few in-depth, honest appraisals of ideological orientation to be found from within the MDC's conservative flank. Its veracity is not questioned, and Cross never offered retractions. Indeed, because the speech so effectively presages the MDC's August 2001 economic policy, it is worth significant attention.

Cross began his talk with a diatribe against the massive state deficits accumulated by the Zanu regime, but failed to disclose that the debt burden was just as much the consequence of Washington loan-pushing, of Harare's cottage industry of *Esap*-promoters, and of domestic financial market failures, as it was of populist politicians pleasing the *povo*. Cross then turned quickly from the critical shortage of forex to the 'totally politically isolated' state in which Mugabe lay. The president's only friends were Laurent Kabila (DRC, subsequently assassinated in 2001), Sam Nujoma (Namibia), Mahathir Mohamad (Malaysia) and Moamar Qaddafi (Libya) – 'providing you don't ask them for money'. He noted the fuel dependency of Zimbabwe upon one company, British Petroleum – but 'you [Mugabe] go and kick them in the teeth. A telephone call to the chairman of BP and we are sunk!'[42]

As for Mugabe's *Millennium Economic Recovery Programme (Merp)*, an update of *Esap* that was never published, Cross railed:

> It is toilet paper. It is worth nothing. Complete junk and if implemented it would simply compound our problems. They talk about exchange controls, they talk about price control, they talk about continuing to maintain controls on the Zimbabwean dollar. They talk control on wages. But nothing in the document to address the fundamental problems, absolutely nothing. I actually met with the IMF team after they had spent four fruitless days in Harare, going through the document, going through the planning with the Government and everybody that the Government could bring to speak to then – including Bernard Chidzero, the ex-Minister of Finance – to plead with them to reconsider their position. They saw me after the process and said that there was nothing in the document that they could take back to Washington. Nothing. They said if they took that back to Washington they would be the laughing stock of the financial community in Washington. And I am afraid that throughout the financial institutions of the world, Zimbabwe is the black sheep.

Similarly, Cross remarked, the controversial trip to Harare by South African president Thabo Mbeki and several key officials in March 2000 generated very little. A threatened cut to Zimbabwe's electricity supply from South Africa's Eskom parastatal due to nonpayment was reportedly deferred pending Eskom's takeover of Zimbabwean state facilities. But a US$120 million loan – hinted at by Zimbabwe and widely reported as a bale-out in the South African press – was hastily denied by the South African Finance Ministry. As Cross interpreted:

> South Africa is terrified of our situation here. When Thabo Mbeki was here he agreed to a programme of assistance with Mugabe and he agreed to a wide variety of other things. Went back to Pretoria and the guys in Pretoria said there is no way on this earth that we are going to allow you to prop up their regime in Zimbabwe. He had to go back to the drawing board, as you know. The financial proposals that were agreed to here in Harare were torn up and the South Africans are giving us very limited assistance.

What, then, did Cross propose to resolve the economic crisis?

First of all, we believe in the free market. We do not support price control. We do not support government interfering in the way in which people manage their lives. We are in favour of reduced levels of taxation. We are in favour of introducing Value Added Tax and we will do so quickly, within six months. We are in favour of a National Revenue Authority, these things are things which the government has been talking about for years. We believe they are sound developments. We would like to cap tax levels, both for individuals and for companies. We would like to reduce the levels of border duties . . . The tax burden is simply not sustainable. It is negative in terms of the way it impacts on our society. Now that means we have got to reduce the size of government and not just talk about it.

On privatisation, Cross was especially brash:

We are going to fast track privatisation. All fifty government parastatals will be privatised within a two-year time frame, but we are going far beyond that. We are going to privatise many of the functions of government. We are going to privatise the Central Statistical Office. We are going to privatise virtually the entire school delivery system. And you know, we have looked at the numbers and we think we can get government employment down from about 300 000 at the present time to about 75 000 in five years.

This agenda was, in effect, the medium-term wish-list of the CZI over several previous years. As Cross reaffirmed: 'There is no doubt in my mind that the only way to grow the economy is on a free-market basis.'

Anti-corporate populism?

Yet Cross was not without the sophistication required to work within a party formed by trade unionists. He talked of 'a mixture of a highly conservative approach to economics and a strong social emphasis on improving the quality of life for the average Zimbabwean'. What kind of politics is this, simple politician-doubletalk, or something more durable?

Going back a few years, it is worth recalling that Southern Rhodesia hosted a peculiar brand of white politics traceable to British working-class immigrants who during the twentieth century brought their successful struggle for a generous social welfare state out to the colonies.

Cross confirmed:

> My father was an alcoholic and I was raised by a single mom. My mother could not afford to pay school fees and I would not have received an education if the government of Rhodesia had not simply treated me like a special citizen and given me a free education of a very high standard.

At first blush, positive references to the IMF and 'international community' may disguise the fact that historically, this political tradition often contested the interests of foreign capital. Indeed, to hazard a label, Cross became a leading post-independence representative of a relatively patriotic white settler-bourgeoisie.[43] Notwithstanding its British-colonial worldview, this class has personal assets more fully developed and cemented within Zimbabwe than anywhere else, thanks mainly to the 1960s–1980s period of rigid exchange controls. (A large degree of capital flight occurred in the 1990s, but Zimbabwe remains an extremely comfortable habitat for wealthy whites.)

The roots of Rhodesian populism are in intra-white struggle against Cecil Rhodes' British South Africa Company (BSAC), which formally ran the colony from 1890–1923. Various factions of the white community expressed such strong grievances – small miners over royalty rights; white unions over wages; settler farmers over their need to block black competition; and the church over social and political relations – that 'self-governing status' was chosen in a 1923 whites-only vote. In 1933, struggling white farmers, artisans, and civil servants elected a 'left'-sounding (yet very racist) Reform Party led by Godfrey Huggins.

Huggins promised to rescind BSAC's mineral rights, to impose protectionism, to nationalise key parts of the economy, to provide unemployment relief and white labour rights, and to establish a central bank for the colony. The election was, as Iden Wetherell observed in his seminal 1975 analysis of white politics, 'fundamentally a populist protest designed to remind the State that its primary consideration lay not with the protection of profit, but with the promotion of institutional safeguards that would insure against a repetition of the recent experience'.[44]

After Huggins drifted towards establishment interests, angry white men re-appeared on the political scene in 1962, when the Rhodesian Front came to power. Ian Smith's broad coalition of white Rhodesians included not only those racists fearful of British decolonisation, but others who were adversely affected by the colony's early 1960s economic crisis. Indeed, the 1965 Unilateral Declaration of Independence, according to sociologist Giovanni Arrighi, 'was directed as much against large-scale capitalism as against the Africans. The populist undertones of the UDI campaign were very noticeable.'[45] Those undertones harked back to the 1933 Reform Party victory, Wetherell insisted, since Smith's intention was 'undoubtedly to conserve a system of safeguards that the radicals of the 1930s fought so hard to establish . . . The inheritors of the pre-war populist or "left-wing" legacy [were] now self-defined as "right-wing".'[46]

It is this uneasy combination which Cross appears to have inherited. It combines 'conservative' economic policies that meet the needs of the white-dominated big business sector, with the memory of state support for a then-white, now-black working class. For even while punting rapid privatisation, Cross adds an anti-monopolistic flair:

> An MDC government will sell our shares in the Dairy Board [the partially-privatised national milk and cheese marketing board] immediately, use the proceeds to retire debt and we will work actively to encourage competition. What about all the other cozy monopolies? What about Anglo American Corporation and their stranglehold on the sugar industry in Southern Africa? Let us open our border posts . . . It is competition that will sort out the fat cats in the private sector.

Cross was especially scathing of his CZI colleagues:

> They have been too complacent, they have been playing footsie-footsie with this government for too long. They need to be tougher. This *Millennium Reform Programme* – we see leaders of the private sector saying it is a good programme! It is, well I was going to use a rude word but I won't. It is absolutely nonsense.

He was not only critical of fat cats living off ultra-cheap Zimbabwe labour and acquiescing to Mugabe. Cross added two additional pillars – corporatist industrial relations and an expanded social plan – to the foundations of the MDC programme:

> On the social side we are going to re-visit the issue of minimum wages. Now I am an industrialist and I am well known in industrial circles for actually following this political strategy. I do not believe in low wages. I do not believe in an industrialist or anybody else

being allowed to pay wages which are well below the basic cost of living in cities . . . So we will, as a Government, and with the private sector through a social contract, and working with the trade unions and employers, work towards a situation where we will pay much higher wages in industry, even if it means losing jobs, so that people working in the cities will be able to afford to live in those cities on a whole family basis. He will be able to send his children to school, he will be able to rent or own accommodation which means he can live there with his entire family. For us that is fundamental.

In addition to 'attacking that [migrant labour] system with everything at our disposal' – in part because of migrancy's contribution to the spread of HIV/Aids – Cross set out impressive social promises:

Education is the key and seven years of compulsory free education – free education – and free, not in the way we are doing it at the moment [with parent fees]. We mean free, parents will not be required to pay for it. And you ask, 'Can we afford that?' Yes, we damn well can, we damn well can! And the international community has the resources to help us build that system and they are willing to do so . . . We have a programme for housing – we are going to give tenure, freehold tenure, to everybody who holds tribal trust land leases, immediately we come to power . . . The government has been talking about this for the past ten years, we are not going to talk about this, we are going to do it and we are going to fast-track the administration procedures through massive housing schemes, to provide site-and-service schemes in all our cities for the entire backlog of housing within five years. And you say, 'Can we afford to do it?' Yes, we can! Yes we can, and the international community is prepared to help us with a programme like that . . . We have got to have primary health care throughout the country. We have got to get our hospitals back on their feet . . . Our social programme is going to be strong and it is going to be dynamic and it is going to be directed at the absolute poor, and there's no compromising that. We are totally committed to that, and you need to know it – this is not a rhetorical commitment, this is not a party of the 'haves', this is not a party on the gravy train.

Beginning around 1990, Zimbabwe's have-nots were ferociously pummelled not only by Mugabe and his then labour minister John Nkomo – who tried often enough to fracture the trade union movement

– but by the IMF and those in the 'international community' who forcefed Zimbabweans the idea that structural adjustment and globalisation would solve their problems. Here, then, arose the central contradiction in Eddie Cross' project: implying that his own ticket to the MDC dance was IMF access. As we see next, this was no idle speculation, for within eighteen months, an MDC document was produced codifying his Book Café talk.

And this leads to the obvious question: if the MDC wins a national election in 2002 or subsequently, what is, and will be, the balance of power within the party when the obvious choice between free education and free markets must be made? That will be the real crossroad.[47]

Esarp: *another* Esap?

The Economic Stabilisation and Recovery Programme (Esarp) was launched as a lengthy and often rambling Executive Summary along with two spreadsheets of the MDC macro-economic model by Eddie Cross and Tapiwa Mashakada in August 2001.[48] As a troubling marker of the struggle over ideas within the MDC, it might not stand the test of time and therefore it may be unfair to attach an acronym, but *Esarp* will have to do.

The differences between *Esarp* and *Esap* are far greater than subtracting 'adjustment' and adding 'recovery'. But the similarities are striking, including *Esarp*'s early announcement that the full programme awaits 'ongoing discussions with multilateral and bilateral donors (*sic*) (particularly the IMF, the World Bank and the European Union)'.[49] And like Chidzero in 1991, Cross/Mashakada in 2001 made some extraordinary promises:

> There is every reason for the economy to enter a phase of sustained high growth of around 10% per annum in normal years and 6–8% per annum in drought years. In the first couple of years of the MDC government, it is tempting to project even higher growth rates because the economy will be recovering from a low base, analogous to a country emerging from war . . . It will not take very large injections of foreign exchange to stabilise the economy and once it is released from the debt trap, the natural vigour and enterprise of its people will reassert itself . . . In this framework, it is confidently expected that, within a decade, poverty can be eliminated altogether from Zimbabwe.

But the promised high growth, escape from the debt trap and eradication of poverty are only achieved if 'large injections' are made. How large? 'A total of US$2.5 billion of official development assistance' is required from 2002–2004 and 'if the level of external support is significantly less than this or is not made available according to the timetable assumed (e.g. US$500 million in 2002), the projected stabilisation will falter.' The debt trap would be unfastened not only through rescheduling, but firstly 'because the external resources will essentially allow the domestic debt to be bought back' (by the state, using new foreign loans) and secondly because the inflowing forex would allow 'the arrears accumulated over 2000–2002 to be paid off and normal levels of imports to resume.' *Esarp* pledges to:

> Use the political changes to win support from the multilateral financial institutions and donors to restructure the national debt. This will involve using grants and concessionary loans to reduce the budgetary gap sufficiently for a 'breathing space' to make it possible for the economy to grow out of the debt trap. The foreign exchange inflows will help restore stability to the foreign exchange markets. Complementary policies will (over time) restore growth in export revenues to rebuild foreign currency reserves and reduce the burden of debt servicing to sustainable levels.

Who will grant and lend the MDC government an average of nearly US$1 billion a year? Zimbabwe's most recent aid inflow peak was just US$310 million in 1995. It is a profound, possibly fatal defect, if *Esarp* requires a begging bowl three times larger than that which Mugabe ever held out, even at a time when *Esap* was considered 'highly satisfactory' by the World Bank and its allies.

If in response, the MDC economics desk argues that some of the funding can come in the form of soft (low-interest) loans, the obvious question is how the World Bank's International Development Association (the main source) can justify lending new money to pay the interest on old loans, when a new Zimbabwe government would start out with US$1.2 billion+ arrears on existing loans? And if a large part of the US$2.5 billion is meant to come in the form of the Bretton Woods Institutions' Highly Indebted Poor Countries Initiative, Zimbabwe should be warned that debt-relief disbursements to even the most Washington-friendly countries (like Mozambique and Uganda) have taken years to materialise and began with peanuts (a few million US dollars per year).

Presumably yet more forex will need to be acquired to finance what in 2002 is projected to be a hugely bloated current account deficit –

nearly 11% of GDP, compared to just over 4% from 1996–2000, as another US$110 million trade deficit is anticipated along with the MDC's promised attempt to settle loan arrears as quickly as possible. Moreover, a great deal of the increased state spending on infrastructure and social programmes that *Esarp* promises must also come from foreign donors (though how much is not specified). And if 'the external resources will essentially allow the [existing] domestic debt to be bought back', that will add another US$1 billion+ to the required-financing intray.[50] Although *Esarp* talks of its 'carefully co-ordinated technical details', the number-crunching looks simply impossible from nearly any vantage-point.

It gets more difficult yet, when the meaning of how to 'use the political changes to win support from the multilateral financial institutions' becomes clear. What new pound of flesh is required from the Zimbabwean masses? The hints were clear in March 2000 at the Book Café, and Cross apparently had a free hand in writing *Esarp* to his earlier recipe. The most startlingly neoliberal formulation comes in the form of marching orders to new directors of state companies within the first 100 days of an MDC government: 'the privatisation of all parastatal activity within two years.'

The details, sketchy as they are, remain of interest. As Cross put it during the Book Café talk, 'It is competition that will sort out the fat cats in the private sector'; similarly, *Esarp* promises that privatisation 'will be done in such a way that the resulting arrangements are competitive in character and provide consumers with real choice'. Yet because 'special attention is to be given to the largest privatisations – Posts and Telecommunications, Zimbabwe Electricity Supply Authority and National Railways of Zimbabwe' – and because these are classically considered 'natural monopolies'.[51] it is impossible to fulfill the competition/consumer-choice pledge.

In a bizarre add-on paragraph that recognises 'limited net returns for the fiscus' due to vast existing parastatal debts, *Esarp* continues: 'In any event, the MDC approach will be to give primary weight to the social and broader economic objectives of privatisation, as these will lock in the longer-term gains . . .' But the opposite is more true: huge socio-economic costs are associated with selling state assets to for-profit companies – assets that could instead be used for the broader public good. International experiences of electricity, water and tele-communications privatisations, among others, show that the lowest rungs of society are prone to be denied access, as for-profit firms 'cherry-pick' the market to serve those who have no affordability constraints.[52]

Likewise, nothing is said in *Esarp* about the trade union role (just one mention of 'employee share ownership schemes' to be 'pursued'), although the ZCTU affiliates have already fought long and hard against rail and postal privatisations.

Nor does *Esarp* mention a state regulatory function, perhaps because alleged competition will solve all consumer problems. The commodifying, neoliberal orientation of *Esarp* reaches as deep as any structural adjustment programme into the social sector. For example, *Esarp* specifies as one of its core objectives that the state will 'provide educational opportunities to all children to a level that will enable them *to compete*' (emphasis added), an extremely disturbing formulation. But more chillingly, the document continues, 'In respect of the teaching and health sectors, it is anticipated that these will be restructured so that the majority of personnel currently employed in these areas will become the responsibility of the private sector supported by a per capita grant scheme funded by government.' Fortunately, outsourcing education is a fantasy, because of the residual power of teachers' unions, parents and students. The student uproar faced by state tertiary education officials because of services outsourcing is just one early warning.

A variety of other hard-core liberalisations are planned, including free trade, notwithstanding the damage done during the 1990s to the manufacturing sector. *Esarp* proposes the rapid demise of 'massive distortions in interest and exchange rates [which] will remove the artificial premium in the parallel market rate, bringing down general import prices quite sharply'.[53] Later, 'all remaining restrictions on foreign exchange will be reviewed with a view to moving towards fully liberalised conditions in money and capital markets.' *Esarp* is so behind the international economics curve, that its authors failed to notice how the 1990s-era demand by Washington for capital-account liberalisation was dropped after the Asian crisis. Even the IMF now recognises the merits of exchange controls.[54]

Occasionally the neoliberal mould is broken, when it is clear that market failures and investor confidence are too far beyond self-correction. Wage and price controls are advocated so as to bring down inflation. To do so requires the ZCTU's return to corporatist mode, in the form of a 'Social Contract involving government, organised business and the Zimbabwe Congress of Trade Unions'.

There are several more admirable points, mainly brought in from other MDC portfolios. If the MDC wins the 2002 election, it will be to their great credit to accomplish within the first 100 days the promised:

- orderly withdrawal of troops from the Congo;
- renegotiation of contracts for military hardware;
- reduction in the number of ministries to fifteen and abolition of deputy minister posts; and
- elimination of provincial governorships.[55]

But on social issues, some of the fine-sounding humanistic commitments are offset by the outsourcing philosophy. To illustrate, *Esarp*'s approach to gender is brutally frank:

> The MDC government will *not* have a gender ministry, nor a gender portfolio in the president's office . . . MDC will ensure that gender perspectives inform policy-making and implementation in each and every ministry, thereby giving prominence to the party's commitment to gender equity in every sphere of public life. (original emphasis)

After a statement of this great conviction, it would be reasonable to do a gender-equity check on *Esarp* itself. Women's needs are mentioned precisely once, in a throwaway line very late in the document about women benefitting from training programmes.

For such reasons, it is hard to take seriously another bald statement: 'There is full political commitment within the party to the Programme, giving assurance that it will be implemented with rigour and determination once MDC is in power.' Given that the programme was not made available *en masse* to MDC members, aside from those who could download it from the Internet, and that the debate has not even really begun over a post-Mugabe economy amongst Zimbabwe's democratic political and social movements, 'full political commitment' is really a codeword for Eddie Cross getting his way in the MDC back office and website.[56]

And if not the MDC? *Esarp* claims, 'Even on the most optimistic assumptions but no change of government, Zimbabwe would be saddled with debts several times the current levels by 2004.' This is an assumption that is worth taking forward into the final chapter of the book, where we consider the *real* options in dealing with the debt-laden Zimbabwean economy. Between *Esarp* and whatever Zanu's newest version of *Esap* turns out to be, the choices on offer are likely to be considered thoroughly unacceptable to the Zimbabwean polity.

Conclusion: Will a debate begin?
This chapter has laid bare some of the core contradictions associated with diverse forms of political rhetoric in Zimbabwe, including radical

arguments by presumed 'left-nationalists' and presumed pragmatic arguments by MDC neoliberals, and has found them both wanting. The resolution to this confusion can only be found at a deeper, structural level, which is the subject of the final chapter. But at the very least, Zimbabweans should expect that the ongoing political debate will also shed more light on the implications of a Washington-centric economic policy, whether that of the 1990s or one that is looming.

Matters may become yet more confusing, the more the ruling party searches desperately for scapegoats, and the more that people of good will reject Zanu's dictatorial tendencies and misinformation with revulsion. For example, on his retirement from government in June 2000, outgoing trade/industry minister Nathan Shamuyarira – still Zanu's information officer – first publicly admitted that *Esap* was Zanu's worst mistake. A few months later, vice president Simon Muzenda confirmed the same. Jonathan Moyo has strongly condemned *Esap*, and Mugabe vowed never to return to structural adjustment in October 2001. Given the overwhelming evidence presented in Chapter Two, it is important not to discount the possibility that albeit for their own reasons – not necessarily in search of a progressive way forward – Zanu elites may actually be right: they were truly in an economic cul-de-sac. Managing an untransformed capitalist economy on the semi-periphery of a stagnant world economy, offered profound constraints to social progress.

In the hurly-burly of Zimbabwe's political debate, elite opinion-makers seemed to sense the importance of this ideological conflict, as well. By early 2001, two columnists of the influential *Zimbabwe Independent* argued the merits of neoliberalism with rhetorical antagonism designed, it seemed, to nip any dissent from orthodoxy in the bud. Wilbert Mukori scornfully recalled 'Tsvangirai's ZCTU days' when 'the trade union movement's economic policies were at best a confused rehash of Zanu's socialist trash . . . The MDC would best be advised to adopt whatever revision of the *Esap* the IMF/World Bank has to offer.'[57]

And the country's main business commentator, accountant Eric Bloch, defended that failed strategy on grounds that

> *Esap* was, to a very great degree, implemented only as a matter of lip-service. Government had no substantive commitment to, or conviction in, *Esap* and therefore only implemented the programme partially. Patients who take prescribed medication erratically,

inadequately and in disregard for the prescription directions, rarely recover . . . It is government which alienated IMF support, and also that of most international monetary organisations, the support of donor nations, and the support of aid agencies.[58]

It may be self-satisfying to say, 'Washington was right but Zanu didn't implement *Esap*.' Yet as noted in Chapter Two, not only did the World Bank give *Esap* its highest mark in 1995.[59] The same year, a rather more pro-government Bloch was celebrating 'significant reductions in direct taxation, the liberalisation of trade and virtual elimination of import controls with a consequential elimination of most shortages, the immense relaxations of exchange controls' and other 'indicators of the achievements of *Esap* to date'.[60] Presumably, the Zimbabwe elites' 1990s splurge on luxury good imports and successful expatriation of Rhodesian-era capital was real, not just 'lip-service'.

The revisionist Bloch argued that an important exonerating factor for neoliberalism was that 'Zimbabwe's economy was in an appalling state and a horrific mess before *Esap* was embarked upon. It was the devastatingly shattered state of the economy which motivated government to consider *Esap* in the first instance.'[61] The concluding section of Chapter Two offers documentation to the effect that according to every single economic variable, Zimbabwe performed far better before *Esap* – and although mired in stagnation borne of the 1970s overaccumulation crisis, was nowhere near 'devastatingly shattered' – than it has since. Upon receipt of this information,[62] Bloch revised again, insisting that

> only two relatively progressive economic growth years occurred, being 1994 and 1995, when government belatedly developed some commitment to *Esap*. In the first three years, *Esap* was embarked upon most half-heartedly, with consequential inadequate contribution to economic growth and moreover, Zimbabwe was afflicted in 1991–1992 with the worst ever drought that it had experienced.[63]

What, then, was *Esap's* record prior to the 1991–1992 drought, which formally began when the rainy season failed (November 1991)? The policy was, from early 1991, implemented rapidly as trade and finance were liberalised, monetary policy was tightened, interest rates soared, the currency was devalued by 35%, and key price controls were dropped. Yet according to the ZCTU, 'Exports fell by over 3% in 1991 before any impact of the drought could be felt, whereas in the comparable drought

year of 1987 they had actually risen.'[64] Inflation began to roar by mid-
1991, quickly doubling average 1980s levels. IMF/World Bank teams
were by then running all over Harare, and on 5 September persuaded the
Reserve Bank to let short-term interest rates soar from 27.5% to 44%.
Immediate results included a massive credit crunch (e.g. no home
mortgages were available), a sustained property market downturn,
disastrous pension fund returns, major corporate financial crises, and a
sudden 30% crash of the Zimbabwe Stock Exchange. All this happened
before the onset of the 1991–1992 drought, and because of *Esap*.

Debating establishment representatives like Bloch – who see in
Zimbabwe's ongoing crisis a chance to repackage neoliberalism – is as
frustrating, we find, as debating the exhausted nationalists. Here again,
Fanon is prescient, because he recognised that in the fight against
colonialism – and in early twenty-first century Zimbabwe, we need
only replace 'decolonisation' with 'democratisation' – the problem of
creeping bourgeois control of the ascendant political party (in our
updated case, the MDC) would be disguised by calls for 'unity'.

> . . . in the thick of the fight, more than a few militants asked the leaders
> to formulate a dogma, to set out their objectives, and to draw up a
> programme. But under the pretext of safeguarding national unity, the
> leaders categorically refused to attempt such a task. The only worthwhile
> dogma, it was repeatedly stated, is the union of the nation against
> colonialism. And on they went, armed with an impetuous slogan
> which stood for principles, while their only ideological activity took the
> form of a series of variants on the theme of the right of peoples to self-
> determination, borne on the wind of history which would inevitably
> sweep away colonialism. When the militants asked whether the wind of
> history couldn't be a little more clearly analysed, the leaders gave them
> instead hope and trust, the necessity of decolonisation and its
> inevitability, and more to that effect.[65]

An entirely different approach is called for, drawing on the best traditions
of internationalism. We argue in our final chapter that Zimbabweans
have a great deal to learn from the constraints to social development
that accompany the Washington Consensus – or more popularly,
'globalisation' – virtually everywhere, just as they have much to learn
from the inspiring resistance that likewise is emerging virtually
everywhere. And in addition, of course, the world, and the region,
should at the same time learn a great deal from Zimbabwe's politico-
financial experiences.

Notes

1. One of us was a BBC commentator during the June 2000 parliamentary election and was stunned at the interviewer's lack of professionalism, as this was asked of unqualified guests on camera.

2. For useful contemporary political analyses, see Kriger, N. (2000), 'Zimbabwe Today: Hope against Grim Realities', *Review of African Political Economy*, 27, 85; Moore, D. (2000) 'The Alchemy of Robert Mugabe's Alliances', *Africa Insight*, 30, 1; and Moore, D. (2001), 'Democracy is Coming to Zimbabwe', *Australian Journal of Political Science*, 36, 1.

3. Fanon, F. (1963)[1961], *The Wretched of the Earth*, New York, Grove Press, pp. 181–182.

4. Fanon, *The Wretched of the Earth*, p. 204.

5. Moore, D. (1991), 'The Ideological Formation of the Zimbabwean Ruling Class', *Journal of Southern African Studies*, 17, 3.

6. *Red Pepper*, May 1998.

7. Nest, M. (2001), 'Ambitions, Profits and Loss: Zimbabwean Economic Involvement in the Democratic Republic of the Congo', *African Affairs*, 100, 4.

8. It has been pointed out to us, though, by Zimbabwe/DRC expert David Moore, that in the wake of Kabila Sr's assassination, the US government may have in reality shifted position on Zimbabwean troops in the DRC, because Kabila's more pliable son may require their support in order to stabilise a situation that is increasingly favourable to Western interests.

9. The idea was not outlandish: see for example, the 'Suharto Scenario' as painted in Alexander, P. (2000), 'The Zimbabwean Working Class, the MDC and the 2000 Election', *Review of African Political Economy*, 27, 85.

10. Here we mainly refer the reader to far more expert specialist accounts, for recent general analysis of the land question, for specific studies of extremely diverse situations, and for policy options: Bowyer-Bower, T. and C. Stoneman (eds) (2000), *Land Reform in Zimbabwe: Constraints and Prospects*, Ashgate, Aldershot; Hansungule, M. (2000), 'Who owns Land in Zimbabwe? In Africa?', *International Journal on Minority and Group Rights*, 7, 4; Harts-Broekhuis, A. and H. Huisman (2001), 'Resettlement Revisited: Land Reform Results in Resource-Poor Regions in Zimbabwe', *Geoforum*, 32, 3; Hoogeveen, J. and B. Kinsey (2000), 'Land Reform, Growth and Equity: Emerging Evidence from Zimbabwe's Resettlement Programme – A Sequel', *Journal of Southern African Studies*, 27, 1; Izumi, K. (1999), 'Liberalisation, Gender, and the Land Question in Sub-Saharan Africa', *Gender and Development*, 7, 3; Kinsey, B. (1999), 'Land Reform, Growth and Equity: Emerging Evidence from Zimbabwe's Resettlement Programme', *Journal of Southern African Studies*, 25, 2; Moore, D. (2001), 'Is the Land the Economy and the Economy the Land? Primitive Accumulation in Zimbabwe', *Journal of Contemporary African Studies*, 19, 2; Nyambara, P. (2001), 'The Politics of Land Acquisition and Struggles over Land in the Communal Areas of Zimbabwe: The Gokwe Region in the 1980s and 1990s', *Africa*, 71, 2; and Taylor, S. (1999), 'Business and Politics in Zimbabwe's Commercial Agriculture Sector', *African Economic History*, 27. Papers by Sam Moyo are cited below.

11. Ranger, T. (1985), *Peasant Consciousness and Guerrilla War in Zimbabwe*, London, James Currey; but see, for evidence of ambiguity on this matter, Kriger, N. (1992), *Zimbabwe's Guerrilla War: Peasant Voices*, Cambridge, Cambridge University Press.

12. See for example, Bakker, I. (ed) (1994), *The Strategic Silence: Gender and Economic Policy*, London, Zed Press; Gibson-Graham, J. (1996), *The End of Capitalism (as we Know it): A Feminist Critique of Political Economy*, Oxford, Basil Blackwell; Jackson, F. and R. Pierson (eds) (1998), *Feminist Visions of Development: Gender Analysis and Policy*, London, Routledge; Mies, M. (1986), *Patriarchy and Accumulation on a World Scale: Women in the International Division of Labour*, London, Zed Press; Moghadfam, V. (ed) (1996), *Patriarchy and Economic Development: Women's Positions at the End of the Twentieth Century*, Oxford, Clarendon; Prugl, E. and M.K. Meyer (eds) (1999), *Gender Politics in Global Governance*, New York, Rowman and Littlefield; Sassen, S. (1998), *Globalisation and its Discontents*, New York, The New Press; Shiva, V. (1989), *Staying Alive: Women, Ecology and Development*, London, Zed Press.

13. Moyo, S. (2000), 'The Political Economy of Land Acquisition and Redistribution in Zimbabwe, 1990–1999', *Journal of Southern African Studies*, 26, 1; (2001), 'The Land Question and Land Reform in Southern Africa', Southern African Regional Institute for Policy Studies, Harare.

14. Similarly tragic blame the 'Other' reactions surfaced in South Africa when, also in 2001, more than 10 000 Zimbabweans working on Northern Province farms were sent home.

15. Interview, Wilf Mhanda, June 2000; for more on the questionable character of Mugabe's claim to nationalist war-hero status, see the interview with Mhanda in Helen Suzman Foundation periodical *Focus*, December 2000.

16. Ngwenya, M. (2001), 'A View from the Pan – Farms and Prices', MDC Mailing List, 5 October.

17. *Daily News*, 14 September 2000.

18. *Daily News*, 8 August 2000.

19. *Daily News*, 19 June 2000.

20. *Daily News*, 23 March 2000.

21. *Zimbabwe Independent*, 19 May 2000.

22. *Herald*, 17 April 2000.

23. The statement was immediately retracted, and the mass-action threat was withdrawn by late 2000 when conservative forces in the MDC compelled a tactful retreat, arguing the chance for success was limited. In November 2001, Tsvangirai's court case on charges of inciting violence was thrown out on grounds of the unconstitutionality of the Rhodesian-era law he was prosecuted under, for the statement above.

24. George, S. (2000), 'A Short History of Neoliberalism', in W. Bello, K. Malhutra and N. Bullard (eds), *Cooling Down Capital: How to Regulate Financial Markets*, London, Zed Press.

25. Zanu (2000), 'The People's Manifesto', Harare, pp. 46–47. For a contrary perspective – namely, that 'black empowerment lobby groups and political commentators say the government has failed to achieve its objective of economically empowering the average Zimbabwean through privatisation' – see *Zimbabwe Standard*, 17 October 1999.

26. *Zimbabwe Standard*, 10 September 2000.

27. Ncube, W. (1989), 'The Post-Unity Period: Developments, Benefits and Problems', in C. Banana (ed), *Turmoil and Tenacity: Zimbabwe 1890–1990*, Harare, College Press.

28. Albert Mugabe, brother of Robert, served as secretary-general until his death, which dramatically retarded the movement's development.

29. Tsvangirai, M. (1991), 'What We Need is Mass Action!' (Interview), *Southern Africa Report*, July.

30. The legacy of post-independence trade unionism is documented in three excellent studies: Raftopoulos and Phimister, *Keep on Knocking*; Yeros, P. (2001), *Labour Struggles for Alternative Economics in Zimbabwe: Trade Union Nationalism and Internationalism in a Global Era*, Harare, Southern African Political Economic Series Monograph Series; and Raftopoulos and Sachinkonye, *Striking Back*.

31. ZCTU, *Beyond Esap*, pp. i, 20–21, 58, 61; see Bond, *Uneven Zimbabwe*, Chapter Twelve, for full details. For evidence that a pseudo-neoliberal ideology retained purchase through the 1990s amongst some civil society intellectuals, see Poverty Reduction Forum and University of Zimbabwe Institute of Development Studies (1998), 'Recommendations for the 1999 National Budget', Harare, United Nations Development Program. One suggestion – that 'privatisation and commercialisation of public enterprises should be speeded up in a transparent manner . . . Proceeds from the divestiture programme should be used to retire debt and avoid the debt trap' (p. 29) – is debunked in Chapter Four.

32. Cited in Sachikonye, L. (1998), 'Trade Unions: Economic and Political Development in Zimbabwe since Independence in 1980', in Raftopoulos and Phimister, *Keep on Knocking*, p. 127.

33. We are indebted to John Saul for the phrase.

34. Van der Walt, L. (1998), 'Trade Unions in Zimbabwe: For Democracy, against Neoliberalism', *Capital and Class*, 66.

35. http://www.samara.co.zw/zctu/position.htm

36. http://www.mdc.co.zw/intro-frames.html

37. *The Worker*, 72, September/October 1999; for more on the ideological give and take, see Yeros, *Labour Struggles for Alternative Economics in Zimbabwe*.

38. *Southern Africa Report*, 15, 3, June 2000. These and the following quotes are in original transcript, held by the authors.

39. For example, in wording identical to that in South Africa's 1996 Constitution, the NCA Bill of Rights is extended to 'juristic persons, such as corporations', in a manner that – South Africa's experience suggests – would hinder policy-making in future, and the strong emphasis on property rights will also be debilitating to the cause of social justice.

40. Fanon, *The Wretched of the Earth*, pp. 152–153.

41. *Financial Gazette*, May 1999.

42. Within eighteen months, Qaddafi had indeed come to Mugabe's rescue, with tens of millions of dollars of petrol supplies provided on 'counter-trade' grounds, which at the time of writing remain obscure, but which are rumoured to include a variety of privatisation options and land transfers.

43. This is not to cast aspersions on Cross himself. The media, especially the *Daily News*, have reported extensively on his own bankruptcy problems.

44. Wetherell, H.I. (1975), 'N.H. Wilson: Populism in Southern Rhodesia', *Rhodesian History*, 6, p. 61.

45. Arrighi, 'The Political Economy of Rhodesia', p. 367.

46. Wetherell, 'N.H. Wilson', p. 76.

47. Reliable reports reached us in November 2001 that this question was put to

Tsvangirai by university students who supported a more progressive MDC education policy – announced in September 2001 – than was allowed for in the August 2001 *Esarp*. Tsvangirai allegedly ordered that the education policy be removed from the MDC website.

48. Movement for Democratic Change (2001), 'MDC Economic Stabilisation and Recovery Programme: Executive Summary Covering the Period April 2002– December 2004', Harare. The document is web-based and hence no page numbers are provided in the citations below. We are informed that other key authors included Peter Robinson and Dan Ndlela, who during the 1980s were generally considered to be economists working from a progressive tradition.

49. In Chapter Two, we offered very rare praise to the Zimbabwe government for not repaying the Bretton Woods Institutions. *Esarp* reads the situation differently: 'The inability of the country to meet primary external obligations, including falling into arrears with the IMF, the World Bank and the African Development Bank, is one of the most damning indicators of economic mismanagement and collapse.'

50. *Esarp*'s own projections are that domestic debt will be Z$431 billion at year-end 2002, of which two-thirds is reduced over two years: Z$120 billion presumably bought at the anticipated effective exchange rate of Z$246/US$1 in 2003 (for US$487 million) and Z$165 billion in 2004 at Z$280/$US (US$589 million).

51. There is no point in building another telcoms fixed line, or electricity transmission line or railway line, when one already exists between two places.

52. The best source is the Public Services International Research Institute at University of Greenwich, at http://www.psiru.org; for southern African municipal privatisation experiences, see the Municipal Services Project at http://www.queensu.ca/msp. It is telling that the main attempt to privatise municipal water in Zimbabwe, by the British firm BiWater in 1999, failed because of lack of sufficient customer affordability for the firm to realise the desired profit.

53. The exceptions are fuel and electricity, whose prices will soar when the artificial Z$55/US$1 rate is removed (or if Zanu wins, merely lowered) in 2002.

54. Some of *Esarp*'s most extreme neoliberal commitments are silly: for example, in the field of financial liberalisation, an attempt to kick-start a secondary mortgage market within 100 days of the MDC taking power, when Zanu's finance and housing ministry functionaries, guided aggressively by the US Agency for International Development (US AID), the World Bank and other neoliberal agencies, did not succeed over a *16-year* period. The promise to close Noczim within the first 100 days is also over-the-top.

55. Given the upsurge of 'federalist' sentiment in Matabeleland North and South, it will be interesting to see whether this provision costs votes in that crucial part of the country.

56. It is difficult to project whether Cross would retain such influence after an MDC electoral victory. Potential finance and economic ministers in a Tsvangirai cabinet, with more credibility than Cross or Mashakada, would probably be recruited from the black banking sector, where men like Julius Makoni and Nigel Chanakira established reputations as sound professionals and political moderates.

57. *Zimbabwe Independent*, 12 January 2001.

58. *Zimbabwe Independent*, 12 January 2001.

59. According to Bloch, 'The World Bank assessment was in 1995, when for over

two years Zimbabwe had at last applied some commitment to the implementation of *Esap*. I believe a very different assessment would have been forthcoming in 1991–1992, or again in 1998–1999!' (*Zimbabwe Independent*, 2 February 2001.) In reality, the Bank's project completion evaluations assessed *Esap* in its entirety, for the years 1991–1995. The Bank continually endorsed *Esap*'s trajectory through 1995. And even in 1998–1999, the Bank and IMF were sufficiently satisfied with Zanu's performance and prospects that they continued to offer new loans, albeit with still more conditionality, as discussed in Chapter Two.

60. *Financial Gazette*, 5 January 1995.
61. *Zimbabwe Independent*, 12 January 2001.
62. *Zimbabwe Independent*, 26 January 2001.
63. *Zimbabwe Independent*, 2 February 2001. The record after Zanu allegedly began taking *Esap* seriously is unimpressive. From year-end 1993 to year-end 1995, per person GDP did rise (by $30, from $1910 to $1940 in 1990 currency values). But over those two years, manufacturing's contribution to GDP fell from 18.3% to 16.7%, indicating rapid de-industrialisation. Meanwhile, output from finance/insurance, including accountancy, rose from 7.5% to 7.7%.
64. ZCTU, *Beyond Esap*, p. 61.
65. Fanon, *The Wretched of the Earth*, p. 170.

CHAPTER FOUR

Globalisation's Constraints

1. Introduction

Zimbabweans face a short-term choice in the 2002 elections and a medium-term dilemma. Zanu's continuing rule offers Zimbabwe worsening economic crisis combined with dictator-type repression. While presumably more tolerant of dissent and diversity in the political sphere, the MDC's economic strategy is dubious at best, and sufficiently similar to previous neoliberal policies that we can safely predict its failure.

To be sure, the problems that either party would face as government in 2002 and beyond are profound. It goes without saying that for the foreseeable future, Zimbabwe will remain in 'crisis'[1] – a situation whereby socio-economic equilibrating mechanisms have broken down, and some force external to the prevailing systematic logic must be invoked to restore stability. If correct, this implies the need for a much further-reaching process of social and economic change than is apparently envisaged by the two contending political parties, a process dependent upon a 'deglobalisation' strategy that is absolutely not infeasible, nor without historical precedent.

But what is the 'systematic logic' that has now moved beyond mere economic stagnation and decline, into near-meltdown mode? We would term Zimbabwe's logic 'uneven development', and assert that on the periphery of world capitalism in the early twenty-first century after a quarter-century of organic crisis and two decades of exposure to intensifying 'globalisation', the prospects for relatively less uneven capitalist development in Zimbabwe – and virtually everywhere – are grim until decisive world-scale change transpires.

The forces working against global social change are discussed in Section 2, beginning with the demands being made by Washington for Zimbabwe's deepening integration into the world marketplace, and new loan sweeteners to entice a new government. While Washington remains powerful, that is partly due to having stared down previous Zimbabweans who postured on the world stage during the 1980s when a similar opportunity for global change briefly presented itself. At the same time, as Section 3 documents, the threat from neighbouring South Africa is ambiguous, because President Thabo Mbeki's (wavering) status quo political interests in Zimbabwe must be set against his government's subimperialist investment/trade policies, applied to both the region and to the continent through the *New Partnership for Africa's Development*.

2. What Washington wants from Harare

If the sweeping argument laid out above proves to be incorrect, it will be because with the help of Washington and Pretoria, a political deal is hammered out in Zimbabwe, perhaps similar in *modus operandi* to the one that gave South Africa its 'liberation' in 1994. Such 'transitions to democracy' occurred from Southern Europe to the Southern Cone of Latin America to Eastern Europe to East Asia to Africa during the 1970s–1990s. It could be argued that Zimbabwe was at the fore of this wave, in 1980, and that it is time again for such a process in 2002, or later if the presidential election is won by Mugabe.

Limits of the deal

Most transitions to democracy, sadly, were merely negotiated elite power-transfers. Authoritarian groups reliant upon the state's repressive apparatus gave way to popular fronts. Yet these very quickly reverted to neoliberalism. Merely naming the popular leaders demonstrates how common it was for anti-authoritarian critics – whether from right-wing or left-wing backgrounds – to transform into neoliberals: Alfonsin (Argentina), Aquino (Philippines), Arafat (Palestine), Aristide (Haiti), Bhutto (Pakistan), Chiluba (Zambia), Dae Jung (South Korea), Havel (Czech Republic), Mandela (South Africa), Manley (Jamaica), Megawati (Indonesia), Museveni (Uganda), Nujoma (Namibia), Obasanjo (Nigeria), Ortega (Nicaragua), Perez (Venezuela), Rawlings (Ghana), Walesa (Poland) and Yeltsin (Russia).

Most deals done by these men and women did nothing to identify and rectify the sins of prior dictatorships, the Cold War depredations and other imperialist power plays, the deeply-embedded corruption, the patriarchy, the racial/ethnic divide/rule techniques, and so much other detritus that the new elite were meant, somehow, to 'transform'. Most deals could be described as 'low-intensity democracy'. Below the facade of multipartyism, the overall parameters had been set in Washington.[2] Truth and reconciliation commissions were rare.

Most deals left the economic status quo intact, no matter how unequal and unsustainable. 'Dictators left debt to democrats', and only in a few cases – Aquino, Aristide and Megawati – were attempts made to retrieve the stolen loot, although civil society groups in Mandela's South Africa, Obasanjo's Nigeria and the Jubilee South movement worked hard to politicise bank collaboration with the dictators. But the period has been remarkable for how few 'democratic' leaders were willing to challenge their tormentors' 'Odious Debts' – which by international legal precedent they should not have to repay. Is there a more poignant reflection of malevolent, long-lasting international financial power relations than Mugabe's spinelessness over the inherited Rhodesian debt?

As a result, most such transitions replaced the repression of the generals/politicians with neoliberal policies favoured by the bankers/businessmen. The new ruling clique of 'democratic' politicians either went along for the ride, perhaps complaining a bit, or they mindlessly bought into the Washington Consensus ideology. In turn, in most cases, economic austerity and sometimes severe financial crises bred more intense class and gender inequity than before. Only very few countries in Europe (e.g. Spain and Portugal) and Asia (Taiwan) remain as durable success stories of these elite transitions, combining democratisation, growth and expanding opportunities for the majority of citizens. Even South Africa's lauded 'miracle' already appears to be failing in ways that are all too similar to Zimbabwe's independence.[3]

For the next few years in Zimbabwe, an elite consensus will not be easy to locate, given how much of its existence Zanu has invested in the spoils of state control, and given the small margin in the numerical battle for votes – albeit never under free/fair conditions – since February 2000. A power-transfer deal cooked up in some new Lancaster House would neither solve nor survive the most profound socio-economic contradictions. Nor would a close MDC electoral victory in 2002 – within 100 days restoring the most devastating early 1990s neoliberal economic policies – be tenable for more than a few honeymoon years, before conflicts ensued. Nor can Zanu continue along the current course.

The neoliberal agenda

As if to prove the latter point, at least a dozen areas of strife emerged by the late 1990s, between Washington, Harare and the interests of the broader Zimbabwean society. What were Washington's key priorities amongst the list on Table 5? Typically, it is impossible for the public to

Table 5   Who wins and who loses from neoliberalism?

Washington's dictates	Progressive rebuttals
Relax foreign currency controls, beginning with corporate and personal forex accounts that permit a full 100% retention of hard-currency earnings.	Exchange control liberalisation would ultimately permit wealthy Zimbabwean individuals and corporations to decapitalise the country, which they would surely do given the lessons learned in 1997 about their government's capacity to stay the neoliberal course. Even a governing MDC – whose constituents in the urban proletariat loudly clamour to be lifted from poverty – would not offer a sufficiently convincing change to prevent capital flight.
Retract luxury-goods import taxes.	Zimbabwe already imports beyond its means, requiring the unethical use of good land and irrigation for export crops (especially tobacco) instead of for food production, in order that the economy has sufficient foreign exchange to serve rich Zimbabweans' First World tastes. Moreover, a return to the 1990s heyday of conspicuous consumption would generate yet more class antagonism and instability.
Abolish price controls.	Under conditions of relatively monopolistic supply, there was during 2000–2001 an inordinate rise in prices for basic essentials. Mugabe's 1998–2001 imposition of controls was generally not well considered. Yet while price controls are no long-term strategy, and while further interventions (even state supply) are required to assure that there remain supplies of basic price-controlled essentials, they were necessary to stave off starvation (and were supported by the ZCTU). It is worth recalling that ending more wide-ranging price controls in 1991 caused the onset of the inflationary era that lasted the whole decade.
Restore full private property rights as the basis for land redistribution, and impose land titles in Communal Areas.	As with the 1980s–1990s willing-seller/ willing-buyer policy, land holdings would concentrate in the hands of the wealthy. Redistribution would again be delayed.

Washington's dictates	Progressive rebuttals
Cut the enormous budget deficit (but not necessarily by lowering debt repayments or by bringing home the boys from the DRC).	Nearly invariably, fiscal shrinkage affects women-headed households and other vulnerable groups most, because they typically are the least powerful when it comes to budget-related advocacy and pressure, and bear the burden of reproducing society.
Repay foreign debt.	The debt should be repudiated and cancelled, as it has been repaid due to declining terms of trade and compound interest, and because joint creditor liability should compensate: i.e. lenders owe Zimbabweans for *Esap's* profound failure.
Devalue the Zimbabwe currency to the parallel market rate.	Full devaluation – of a factor of 6 in late 2001 – would result in massive imported inflation via petrol and electricity.
Restore a positive real interest rate.	To raise interest rates by at least 85% so as to achieve a positive real (after-inflation) rate, would cause an immediate financial crisis for debtors, which in turn would undermine the health of many local financial institutions when debts come due.
Impose wage restraint.	Zimbabwe's workers already took the brunt of the failures associated with structural adjustment, and their combined direct and social wages fell by far more than did profits and upper-income salaries.
Privatise parastatal corporations.	Parastatals are inefficient and corrupt, yet it has not been established who (if anyone) might buy the companies, what degree of job loss (and related social costs) would occur, and whether the 'public good' aspects of state assets would be lost in the process (e.g. subsidies for rural electricity).
Cut the civil service and outsource state functions.	To genuinely develop Zimbabwe, a larger not smaller civil service will be required.
Promote free trade in regional and international forums such as the World Trade Organisation.	Zimbabwe was one of the few countries that stood up against the North – and South Africa – in Seattle and related venues, and should continue doing so for its own sake and on behalf of the Third World.

learn what demands are being made on their elected leaders. Even in 2002, World Bank reports carry the following warning in an intimidating front-page note: 'This document has a restricted distribution and may be used by recipients only in the performance of their official duties. Its contents may not otherwise be disclosed without World Bank authorisation.'

However, as discussed earlier in Chapter Two, readers of the *Financial Gazette* were aware of IMF Africa official Michael Nowak's primary objectives in 1999 (the first three) and of what his boss Stanley Fischer told Simba Makoni in 2001 (the fourth). In late 2000, another IMF team visited and publicly insisted that 'fiscal consolidation and exchange rate re-alignment – the main pillars of the proposed package – should be buttressed by a re-orientation of public spending to priority sectors, tight monetary and wage policies, and expedite (*sic*) structural reforms especially privatisation, civil service reform and trade liberalisation,' the *Herald* reported. According to the same source, government would be compliant:

> Fiscal consolidation would be achieved by reducing the budget deficit from an estimated 23% to 15.5% of the gross domestic product in the 2001 national budget presented by Dr Simba Makoni last month. The deficit would be curtailed to 8% in 2002 and 3% in 2003. The wage bill will also be limited from 16.7% to 12% of GDP, which refers to the total value of goods and services produced in Zimbabwe, through the rationalisation of the civil service . . . Zimbabwe is also in the process of eliminating foreign currency and exchange restrictions, stimulate (*sic*) the export sector, paying off its debts and improve (*sic*) the collection of statistical data . . . But the IMF remained saddened by slow progress in rationalising the civil service and disposing of Government stake in public enterprises.[4]

Lending lines

Washington also intends to push more loans on Zimbabwe. A list of pipeline credits remained on the World Bank website through the dark days of 2000–2001, as depicted in Table 6.

Even prior to loans being granted or conditionalities revealed, there are several reasons to critique the premises:

(1) the fundamentally unsound practice of using hard-currency financing (US$) to pay for goods/services that have no (or very little) import cost;

(2) the fact that the Bank's previous Zimbabwe project loans in many of these areas were disasters;

(3) the Orwellian discourse associated with decentralisation – typically meaning, in the context, more responsibilities but fewer resources, hence certain failure;

(4) the spectre of privatisation, cost-recovery and even US-style 'managed care' problems – especially healthcare access for poor people and women – associated with commodification and a 'public/private mix'; and

(5) the need for an alternative to borrowing from the Bank to buy imported drugs (in the form of high-priced international pharmaceutical products typically on patent): namely, local generic production of anti-retrovirals and other essential drugs, at a fraction of pharmaceutical corporation prices.[5]

For example, taking on a hard-currency loan so as to downsize the (coal-powered) rail sector would be especially daft, in the midst of a petrol

Table 6   Next-generation World Bank loans to Zimbabwe?[6]

Title	Amount	Loan purposes (and reference to critique on pp. 118 and 119)
Structural Adjustment	US$140 m	• Restructure public expenditures (1) (2) • Reduce domestic debt (1) (2) • Privatise state enterprises (1) (2) • Initiate land reform (1) (2)
Transport (roads)	US$100 m	• Rehabilitate and maintain roads (1) • Co-ordinated plans, policy and institutional reforms (1) • Programming of rehabilitation and maintenance (1) • Private sector participation (1) • Human resource development (1)
Transport (rail)	US$60 m	• Staff retrenchment and rationalisation (1) (2) • Infrastructure rehabilitation (1) (2) • Studies and technical assistance (1) (2) • Training and counselling (1) • Assistance to retrenched staff (1)
Public Sector Management	US$50 m	• Infrastructure financing (1) (2) • Local government capacity building support (1) (2)
Population, Health and Nutrition	US$50 m	• District health decentralisation (1) (3) • Public/private mix (4) • Provision of drugs (5) • Personnel reform (1)

crisis which should logically shift deliveries and even passenger traffic from road to rail. Railways trade unionists have opposed downsizing and public-private partnerships, and point to the Bulawayo–Beitbridge Railroad as an example of the patronage-based, corruption-ridden privatisation that must be avoided.

World Bank loans for health crises, especially HIV/Aids and malaria, deserve special consideration. Bank president James Wolfensohn has identified 'global public goods' as a rationale for future increases in Bank lending that cannot be otherwise justified. Zimbabwe will be pushed to participate in an Aids Fund whose origins in 2000–2001 reflected the shifting balance of power between international pharmaceutical corporations and their host governments (especially the United States and European Union states) on the one hand, and progressive activists South and North on the other. A post-Zanu Zimbabwe – or even one in which a modicum of effort is made to pay back arrears, in the event Mugabe wins – will be a prime candidate.

Yet the Bank's record on HIV/Aids and other health crises does not inspire confidence. In 1992, the US Center for Disease Control condemned World Bank and IMF structural adjustment programmes for exacerbating the spread of Aids in Africa. Notwithstanding this early warning, Bank-imposed user-fees were subsequently required in nearly three quarters of the Bank's health projects in sub-Saharan Africa. Health utilisation rates plummeted in virtually all cases.

After enormous destruction to Third World health systems, the World Bank responded to the African Aids crisis by offering hard-currency *loans* of $500 million in 2000. Ethiopia and Kenya were the first to accept. Yet virtually all spending associated with those Aids programmes covers interventions such as education that could be paid for with local currency, instead of adding a hard-currency liability. Moreover, the most important single external intervention that would help Africa deal decisively with Aids – relaxation of pharmaceutical corporate patents – remained off the Bank agenda. In December 2000, the Bank joined six international agencies to argue that 'anti-retroviral therapy is still unaffordable for most developing countries'.[7] The Bank and its allies sided with the pharmaceutical corporations most responsible for the unnecessary deaths of millions of people, so as to assure that the firms continue to reap billions of dollars in profits.[8]

The holocaust-style suffering caused by Aids has now killed more people than any other illness since the Black Plague of 1347, which it will soon overtake. Millions of Zimbabwean lives will be lost, decades too early. Yet in the United States, what was inexorably fatal has been transformed into a chronic illness comparable to diabetes, thanks to anti-retroviral drugs. Because the price of such treatment was, during the 1990s, in excess of US$10 000 per patient each year, it was inconceivable to offer all HIV-positive Zimbabweans the necessary drugs. Yet by 2000, generic production – and effective administration – of a standard anti-retroviral drug cocktail became a reality in Brazil, India and Thailand, for approximately US$1 per day per patient.

Instead of embracing the possibility of violating the pharmaceutical corporations' monopoly patents so as to bring treatment costs down, the Bank's Aids lenders simply rejected treatment. This would not impress either southern African health professionals or social-justice activists. As Zambia's Jubilee 2000 pointed out:

> Loans will not solve the Aids/HIV pandemic that Zambia is currently facing. As Jubilee-Zambia, we are concerned with the World Bank's insistence that Zambia should acquire loans to tackle the Aids problem. The World Bank should realise that Zambia is actually losing more lives as a result of servicing debts for the loans that we are being encouraged to borrow.[9]

Can Washington reform?

IMF and World Bank loans, policy advice, and conditionality could well return to Zimbabwe if there is a future MDC government – either elected in 2002, or possibly at some stage in the future – or even to another Mugabe-led government, if it again zig-zagged back towards neoliberalism. Have the Bank and IMF made a turn towards 'pro-poor' strategies over the decade since *Esap* was introduced? Do the Poverty Reduction Strategy Papers signal a more humane approach?

Table 7 provides a rough political mapping of the balance of forces required to answer such questions. By the end of 2001, the bloc of neoliberal international elite managers appeared to be holding the Washington Consensus line, notwithstanding the temptation of many on the far Right – like George W. Bush – to apply proto-fascist formulae to both geopolitics and economics. The US economy had begun a severe recession well before the 11 September catastrophe, with potentially devastating consequences for those exporters which had grown dependent upon American hedonistic consumption norms.

Helping to bolster the sole superpower's claim to economic predominance was ally Tony Blair and his chancellor of the exchequer, Gordon Brown. The Federal Reserve Board's chairperson, Alan Greenspan, lowered interest rates urgently, while US treasury secretary Paul O'Neill

Table 7   Five reactions to the global crisis: An international snapshot (~2002) highlighting Zimbabwean locations.[10]

Tendency → issue ↓	Global justice movements	Third World nationalism	Post-Washington Consensus	Washington Consensus	Resurgent right-wing
Main arguments	Against globalisation of *capital* (not *people*) and debt repayment, for 'people-centred development'.	For more global integration: i.e. join (not change) the system, but on fairer terms (debt relief, more market access).	Reform the 'imperfect markets' and add 'sustainable development' to neoliberal framework.	Slightly adjust the status quo (transparency, supervision and regulation) and establish effective bale-out mechanisms.	Restore US isolationism, punish banks' mistakes, and reverse the globalisation of people.
Key institutions	Social/labour movements; environmental advocacy groups; radical activist networks; regional and national progressive coalitions; left-wing think-tanks; ***Zimbabwe Coalition on Debt and Development.***	Self-selecting Third World governments: Algeria, Argentina, Brazil, China, Cuba, Egypt, Haiti, India, Malaysia, Mexico, Pakistan, Russia, Venezuela and ***Zimbabwe.***	Most United Nations agencies; governments of France, Japan and sometimes South Africa.	US agencies (Treasury, Federal Reserve, US AID), World Bank IMF, WTO, centrist Washington think-tanks, British and German governments and sometimes South Africa; ***MDC Economics Desk.***	Populist and libertarian wings of Republican Party, American Enterprise Institute, Cato Institute, Manhattan Institute, Heritage Foundation.
Key proponents	Amin, Bello, Bendana, Bordieu, Bove, Brutus, Chalmers, Chomsky, Danaher, Galeano, George, ***Gokova, Gwisai,*** Kagarlitsky, Khor, Klein, Lula, Maathai, ***Malungisa,*** Marcos, Nader, Ndungane, Negri, Ngwane, Njehu, Patkar, Pilger, ***Raftopoulos,*** Shiva, ***Tandon.***	Aristide, Castro, Chavez, Mahathir, ***J. Moyo, Mandaza, Mugabe,*** Obasanjo, Putin, ***Shamuyarira.***	Annan, Jospin, Krugman, Mbeki, Sachs, Schroeder?, Soros, Stiglitz, ***Tsvangirai?***	Blair, ***Bloch,*** Brown, Bush?, ***Cross,*** Greenspan, Koehler, ***Makoni?,*** Moore, O'Neill?, Wolfensohn.	Buchanan, Bush?, DeLay, Haider, Le Pen, Lott, ***I. Smith?***

gave rich individuals and large corporations huge tax cuts to keep happy and keep spending. The leaders of the Bank, IMF and World Trade Organisation (WTO) – James Wolfensohn, Horst Koehler and Michael Moore – maintained their devotion to corporate and banking power, and often specifically US economic interests. Neoliberal apologists appeared generally unmoved by the unfolding economic crisis.[11]

Genuine reform under the leadership of this crew appeared impossible. In the wake of the September 1999 firing of Bank chief economist Joseph Stiglitz, it is hard to take seriously any notion that the Bretton Woods Institutions can make fundamental changes from within. At that point, two years before he won the Nobel Prize in economics, Stiglitz had criticised IMF structural adjustment policies and crisis-management in East Asia and Russia. Bill Clinton's treasury secretary, Lawrence Summers, immediately met with James Wolfensohn over the latter's desire for a second five-year term, and soon thereafter Stiglitz was dismissed 'with a fig leaf', in the words of Jagdish Bhagwati: 'a sorry episode'. Insiders say that Summers insisted that Stiglitz simply had to leave if the US was to support the Wolfensohn re-appointment.[12]

The short-lived 'post-Washington Consensus' philosophy that Stiglitz introduced was not particularly radical, as it simply posed the need for state intervention in the event of market failure and for more attention to 'sustainable development' goals like equity and environmental protection. But the 2001 Nobel award he shared with two other US economists recognised Stiglitz's 'information-theoretic' approach to markets, which does fundamentally undermine the neoliberal faith in self-correction, deregulation and growth.[13] While not a movement-builder himself, Stiglitz won a following from other economists who pushed slightly heterodox viewpoints, but squarely from within the general framework of neoliberalism.[14] Other international reformers were aware of widescale market failure. Financier/philanthropist George Soros, at least one national G-7 leader – France's Lionel Jospin[15] and UN secretary-general Kofi Annan all suggested imposition of a 'Tobin Tax' on international financial transactions.[16]

This was not merely an abstract theoretical problem, at a time – late 2001 – that Argentina defaulted on its foreign debt, in the wake of other high-profile national bankruptcies: Ecuador (2000) and Russia (1998). Just as worrisome, a currency crisis emerged close by Zimbabwe, when South Africa's allegedly 'sound macro-economic policy' was also reduced to rubble during 2000–2001: the value of a rand slipped 55% (from US$0.17 to US$0.08) due to both short-term speculation and to outflows of profits and dividends to the new London headquarters of Anglo American Corporation, Old Mutual, South African Breweries, Gencor/Billiton and Didata. Restoring tough exchange controls against the unprecedented capital flight, so as to deter rich white people from expatriating their apartheid-era wealth from the New South Africa, proved just too trying a challenge for Thabo Mbeki, as a function of the prevailing ideology and power relations discussed below.

The resurgent far Right, meanwhile, proved to be just as durable an affliction as economic crisis, and the more the latter spread the happier the former appeared. This political tendency gained great momentum in Washington when the Supreme Court selected Bush as US president in December 2000. The five justices who outvoted the citizens of Florida and the majority of US voters in that election were all chosen by the new president's father a decade earlier. Bush had a right-wing flank of his own to worry about, led by commentator and perpetual candidate Patrick Buchanan, and a powerful reactionary Republican bloc in the US Congress centred around Tom DeLay, Jesse Helms and Trent Lott – who all mainly saw the World Bank and IMF as agencies behind a socialist plot to promote cheeky Third World leaders like Robert Mugabe. Internationally, Jorg Haider in Austria and Jean-Marie le Pen in France mirrored this bizarre, reactionary tendency.

By late 2001, the far Right was dangerously resurgent, along with the military-industrial complex, thanks to the lunatic-fundamentalist Islamic group Al-Qaeda which hijacked four airplanes on 11 September. While on the surface it first appeared as a blow to official US morale, the terrorist attacks soon provided justification for establishing something akin to a police state, which Bush and his big business allies warmly welcomed.[17]

Aside from Mbeki, what were Third World elites up to at this stage? As Table 7 suggests, there were a few nationalist leaders – Jean-Bertrand Aristide, Fidel Castro and Hugo Chavez in the Caribbean corner of Haiti, Cuba and Venezuela, respectively – who regularly spoke from the Left. Most notably, perhaps, Mugabe's Malaysian ally Mahathir Mohamad – an anti-Semitic authoritarian – showed in 1998 that capital controls could be implemented in a major emerging market without the threat of US military intervention. Nigeria's Olusegun Obasanjo made some anti-systemic sounds as head of the Group of 77 developing nations and Vladimir Putin appeared anxious to break from the lock-step of Russian neoliberalism. Some of the world's most indignant nationalists and anti-imperialist rhetoricians were to be found in Harare.[18]

But after adding up a variety of small-scale nationalist projects, the sum is not yet sufficiently impressive at the global scale to merit much attention. The hope that India would lead a Third World revolt against the WTO – as Zimbabwe had done in Seattle in December 1999 – was dashed in Doha, Qatar in November 2001. As Washington's economic crisis-management morphed into a broader geopolitical 'coalition against terrorism' and back via the WTO, nothing the nationalists tried appeared to work. Their most important spokespeople – especially from South Africa – were led, by late 2001, to merely concede the logic and power of Washington's dictates.

Who, then, can catalyse substantial social change in an era of disempowered states, extreme international economic chaos and additional military-induced suffering? Little hope appeared from those immediately to the Left of Washington: the existing set of national rulers and nationalist leaders, conscientious establishment intellectuals and philanthropists, or international agencies. Instead, the column in Table 7 of greatest interest is further left: the 'global justice movements', whose dynamics are addressed in more detail below.

And what of Zimbabwe? In particular, what lessons did men like Robert Mugabe bring from past encounters with Washington? The desperate straits in which Mugabe, Moyo, Makoni and other government figures found themselves at the turn of the millennium, should not lead us to forget a prior moment when Washington was relatively weaker, and when Zimbabwe was more capable of rallying international allies to its defense: the early 1980s.

At that point, Zimbabwe had recently won independence. Rising international interest rates and global-scale economic recession were putting unprecedented pressure on Third World economies. The Third World debt crisis broke out in August 1982 when Mexico was forced into a near default. As noted above, a wave of political transitions, allowed the brief convergence of 1970s-era radical nationalist discourses – 'We want a New International Economic Order!' – and true legitimacy for young democracies across the Third World. Surely reform was possible then? And if not, how do we analyse the international circumstances in which so many loans were showered upon independent Zimbabwe, with so little to show for it?

Zimbabwe's prior inability to resist
As noted in Chapter Two, on several occasions in world history, sovereign debt was the scourge of international economics. During the early 1980s, too, debt not only threatened the stability of major money-

centre banks, but also reached mythical proportions in anti-imperialist discourse. Tanzania's Julius Nyerere labelled the IMF 'a neocolonial institution which exploits the poor to make them poorer and serves the rich to become richer'.[19]

Such complaints had little effect. Following appeals by Nyerere and Fidel Castro in 1983 for a Third World debtor's cartel – considered far too radical by many leaders with substantial personal foreign bank accounts – IMF and World Bank pressure on Latin nations intensified in the mid 1980s in order to avoid a major case of debt repudiation, no matter what the social cost. At the 1985 World Bank/IMF meeting in Seoul, for example, the 'Baker Plan' was introduced, and won Zimbabwe finance minister Bernard Chidzero's praise, even though it would not apply to Zimbabwe due to the latter's then relatively higher average incomes.

Soon thereafter, Robert Mugabe won – and then decisively squandered – significant opportunities to resist the power of international finance, for the sake of both Zimbabwe and its allies in the Non-Aligned Movement (Nam), which Mugabe chaired from 1986–1989. Chidzero also chaired the seventh session of the United Nations Conference on Trade and Development (1987) and the IMF/World Bank Development Committee (1987–1990). Immediately following Mugabe in the hierarchy of the 1986–1989 Nam was Peruvian President Garcia, an enthusiastic though unsuccessful promoter of a unilateral debt repayment limitation of 10% of foreign currency earnings.

Expectations were high, particularly given the militant profile of Castro at the 1986 Nam conference in Harare. But strong rhetoric led to nothing in the way of collective action on the debt. As Morgan Tsvangirai later complained, 'At the time of Zimbabwe's leadership of the Nam, this was our worst period for debt servicing. We paid 35% of our forex earnings to the banks. But the government's priorities of that time were misplaced, so we missed the opportunity to lead the Third World.'[20]

Probably because of Zimbabwe's gentle Nam stewardship, Chidzero was quickly offered the chair of the 22-member IMF-Bank Development Committee at the institutions' October 1986 annual meetings. In taking the post, Chidzero noted the obvious: 'Developing countries are exporting capital back to the industrialised countries, almost subsidising them. We will have to do something dramatic about this.'[21] In fact, nothing 'dramatic' to halt reverse flows of capital was done, and instead the Development Committee's executive secretary travelled to Harare

in 1987 to bask in what he termed the 'new era in co-operation between developing countries, donors and the IMF and World Bank'.[22]

Capitulating to initiatives from international financial centres,
Chidzero accepted an inferior European Community debt relief proposal
(later approved by the G-7 countries in Toronto) for the rest of Africa
during his first Development Committee meeting in early 1987 – and
he ruled out the possibility of debt relief for Zimbabwe. He advocated
moderate reforms such as the 'menu approach' with its exit bond buy-
backs, debt-equity swaps, and interest caps. Chidzero was clearly opposed
to even raising the possibility of stronger relief, debt repudiation or
Third World solidarity in the form of a debtors' cartel.

Another opportunity for action arose while Chidzero chaired the
seventh meeting of the UN Conference on Trade and Development
(Unctad) in 1987. Across the Zambezi, Kenneth Kaunda was witnessing
the beginning of the end of his 27-year rule in the form of 'IMF Riots'.
Zambia necessarily fell behind on debt payments, attracting the wrath
of the IMF. Chidzero ensured that, 'contrary to what some people
expected, there was no confrontation between the developed and
developing countries' at the Unctad meetings. Shortly afterwards, at the
September 1987 meetings of the Commonwealth group of nations,
British finance minister Nigel Lawson announced a plan to reduce
interest rates on Third World debt, and IMF managing director Michel
Camdessus promised to search for more fresh money for loans from
central banks. Chidzero overstated the gains from these inconsequential
initiatives: 'Even though the new solutions were not always perfect,
they generated a feeling of optimism among developing countries.'[23]

There were many promises for 'responsible' debtors – new direct
foreign investment, new flows of financial capital, better interest rates
and borrowing terms, greater power and respect within international
economic forums, a return to economic growth, etc., etc. – in exchange
for punctual repayments and endorsement of structural adjustment.
The promises were generally not honoured. As the international debt
crisis was judged 'resolved' from the standpoint of Northern banks (if
not Third World countries), Chidzero attended the 1989 IMF/Bank
annual meeting and reported back to a regional news magazine,
'Curiously enough, debt was not the central issue. It was at the back of
everyone's mind. But those who are primarily concerned with the debt
issue have been saying: Look, the game is being played. Don't upset the
apple-cart too much.'[24]

Meanwhile, however, the commercial bank loan tap had been
turned off and even conditional aid to the Third World was slowing by

the end of Chidzero's reign as Development Committee chair in 1990. Indeed, the transfer of net financial resources from South to North soared from nothing in 1987 to in excess of US$50 billion in 1989. The full name of the Development Committee, ironically, is the Joint Ministerial Committee on the Transfer of Real Resources *to* Developing Countries.

By the time Zimbabwe surrendered its leading positions in most of the international forums where the debt problem could be raised, Third World external finances were in such tatters that what had seemed unreasonable and excessively cheeky in the mid 1980s – namely, stating the absolute impossibility of foreign debt repayment – was obvious. The United Nations *New Agenda for Development of Africa in the 1990s* even argued that the US$270 billion African debt should be cancelled outright.

By the mid-1990s, debt relief was finally embraced by the World Bank. But Wolfensohn's chosen vehicle was the Highly Indebted Poor Countries (HIPC) initiative which was cited by Jubilee South as being 'too little, too late', and ultimately more harm than good because of the brutal conditions attached.[25] The financial markets – and the multi-lateral institutions that guided them – would not tolerate debt relief unless it was accompanied by tighter adherence to structural adjustment conditions. And yet structural adjustment programmes were themselves accompanied by massive and usually untenable increases in new foreign debt.

The explanation for Zimbabwe's extremely poor record of top-down interventions in the debt debate must lie, in part, in the interests and ideologies of those leading the Zimbabwe government, especially Chidzero's *compradorism*. Prior to falling ill during the early 1990s, Chidzero reached the peak of his career when he took a close second place in the October 1991 race for United Nations secretary-general. Boutros Boutros-Ghali was chosen, as Chidzero claimed, because 'the industrialised countries would like to control the United Nations in a more subtle manner than through the veto in the Security Council.'[26]

The disappointing late 1980s experience of official resistance by Zimbabwe, Africa and the entire Third World, suggests that the struggle against debt and economic oppression is not easily waged from the top of state bureaucracies. Conditions in Zimbabwe then deteriorated dramatically, as Chidzero, Mugabe and the cabinet succumbed to Washington's economic snake-oil. As one of the world's basket cases, there is today no chance that any Zimbabwe representative would be permitted such high-profile platforms until a new government is elected.

However, the neighbours immediately to the south – where political leaders presided over the Nam, Unctad, the Commonwealth, Organisation of African Unity (OAU), Southern African Development Community (SADC) and the World Bank/IMF Board of Governors during the late 1990s and early 2000s – appear as logical inheritors of the *comprador* tradition.

3. Factoring in Pretoria

Just after his return from launching the *New Partnership for Africa's Development*, on 24 October 2001, a sarcastically-inclined Thabo Mbeki was confronted by a tough question in parliament. Mugabe's throw-away line, at the funeral of a liberation hero, that now Zimbabwe 'would return to socialism', prompted a comment from an ex-apartheid member of the then-opposition New National Party:

> Boy Geldenhuys: My question to the honourable President is, in your view sir, Zimbabwe's announced return to socialism – What impact will that have on the New African Initiative?
> Thabo Mbeki: I have a bit of a problem with regard to this, Madam Speaker, because unlike the honourable member, I do not know what is meant by socialism in this particular context and therefore have no way of measuring what its impact would be on these processes that we are dealing with, with regard to the African continent. If I knew a bit more, perhaps as much as he knows about this matter, I might be able to comment on this.
>
> But I think that what is critically important with regard to Zimbabwe, is that Zimbabwe must address all of these questions that have been raised: of peace and stability in this country; of an end to the conflict; dealing with the issue of the land redistribution within the context of the law; absence of conflict; and addressing these very, very serious issues that face the economy of Zimbabwe, in a serious way. It is important that all of those matters are addressed in Zimbabwe. I think they are important for the people of Zimbabwe in the first instance, and certainly as this government we are very interested that the Zimbabwean government does deal with those questions.
>
> As to what socialism in this context means, I haven't the slightest idea, and I wouldn't know what impact it would have on the processes of the renewal of the African continent.[27]

Being evasive is one of Mbeki's traits, especially on the matter of

Zimbabwe. In mid-2001, he told the British television show 'Hard Talk' that he had tried persuading Mugabe to reform, but that the Zimbabwean ruler 'didn't listen to me'. By November, Mbeki publicly attributed Zimbabwe's severe problems to 'twenty years of economic policies' (with no details – e.g. was *Esap* included?). Likewise, African National Congress (ANC) president's spokesperson Smuts Ngonyama blamed the Zimbabwean economic mess on too many 'subsidies'. Deputy president Jacob Zuma also chimed in during a tour to South Africa's Northern Province, not far from the Beitbridge border crossing, according to a press report:

> Zuma gave a brief lecture on Zimbabwean political economics: President Robert Mugabe's government embarked on a huge social spending spree without analysing social needs, which caused inflation to spiral. 'We do not want to follow the same route,' said Zuma. 'We have a responsibility to more than just the sectarian [*sic*] needs of the union movement. We have to serve the broader population as a whole.'
>
> Zuma's loss of cool clearly underlined how heated the debates were during the government's programme to meet communities. Betty Khoza, 66, summed up the feeling of the locals when she commented that the meeting had brought both hope and confusion about government programmes to address rural poverty. Khoza said: 'They did provide us with some answers, although not all of them were convincing.'[28]

Khoza is right: Pretoria was not convincing – about rural poverty in South Africa *or* Zimbabwe. Mugabe's 'huge social spending spree' was, in reality, a brief period of rising education and health expenditures, followed by systematic cutbacks and deprivation under IMF and World Bank guidance.

To misread the Zimbabwe situation so blatantly was reminiscent of the case of former ANC land minister Derek Hanekom, who also used Zimbabwe as a whipping boy in 1997. At that stage, land hunger was causing organic (not war veteran-induced) land invasions and farmworker strikes. In November that year, Mugabe announced that the Land Designation Act would finally be implemented.

Down south, the spectre of large-scale land reform would have been terrible for investor confidence at a time when Mbeki's own Washington-centric *Esap* – the misnamed Growth, Employment and Redistribution strategy – was already failing noticeably. Hanekom was inclined to periodically clarify that, unlike Zimbabwe, South Africa was proceeding with land reform on a willing-seller/willing-buyer basis. Hence, no white South African farmer need fear the breakdown of rural law and order, as was beginning in Zimbabwe. Of course, nor would black South African farmers gain access to land stolen from them in living memory, given Hanekom's emphatic endorsement of the same World Bank strategy that had failed so miserably to redistribute land in Zimbabwe.[29]

South African schizophrenia in relation to Zimbabwe has several features. In early 2000, as Mugabe appeared to have squandered both political popularity and the legitimacy to govern, the ANC leadership must have looked north and observed the following:

- a liberation movement which won repeated elections against a terribly weak opposition, but under circumstances of worsening abstentionism by, and depoliticisation of, the masses;
- concomitantly, that movement's undeniable failure to deliver a better life for most of the country's low-income people, while material inequality soared;
- rising popular alienation from, and cynicism about, nationalist politicians, as the gulf between rulers and the ruled widened inexorably and as more numerous cases of corruption and malgovernance were brought to public attention;
- growing economic misery as neoliberal policies were tried and failed; and
- the sudden rise of an opposition movement based in the trade unions, quickly backed by most of civil society, the liberal petit-bourgeoisie and the independent media – potentially leading to the election of a new, post-nationalist government.

If all such bullets were fired in Zambia roughly a decade earlier, and if all but the last bullet were also loaded in South Africa, then it was logical for ANC leaders to look out from their headquarters at Albert Luthuli House in Johannesburg – and to panic. At that point, two options emerged: hunker down and mindlessly defend the Zanu government against its critics; or move into 'constructive-engagement' mode that might serve as the basis for an 'honest-broker' role on some future deal-making occasion. A third option – actively support Zimbabwe's democratic movement, perhaps through sanctions or other pressure techniques, so as to ensure the government held free and fair elections – presumably did not warrant attention, for fear that the last bullet would inspire South African trade unionists to do the same, in the near future.[30]

The ANC leadership moved from the first to the second strategy. Attempts during 2000 by ANC parliamentary leader Tony Yengeni, ANC secretary-general Kgalema Motlanthe and other nationalist ideologues to stitch together the Old Boys of Southern African liberation movements in a regional grouping, and Yengeni's own June 2000 SADC parliamentary electoral observation mission – characterised by blatant pro-Zanu utterances – came to naught. Perhaps the key incident that facilitated the move was the overreach by war veterans in April 2001, when for the first time they started occupations not simply of white Zimbabweans' rural farms, but of white South Africans' Harare factories.

An additional, related factor may have been intensifying pressure from South African investors in Zimbabwe. Amongst the highest-profile were the major retail groups: Shoprite, Pick 'n Pay and Massmart (Makro). All took advantage of the *Esap* years by opening shops in what was then a forex-rich Zimbabwe, and importing mass-produced consumer goods from their own South African supplier networks, to replace goods which were previously made locally in Harare or Bulawayo.[31] But Zimbabwe's de-industrialisation meant that when forex began to dry up in 2000, it became more difficult to source those same goods; no local alternatives were available. Moreover, when in October 2001, price controls on basic foodstuffs were imposed by Mugabe, the retailers began complaining.

Then, when foreign exchange controls were tightened, the South Africans were not able to repatriate their earnings. Tellingly, however, Massmart's deputy chief executive, Dan Barrett, bragged to *Business Day* about profit rates that still prevailed under conditions of scarcity and inflation:

> In spite of the difficult trading conditions, Barrett said that there was no 'financial risk on (the group's) investment'. Massmart did not bring back the profit made by its Makro stores to SA. He said that Zimbabwe's shortage of foreign currency was the main reason for this. Ironically, the stores were quite profitable when measured in Zimbabwean dollars. High inflation meant the stores merchandise were gaining value 'by sitting on the shelf', Barrett said.[32]

All of these factors would have weighed heavily on Mbeki's mind, and business pressure combined with increasingly shrill anti-Zimbabwe rhetoric from the white opposition – Marthinus van Schalkwyk and Tony Leon – had to be factored into the South African domestic political situation.

Civil society groups in South Africa, meanwhile, remained confused about Zimbabwe. There were few specific calls for solidarity emanating from allies within Zimbabwean civil society. By late 2001, MDC leader Tsvangirai supported the idea of smart sanctions against Mugabe and his top cronies – some of whose personal assets were located in South Africa – but mass-based organisations in either country rarely if ever discussed the issue. Crucially the Zimbabweans failed to make a coherent call for support, similar to the ANC's and South African United Democratic Front's 1980s-era sanctions campaign. Many South African workers and urban poor residents suffered, instead, from a vicious strain of xenophobia that often resulted in the murders of SADC immigrants.

The Southern African Trade Union Co-ordinating Council had been hostile to Mugabe for many years. But under the influence of Tsvangirai, the trajectory of the MDC during 1999–2000 was as disturbing to the Congress of South African Trade Unions (Cosatu) as was Frederick Chiluba's metamorphosis from Zambian union boss to neoliberal authoritarian a decade earlier. When Tsvangirai visited Cosatu in 2001 in search of solidarity, he was treated with contempt by the left-leaning unionists. Cosatu leader Zwelinzima Vavi did not see eye to eye with the ZCTU on various issues, especially regional trade relations and whether to reform the World Trade Organisation using 'Social Clause' provisions, which the ZCTU officials rejected and Vavi supported. But Vavi spoke out periodically against Mugabe, which in turn pulled the ANC further away from Mugabe.

Pretoria's own self-perceived interests apparently remained fluid. As Mbeki's spokesperson, Bheki Khumalo, told the press in December 2001, 'We as a government are opposed to any form of sanctions against Zimbabwe. What we can only do and will do is engage with Zimbabwe in the context of the SADC Task Force, of the Commonwealth initiative, as well as government to government as well as party contacts.'[33]

But it was obvious by that time that the international effort to armtwist Mugabe was going nowhere. SADC, led by Malawian president Bakili Muluzi, repeatedly soft-peddled Zimbabwe's problems. The Commonwealth's highly-publicised September 2001 Abuja Agreement to end farm invasions was a damp squib. The various international human rights groups active on Zimbabwe – Amnesty International, Human Rights Watch and the International Crisis Group – had made little impact. The US Zimbabwe Democracy and Economic Recovery

Act of December 2001 was mainly symbolic, although it raised expectations that an MDC victory would lead to an aid/loan bonanza.[34]

But if such expectations existed, it would be useful to recall Henry Kissinger's US$1 billion promise a quarter-century earlier, if only a deal was cut – but when it was at Lancaster House, the Kissinger promise was not honoured by the US government.

In short, just as we observed in relation to simultaneous efforts at reforming Washington Consensus ideology and institutions, an elite-reformist gambit in Zimbabwe was doomed to fail. *Nothing was really on offer.* South African officials must have sensed this, and kept their options somewhat open in the event Mugabe remained president after March 2002. Thus in late 2001, South Africa's deputy director-general of foreign affairs Welile Nhlapo hinted at Pretoria's ongoing ideological alignment with Harare when, in the wake of his apparent attack on the MDC, he claimed that he was merely:

> quoting verbatim from information supplied by the Zimbabwe government which insinuated that the opposition Movement for Democratic Change was the recipient of funds from the UK's Westminster Foundation . . . On the basis of the false information, Nhlapo said western countries were 'causing further problems in Zimbabwe in their eagerness to assist the troubled country' . . . Asked whether the South African government believed the essential problem in Zimbabwe was Mugabe's clinging to power at all costs, Nhlapo said 'the problem is clearly defined', but South Africa was not prepared to contribute 'to what Zimbabweans detest' by saying Mugabe was the cause of all of the country's problems. [35]

Confusing though this might have sounded, nevertheless a great deal of progress had been made in adding democracy to South African foreign policy formulation. Consider a starting point in early 2000, when ANC leaders defended the besieged Mugabe with full-fledged nationalist myth-making, and a mid-point in December 2001, when the South African leadership criticised Zanu quite openly.

The storm continued to gather. By year-end 2001, editors at the government-controlled *Herald* newspaper – probably with the encouragement of Jonathan Moyo – were frustrated to the point of paranoia:

> A clear pattern is now emerging of a build up against Zimbabwe and South Africa's complicity in the plot to overthrow the ruling

Zanu government from power. What is even worse and a bit sickening is how President Mbeki is reported to be in the same bed with the same architects of apartheid . . . in the fight against Zimbabwe . . . President Mbeki's alleged utterances neatly dovetail into Britain's grand plan for a global coalition against Zimbabwe similar to the one adopted by America in its fight against terrorism in Afghanistan.[36]

There was one point in which virtually all mainstream commentators, think-tanks and human rights organisations, as well as the ANC political leaders' arguments, did appear complicit: their neoliberal economic presumptions. This was the basis by which we conclude that something even more profound than local political dynamics had changed between early 2000 when the MDC burst onto the scene, and late 2001. The key intervening factor required to fully grasp Mbeki's evolving Zimbabwe policy may well be the *Nepad*: the programme with which he aims to lift Africa from poverty, marginalisation and instability.

Map/Nai/Nepad, *no thanks*

Well above and beyond the Zimbabwe quagmire, a major question had emerged in the context of early twenty-first century international economic turmoil: could the increasingly delegitimised World Bank and IMF be trusted to sell neoliberalism in Africa, or was a new group of Africans – and a new name for structural adjustment – required? Evidence of the latter mounted, and not only through the Poverty Reduction Strategy Programmes (PRSPs) of cynical Washington spin-doctors.

An allegedly home-grown, African socio-economic strategy dawned in 2000–2001: the *Millennium Africa Recovery Plan* (with the acronym *Map*, from mid-2000 to mid-2001); a *New African Initiative* (*Nai*, from July–October 2001); and finally a *New Partnership for Africa's Development* (*Nepad*), launched in Abuja, Nigeria by several African heads of state in October 2001. These different names referred to the same plan, but for various reasons – including the Afrikaans translation of 'naai', i.e. to 'totally fuck over' – the Abuja meeting settled on *Nepad*.

In the wake of the 11 September terrorist attack on the United States, it was suddenly trendy to gurgle sympathetically about how Africa needed special elite attention, so as to offset – with vague hopes for 'economic integration' – the festering conditions of poverty upon which Islamic fundamentalism bred.[37] The European Union (EU) quickly endorsed *Nepad*. The November 2001 World Trade Organisation summit in Doha echoed with the alleged urgency for Africa to get more access to international markets, especially in agriculture. Notwithstanding his own Aids policy disasters, Thabo Mbeki was seen as Africa's most legitimate, self-confident and fundamentally pro-Western leader, and a great ally in fending off both Muslim terrorists and cheeky idealists protesting in the North's streets outside elite meetings, allegedly on behalf of Africa.

From the late 1990s, Mbeki embarked upon an 'African Renaissance' branding exercise with poignant poetics. The contentless form was somewhat remedied in the secretive *Millennium Africa Recovery Plan*, whose powerpoint skeleton was unveiled to select elites in 2000, during Mbeki's meetings with Bill Clinton in May, the Okinawa G-8 in July, the UN Millennium Summit in September, and a subsequent European Union gathering in Portugal. The skeleton was fleshed out in November 2000 with the assistance of several economists and was immediately ratified during a special South African visit by World Bank president James Wolfensohn 'at an undisclosed location', due presumably to fears of the disruptive protests which had soured a Johannesburg trip by new IMF czar Horst Koehler a few months earlier.

Thanks to work by a co-author of South Africa's own disastrous 1996 homegrown structural adjustment programme (Stephen Gelb), the content of the 60-page working document was becoming clearer: more privatisation, especially of infrastructure (no matter its failure especially in South Africa); more insertion of Africa into the world economy (in spite of fast-declining terms of trade); more multi-party elections (typically, though, between variants of neoliberal parties, as in the US) as a veil for the lack of thorough-going participatory democracy; grand visions of information and communications technology (hopelessly unrealistic considering the lack of simple reliable electricity across the continent); and a self-mandate for peace-keeping (which South Africa has subsequently taken for its soldiers stationed in the DRC and Burundi).

By this stage, Mbeki had managed to sign on as partners two additional rulers from the crucial West and North of the continent: Abdelaziz Bouteflika and Olusegun Obasanjo from Nigeria. Unfortunately, both continued to face mass popular protests and widespread civil/military/religious bloodshed at home, diminishing their utility as model African leaders. Later, to his credit, Obasanjo led a surprise revolt against Mbeki's capitulation to Northern pressure at the World Conference Against Racism in September 2001, when he helped generate a split between European Union and African countries over reparations due the continent for slavery and colonialism. Tellingly, even loose talk of reparations was not found in *Nepad*, and the South African host delegation was furious at Obasanjo's outburst because it nearly scuppered a final conference resolution.

But that incident aside, 2001 was a successful year for selling *Nepad*. Another pro-Western ruler with a deplorable recent human rights record, Tanzania's Benjamin Mkapa, joined the New Africa leadership group in January 2001 in Davos, Switzerland. There, Mbeki gave the world's leading capitalists and state elites a briefing, which was very poorly-attended. A few days later, an effort was made in Mali to sell West Africans to the plan, with on-the-spot cheerleading by Wolfensohn and Koehler. The July 2001 meeting of the African Union in Lusaka provided the opportunity for a continent-wide leadership endorsement, once Mbeki's plan was merged with an infrastructure-heavy initiative – the 'Omega Plan' – offered by the neoliberal Senegalese president, Abdoulaye Wade, to become the *New African Initiative*. A few days later, the Genoa G-8 summit offered soothing encouragement. With 300 000 protesters outside the conference accusing the world's main political leaders of running a destructive, elitist club, Mbeki was a useful adornment.

Likewise, Mbeki's October visits to Japan and Brussels confirmed his elite popularity, perhaps because there was no apparent demand for formal monetary commitments. The same month, enthusiastic endorsements of *Nepad* were published in the *Financial Times* by Johannesburg capital and Washington multilateral banks: the heir to Anglo American Corporation (and former head of its Zimbabwe division) Jonathan Oppenheimer and South Africa's main international think-tank intellectual Greg Mills, and the highest-ranking Africa officials at the IMF and World Bank, Gondal Gondwe and Callisto Madavo.[38]

To sum up the ideological partnership Mbeki proposed, consider the way that the 1980s–1990s neoliberal recolonisation of African economic policy is explained in *Nepad*:

> The structural adjustment programmes provided only a partial solution. They promoted reforms that tended to remove serious price distortions, but gave inadequate attention to the provision of social services. As a consequence, only a few countries managed to achieve sustainable higher growth under these programmes.[39]

Slippery, this line of analysis, and worth unpacking briefly. One test of robust analysis is to pose the opposite premise, and to see whether the subsequent hypotheses are worth exploring:

- What if structural adjustment represented not 'a partial solution' but instead, reflecting local and global power shifts, a profound defeat for genuine African nationalists, workers, peasants, women, children and the environment?
- What if the structural adjustment programmes of the 1980s–1990s were the result not of independent Africans searching honestly for 'solutions', but instead mainly reflected the dramatic shift in power relations at both global scale (where financial and commercial circuits of capital were in ascendance) and within individual African states, away from lobbies favouring somewhat pro-poor social policies and (at least half-hearted) industrial development, towards cliques whose strategies served the interests of acquisitive, overconsumptive local elites, Washington financiers, and transnational corporations?
- What if 'promoting reforms' really amounted to the IMF and World Bank imposing their cookie-cutter neoliberal policies on desperately disempowered African societies, without any reference to democratic processes, resistance or diverse local conditions?
- What if the removal of 'serious price distortions' really meant the repeal of exchange controls (hence allowing massive capital flight), subsidy cuts (hence pushing masses of people below the poverty line), and lowered import tariffs (hence generating massive de-industrialisation)?
- What if 'inadequate attention to the provision of social services' in reality meant the opposite: excessive attention to applying neoliberalism not just to the macro-economy, but also to health, education, water and other crucial state services? And what if the form of IMF/Bank attention included insistence upon greater cost recovery, higher user-fees, lower budgetary allocations, privatisation, and even the disconnection of supplies to those too poor to afford them, hence leading to the unnecessary deaths of millions of people?
- What if 'inadequate attention to the provision of social services' is not anywhere correlated to the inability of countries to 'achieve sustainable higher growth', but rather serves as a nice-sounding justification for 'adjustment with a human face', as UNICEF coined the compromise that *Nepad* apparently seeks?

If these hypotheses are reasonable, and if the implication is to proceed no further with structural adjustment – human face or not – then a central task of *Nepad* was posed: to slip around such arguments without reference to their relevance. In doing so, *Nepad* fits into the globalisers' modified neoliberal project, by which it was even more vigorously asserted, ever more incongruously, that integration into global markets solves poverty, and that therefore an alleged 'Development Agenda' should be adopted by the WTO.

Nepad's feedback loop

There was great neo-colonial/*comprador* trickery afoot when IMF/Bank African leaders Gondwe and Madavo promoted free trade as Africa's saviour: 'The most effective help for self-help will come from trade. Africa needs better opportunities for trade.' Yet projections from the last major study (by the World Bank and the Organisation for Economic Co-operation and Development) of the benefits of the previous liberalisation – the Uruguay Round – were a bit less sanguine: Africa would lose billions of dollars in annual output by 2002, as a result of imports swamping the uncompetitive industries which struggle under inefficient scale-economies.

The process of liberalisation had actually been underway for a long time, reducing Africa's ability to earn income from trade over the past two decades, and forcing economies to switch from meeting basic needs to generating more – and ever less valuable – export outputs. Given the structure of international commodity trade, the results were inevitably to cheapen imports for already-wealthy Northern consumers, harm millions of small farmers North and South, compel further switching of Southern food production to export cash crops, and concentrate more resources in the clutch of a few monopolistic firms.

As discussed below, the WTO deal offered to the South in 2001 included fewer restrictions on pharmaceutical patent violation, the potential for slightly freer trade in crops and a few light manufacturing sectors (paid for by yet more opening of African markets), deeper-ranging intellectual property provisions, competition policies drafted in the interests of multinational corporations, and extension of liberalisation to water, electricity, banking and other crucial services through the General Agreement on Trade in Services. The reality of international trading power was that both the US and South Africa imposed ever-tougher anti-dumping penalties against impoverished trading partners such as Zimbabwe.

Gondwe/Madavo confirmed, 'The IMF and the World Bank are doing everything possible to play a part [in *Nepad*]. The initiative expects the IMF and World Bank to make a contribution on the basis of the poverty reduction strategy adopted in 1999.' That meant continuing on the path of the Highly Indebted Poor Countries debt-relief initiative, which civil societies and less supine governments have rejected vociferously. With only 13% of the promised $100 billion in debt reduction promised at the June 1999 G-8 meeting in Cologne, why should this initiative retain any credibility in late 2001? Mozambican president Joachim Chissano, for instance, publicly complained at that point that the near-total destruction of the cashew-processing industry was the pain the World Bank required for meagre gain: a few HIPC breadcrumbs. We consider African civil society's rejection below.

Yet for Gondwe/Madavo, *Nepad* appeared as a crucial vehicle to solidify existing financial-dependency relations: 'Credit is crucial for economic development. That is why, in the longer run, African countries need to retain the trust of investors in their ability and willingness to repay what they borrow. Therefore the IMF, the World Bank, and other development partners are working to help African countries create sound domestic financial sectors and, eventually, integrate into international financial markets.'

More trickery. The IMF and Bank worked for at least two decades, since adopting the Berg Report, to undermine domestic African finance by demanding excessive deregulation at a time of structural adjustment austerity, leading to banking crises across the continent. The words 'eventually integrate' are deceitful, given that one of the key dictates of the IMF and Bank was the lifting of capital controls, with virtually no African states daring to put them back on – save Robert Mugabe's Zimbabwe.

In most mainstream analysis, Mugabe also stood out as the primary political negation of *Nepad*. For example, Mills' South African Institute for International Affairs promoted *Nepad* using a slick video which, by way of balance, showed a manic-looking Mugabe engaged in his most dictatorial posturing, presumably to warn Mbeki that he must work harder on his northern neighbour.[40] Mills also hosted two major conferences in late 2001 focused on the liberal political processes and economic interests in Zimbabwe that were dear to South African elites.

In such circumstances, Mugabe was continually portrayed as the obstreperous African who rejected partnership and made only financial demands on the North. An especially sore point was the sabotage that his officials accomplished at the 1999 Seattle WTO summit, by persuading the Organisation of African Unity (OAU) caucus to issue a statement withdrawing consensus: 'There is no transparency in the proceedings and African countries are being marginalised.' African trade expert Yash Tandon reported on Zimbabwe's role immediately after the OAU revolt:

Now in panic, the US State Department sent its most skilled negotiators to pacify the Africans. They tried to co-opt Zimbabwe's industry minister [Shamuyarira] (by now identified as the chief spokesperson for the Africa group) into the process by offering to consider a draft declaration that would satisfy the Africans. This was the first serious effort made by the US to bring in the Africans. However, the Zimbabwe minister was not persuaded, and he refused to join in the 'Green Room' consultations.[41]

Shamuyarira's main allies came from the 'Like-Minded Group' of countries: India, Pakistan, Egypt, Uganda, Indonesia and the Dominican Republic. On the other side in the Green Room (and its twenty leading negotiating teams), expressing immense frustration at the WTO's apparent breakdown, was South Africa's minister of trade and industry.

Ironically, Alec Erwin was born in Bulawayo, but he moved to Durban at a young age and was radicalised in the anti-apartheid struggle. He became a heroic trade unionist during the first Durban strikes of 1973, and was regarded as organised labour's premier Marxist intellectual during the 1970s–1980s. By the 1990s, however, his politics shifted rapidly rightward, and as Pretoria's trade minister from 1996, he was especially tough during South Africa/Zimbabwe trade negotiations, and especially insensitive to Zimbabwean concerns over the growing trade deficit and further regional de-industrialisation caused by the South African/European Union free-trade agreement.

After losing face and the mantle of African leadership in Seattle, Erwin pushed even harder for a new WTO round. In Freetown, Cairo and Mexico City in 2000–2001, he unsuccessfully lobbied African trade officials to support Pretoria's international trade strategy. Zimbabwean officials remained the main cause of Erwin's headaches for a few more months, but Shamuyarira retired in June 2000. His replacement as Zimbabwe's trade/industry minister, the neoliberal ex-banker Nkosana Moyo, was frightened by how little influence he had over Mugabe, when trying to end the April 2001 factory invasions, and he soon fled the country (to work at the World Bank). For Erwin, his northern neighbour's massive domestic troubles offered an excellent opportunity to split SADC members away from the rest of Africa, and to assure that a repeat of the uncooperative African delegation at Seattle did not transpire at the Qatar summit.[42]

A Doha diversion

Less than two months after the 11 September terrorist attacks, the
United States government and its leading multinational corporations
were willing to bend over backwards, stylistically, to maintain the
pretense of international co-operation. But with respect to content, the
Doha agreement amplified the free-trade agenda that had generated
such intense unevenness, inequality, eco-destruction and women's
suffering over the previous decades. Harare-based sociologist Raj Patel
explains that the agreement – which adds many new areas of trade and
investment liberalisation – will have the effect of bullying the world's
weakest countries even more:

> The civil services in the poorest countries have been pared to the
> bone by World Bank structural adjustment policies. Many cannot
> afford to have even one delegate in Geneva to monitor, negotiate
> and resist these organisations. Negotiating several issues at once is
> well beyond the means of most poor countries. The mere demand
> that these wrecked bureaucracies 'negotiate' a cluster of new issues
> effectively guarantees their detonation.
>
> Why, then, did developing countries agree to sign? Part of the
> reason lies in the magic of advertising. The new round hasn't been
> called a round. Instead what we have is a new brand round, the
> 'Doha Development Agenda'. This rebranding idea is one with
> which we are all familiar: you tinker with the name, but nothing
> else, in order to make punters believe that you've actually improved
> things. It has worked for corporate giants, it works for the US
> government . . .
>
> In Seattle, Southern governments refused to sign a declaration
> not because they opposed the entrenchment of neoliberalism and
> the elite class bias that comes with it, but because they had been
> roughly treated. Delegates had not been able to enter meetings, and
> the US negotiating team had rubbed Southern inferiority in their
> faces. In other words, the signing of the Doha Development Agenda
> is only a mystery if one thinks that developing country governments
> have recently taken a principled stand against neoliberalism. They
> haven't. The refusal to sign at Seattle was not about indignation at
> neoliberalism, but about the failure to treat elites as they are
> accustomed.
>
> In Doha, by contrast, United States Trade Representative Robert
> Zoellick was a dealer, a broker of accord, a merchant of consensus.
> This new-found humility evidently pushed the buttons of the

developing country elite. So they signed. This should come as no surprise. These are the elites that milk and pimp the majority of people in their countries. It's hard to see why putting them in five-star accommodation and making them feel important might make them less venal.[43]

Patel is correct: most developing country governments had not taken a principled stand against neoliberalism. And yet their officials grappled with the issues and repeatedly pointed out the obvious: neoliberalism was killing their constituents.

For example, even under the uncharismatic, conservative guidance of trade and industry minister Herbert Murerwa (Nkosana Moyo's replacement), Zimbabwe continued as co-ordinator of the Africa Group delegation to Doha, and retained alliances with other Third World nationalist regimes. In the run-up to the ministerial summit, the Africa Group proposed that 'patenting of life forms would be prohibited' and that the Trade in Intellectual Property Rights agreement should not 'prevent Members from taking measures to protect public health'.[44] Thanks in large part to consistent grassroots activist pressure, the latter demand was, at least, conceded by the North.[45]

Zimbabwe's negotiators also joined an unsuccessful attack on the General Trade in Services agreement. Officials from Harare, its Like-Minded Group allies, plus new friends Cuba, Haiti, India, Kenya, Peru and Venezuela, offered an eloquent critique of the services agreement that is worth excerpting at length. It appears a rare case of Third World nationalists speaking truth to power (even if they crumbled under pressure in the final hours):

Developing countries have clearly not received the benefits they thought they would. Developed countries continue to be heavily regulated in the form of maintaining trade barriers especially in several sectors of interest to developing countries. For example, technical standards and licensing in certain professional services, is used to effectively restrict entry by developing countries into the industry . . .

The regulatory initiatives taken by developing countries would already seem to be having a negative impact on them since many developing countries have adopted regulations that have turned out to be more suited to the needs and level of development of services industries of the developed countries . . .

There is the danger that re-regulation as promoted in Article VI could in fact become deregulation [and that this] could be fundamentally incompatible with the requirement or the desire of many governments to provide basic public services for their people, especially since certain sections of their population may not be able to afford to pay market prices for these services . . .

Many services markets are dominated by only a few large firms from developed countries and a number of small players. The top 20 service exporters are mainly from developed countries . . .

Liberalisation under these circumstances of unequal competition has aggravated the alarming divide in supply capacity between developed and developing countries . . .

Developing countries' small suppliers are also disadvantaged in other ways, such as through discriminatory access to information channels and distribution networks . . .

Under conditions of liberalisation, privatisation of services could very easily happen since foreign corporations which are more competitive are likely to enter the new market and take over from the local company. This could have consequences on access to basic services for those who may not be able to afford these commercial prices of services.

In addition, investments, when they come in, have often not been in sectors that could most benefit the host countries . . .

For the rural sectors in many developing countries, these basic services may not even be provided by the state, but by communities and local authorities which use currently common resources, such as water, minerals, fuels . . .

Through marketisation, previously available public goods are put out of reach of many when these are commodified in the process of privatisation. The experience of several developing countries with structural adjustment already shows that large segments of the population are having serious difficulties gaining access to basic commodities and services at prices they can afford.[46]

Another fight picked and lost in Doha – by Zimbabwe alongside the countries noted above, and El Salvador, Honduras, Nicaragua, Nigeria, Senegal and Sri Lanka – concerned agriculture:

These talks remain dominated by the EU on the one hand, and the US and Cairns group of exporting countries on the other. As a result, these negotiations have ignored developing country concerns about the problems our small subsistence farmers are facing . . . Since before Seattle, we have been pushing for a 'Development Box' to be included in the Agriculture Agreement, but our proposal has been sidelined. The WTO is supposed to ensure equity in trade, but the present agricultural trading system in practice legitimises the inequities, for instance, by allowing the dumping of agricultural products from the North.[47]

The Third World bowed to its knees on this occasion. Yet considering all these reasonable critiques of international economic power relations, was Harare's skepticism about a partnership between Africa and the Quad – the US, Europe, Japan and Canada – so unreasonable? *Nepad* correctly observes, in one of its moments of radical-chic critique, that 'the increasing polarisation of wealth and poverty is one of a number of processes that have accompanied globalisation, and which threaten its sustainability.'

The next logical question, 'how do we roll back globalisation?' surely deserved asking.

Nationalists forced to deglobalise

Nepad would not mention the sacrilegious idea of self-reliance, but several contemporary southern African examples stood out whereby nation-states – not only civil-society activists – contested the Washington Consensus and the transnational corporations and banks which are its beneficiaries, in the spheres of trade, finance, investment and procurement. On trade, as noted earlier, the pharmaceutical industry withered before the onslaught of mass popular Africa-solidarity protest around the world, especially in the wake of the March 2001 decision by 39 international drug firms to sue the South African government over the violations of patents required to save millions of African lives.

Financially, Mugabe's fairly tight exchange controls and refusal to repay the IMF, World Bank and African Development Bank, represented a troubling economic model. Though for reasons pointed out in Chapters Two and Three, Mugabe deserved no praise for governance or economic management, some of Harare's technical interventions did suggest that stiffening domestic political will could overcome Washington's neoliberal financial-liberalisation dictates. As discussed already, Mugabe's imposition of a 100% luxury goods import tax, his capture of hard-currency accounts kept by wealthy Zimbabweans who prospered during the 1990s era of structural adjustment, his debt default, his lowering of the real (after-inflation) interest rate from high positive levels during the 1990s to an amazing –85% in 2001, and his ability to keep a currency peg in place at artificially high levels were all techniques that were previously held to be impossible, given financial-industry power and state weakness. Delinking from international financial circuits could be accomplished on a piece-meal basis, Zimbabwe showed, although the country degenerated rapidly because democratic social change was the crucial missing ingredient.

Against transnational corporate investment and procurement, a variety of minor attempts to begin rectifying the power imbalance also deserved mention in any early twenty-first century political-economic initiative from Africa. Amongst them were the Botswana government's decision to 'renationalise' key diamond investments via a highly profitable stake in De Beers in early 2001 – a move which the South African government had to emulate a few months later in the case of its national airline following the bankruptcy of its privatisation partner, SwissAir.

Even more aggressively, the Lesotho government persisted in bringing to book international corporations which from 1988–1998 repeatedly bribed the chief executive of the Lesotho Highlands Development Authority for procurement purposes, in spite of the insistence by the World Bank in 1994 that the man responsible stay in his job. More pressure from southern African states on these firms, including South African firms, would be necessary if the *Nepad* provisions against corruption were to be taken seriously.

In a not dissimilar case of procurement corruption, Mbeki's close confidants were originally thought to be relatively protected from prosecution once Mbeki had the most pugnacious investigator (Willem Heath) removed from his job in early 2001. But by October, at least one high-level arrest – of Mbeki's legislative manager in parliament, Tony Yengeni, for eliciting a half-priced Mercedes from Daimler-Chrysler in exchange for favourable arms-deal interventions – suggested that in spite of Mbeki's obvious desire to push through the R66 billion purchase of high-tech weaponry, enough social pressure existed to demand at least a modicum of good governance.

All of these examples just go to show that the balance of forces is not cemented, and that political pressure ebbs and flows to either welcome or repel globalisation. Favouring the latter are progressive civil society groups which demonstrate their disgust over neoliberal economic policies through mass demonstrations, national stayaways, surgical strikes, lawsuits, lobbying and even merely through conference resolutions, in Mbeki's South Africa, in Zimbabwe and indeed across the world. It is to these forces, and the solidarity support they might give to genuine alternative options for Zimbabwe, that we turn in conclusion.

Notes

1. We favour the definition of Robert Cox (1987), *Power, Production and World Order*, New York, Columbia University Press.
2. See for example, Robinson, W. (1996), *Promoting Polyarchy: Globalisation, US Intervention and Hegemony*, Cambridge, Cambridge University Press.
3. The South African case is considered in Bond, P. (2000), *Elite Transition: From Apartheid to Neoliberalism in South Africa*, London, Pluto Press and Pietermaritzburg, University of Natal Press; and Marais, H. (2000), *South Africa: Limits to Change* (second edition), London, Zed Press and Cape Town, University of Cape Town Press. Like Zimbabwe, the most severe contradictions will be of an urban character, as discussed in Bond, P. (2000), *Cities of Gold, Townships of Coal: Essays on South Africa's New Urban Crisis*, Trenton, Africa World Press.
4. *Herald*, 9 December 2000. However, it seemed that tempers improved over the holidays, for in early 2001, another IMF report was partially published in the press, emphasising the need for devaluation:

   > The International Monetary Fund has urged the Reserve Bank of Zimbabwe (RBZ) to scrap its monetary policy linking rates of interest with the rate of inflation, effectively pegging the bank rate at between 2 to 2.5 percentage points above the rate of inflation. However, the RBZ has been commended by the IMF for its decision, which has not yet been announced in the country, to depart from a fixed exchange rate system. (*Zimbabwe Independent*, 5 January 2001.)

   The IMF had 'commended' too soon, as the decision to depart from reliance on an overvalued Zimbabwe dollar was never announced.
5. Or, at worst, the parallel-import of generic drugs from India, Thailand and Brazil, amongst other exporters.
6. Source: http://www.worldbank.org
7. Cited in *Watching the World Bank in Southern Africa* 2, Alternative Information and Development Centre.
8. The standard excuse that research and development might be harmed by relaxation of intellectual property rights is countered by the fact that key anti-retroviral drugs were developed through US government and university support.
9. Jubilee 2000 Zambia (2001), 'No loans for AIDS!', Press statement reproduced in *Watching the World Bank in Southern Africa* 2, Alternative Information and Development Centre.
10. Adapted from Bond, *Against Global Apartheid*, Chapter Five.
11. In Zimbabwe, at least three public figures – the MDC's Eddie Cross, *Zimbabwe Independent* commentator/accountant Eric Bloch and finance minister Simba Makoni – remained important representatives of overlapping Washington-centric constituencies. The implications of ongoing world economic volatility seemed to pass them by.
12. *Left Business Observer*, February 2001.
13. The main point is that 'asymmetry' between market players can lead to large-scale distortions – and hence Stiglitz-style policy prescriptions are generally limited to more transparency, more competition and a bit more government regulation to eliminate those distortions.
14. Jeffrey Sachs of Harvard, and Paul Krugman of Princeton and the *New York Times* stand out.

15. There was hope that perhaps he would be joined on the Left of the EU by the German premier Helmut Schroeder, in desperate need in late 2001 of maintaining his Green coalition partnership.

16. Would more resolve be found in Zimbabwe, perhaps, if within the slippery 'spaghetti' of the MDC's ideology, Morgan Tsvangirai's own self-styled 'social democratic' agenda was located in the post-Washington Consensus category?

17. Ian Smith was traditionally comfortable amongst this crowd. But whether their 2001 Zimbabwe Democracy Act meant anything beyond far-away baying for Mugabe's blood, and an indirect funding inflow to the MDC and its allies, remained to be seen.

18. Mugabe, Jonathan Moyo, *Zimbabwe Mirror* editor and leading left-nationalist intellectual Ibbo Mandaza, and Zanu information secretary Nathan Shamuyarira.

19. *Herald*, 13 February 1985.

20. *Southern Africa Report*, July 1991.

21. *Herald*, 23 October 1986.

22. *Herald*, 19 December 1987.

23. *Herald*, 5 November 1987.

24. *Southern African Economist*, November 1989.

25. http://www.jubileesouth.net

26. *Southern Africa Political and Economic Monthly*, Dec–Jan 1991–92.

27. Mbeki, T. (2001), 'Answers to Questions in Parliament', SA Presidential website, speech01/011029946a1002.txt, The Presidency, Cape Town, 24 October.

28. *Sunday Times*, 11 November 2001.

29. Hanekom's political mandate, in the 1994 Reconstruction and Development Programme, was to redistribute 30% of the good land within the first five years. By using a willing-seller/willing-buyer approach topped up with a small grant and rural credit, Hanekom virtually copied the Zimbabwe Lancaster House model intact, to the extent of using as a policy advisor the same World Bank economist, Robert Christiansen, who had tried to salvage the failed AFC scheme discussed in Chapter Two. Hanekom ensured that the state was inactive as a land redistribution agent. Because there were practically no black, small-scale farmers who could use the tiny R16 000 state grant to acquire land individually, and because the few cases where farmers grouped their subsidies together were not given sufficient state support and mainly failed, Hanekom's record of land redistribution was less than 1% after five years. He was demoted to back-bench MP in 1999. For details, see Bond, *Elite Transition*, Chapter Five.

30. For a South African insider perspective, see Mbeki, M. (2000), 'Zimbabwe's Troubles', *South African Journal of International Affairs*, 7, 2.

31. Economies of scale allowed production on such enormous runs in South Africa that savings offset the labour-cost differential between the two countries. There were virtually no cases of Zimbabwe being used as an *Esap*-era production site for goods headed for the South African market.

32. When the goods sit on the shelf, they get marked up again and again. *Business Day*, 18 October 2001.

33. *Daily Mail and Guardian*, 4 December 2001.

34. Eddie Cross issued a myopic statement to this effect on 11 December 2001:
     What is much more encouraging in respect to the new legislation, is the commitment by the government of the United States to help Zimbabwe get

back on its feet once we have changed the way we do things and come back to our senses. This is a very significant step forward. Normally a country like Zimbabwe, coming out of a period of delinquency, would have to wait for anything up to a year before the multilateral institutions could resume support . . . The decision of the US House of Representatives to ensure that such help will be forthcoming as soon as we put our own house in order, is the best news we could have had from anyone this Christmas.

35. *Daily News*, 6 November 2001.
36. *Herald*, 3 December 2001.
36. See for example, by South African economists and senior World Bank employees Ian Goldin and Alan Gelb (2001), 'Attacks on US Hurt Africa', *Financial Times*, 10 October.
38. Mills, J. and J. Oppenheimer (2001), 'Partnerships only way to break cycle of poverty', *Financial Times*, 1 October; Gondwe, G. and C. Madavo (2001), 'New swipe at fighting poverty', *Financial Times*, 7 October.
39. South African Department of Foreign Affairs (2001), 'New Partnership for Africa's Development', Pretoria, 23 October.
40. South African Institute of International Affairs (2001), *Breaking the Cycle* (video), Johannesburg.
41. Tandon, Y. (1999), 'A Blip or a Turnaround?', *Journal on Social Change and Development*, 49, December, p. 18.
42. Erwin's manoeuvres were exposed in the *Mail and Guardian*, 9 and 16 November 2001. His own justifications are spelled out in an interview in *New Agenda*, 3, Autumn 2001.
43. http://voiceoftheturtle.org/articles/raj_doha.shtml
44. Africa Group (2001), 'Proposals on TRIPS for WTO Ministerial', http://www.twnside.org.sg, 19 October.
45. However, Patel's Doha article again provides a reality check:
    It turns out that the declaration merely clarifies existing provisions in the WTO patents regime, in which public health criteria can already be used to abrogate patent rights. There's nothing new in the Doha declaration to worry the pharmaceutical companies, as the US Pharmaceutical corporate lobby have recently confirmed. In fact, the WTO's rules are so powerful that even rich countries are wary of them. Nothing else explains the Canadian government's swift about-face on the compulsory licensing of Cipro [the antidote to anthrax]. If the Canadians are afraid compulsorily to license because of the precedent this will set for the pharmaceutical industry, it's unlikely that small developing countries stand much of a chance. Only Brazil has moved ahead with a compulsory licensing initiative, despite US threats of legal action. To have the rich countries affirm what was written into an already unjust law is scant victory.
46. Cuba, Dominican Republic, Haiti, India, Kenya, Pakistan, Peru, Uganda, Venezuela and Zimbabwe (2001), 'Assessment of Trade in Services', Special Communication to the World Trade Organisation, 9 October.
47. Friends of the Development Box (2001), 'Press Statement', Doha, 10 November.

CHAPTER FIVE

Conquering the Constraints

1. Movements for justice

This final chapter makes the optimistic case that world-scale social change has indeed now begun, and that this augers well for genuine democrats and progressives in Zimbabwe. Such optimism will increase in coming months and years if organic intellectuals and grassroots/ shopfloor leaders take up a series of challenges we pose in an exploratory way in Section 1. These translate, in Section 2, into options for feasible 'non-reformist reforms', mainly in the financial sphere that would suit a more profoundly democratic movement for change in Zimbabwe. Section 3 draws out scenarios that lead towards and away from such a movement.

We come now to the groups with which we most closely identify: those arguing for an entirely different approach to international political-economy, sometimes termed 'anti-globalisation', but better described as 'movements for global justice'.[1] Table 7 lists notable individuals associated with these movements, although the main point is that as an 'NGO-swarm' – to cite the Rand Corporation's frightened description – these networks do not have formal leaders who tell followers 'the line' or 'the strategy'.[2]

In general, the diverse movements have this in common: *they promote the globalisation of people and halt or at minimum radically modify the globalisation of capital.* Their demands, campaigns and programmes reflect the work of organisations with decades of experience. Their activists were schooled in social, community, women's, labour, democracy, disarmament, human rights, consumer, public-health, political, progressive-religious, environmental, and youth traditions, spanning an enormous variety of issues, organisational forms and styles. In the Third World, high-profile justice movements at the turn of the twenty-first century included Mexico's Zapatistas, Brazil's Movement of the Landless, India's National Alliance of People's Movements, Thailand's Forum of the Poor and the Korean Confederation of Trade Unions.

After September 11?

In contrast to these non-violent movements whose ambition is social justice, the most important reactionary Third World force that emerged at the same time was an ultra-fundamentalist, violent streak within Islam, whose adherents numbered at least 70 000 trained cadres associated with the Al-Qaeda network. We mention this here merely because although there was absolutely nothing in common between the justice movements and Al-Qaeda's analysis, vision, objectives, strategies and tactics, there did emerge in the minds of some commentators a kind of 'competition' to make an impact – of a very different kind – on the global elite.

For example, James Harding, writing in the *Financial Times* under the provocative title 'Clamour against capitalism stilled', anticipated that in the wake of the 11 September terrorist incidents, global justice movements would be 'derailed'.[3] A spurious reason was 'the absence of both leadership and a cogent philosophy to inspire fellowship'. One counterpoint was obvious: hierarchical leadership is not necessarily a positive attribute for the kind of broad-based opposition to neoliberalism that is required, and that is bubbling up from all corners of Africa and the world.

Still, the death-knell of the 'movement' (really many movements) for global justice was sounded by Harding:

It is riddled with egotism and petty politics. Its actions are sometimes misinformed, sometimes misjudged. It has an inflated sense of its own importance. Its targets keep changing and growing. And it has been robbed of its momentum. Counter-capitalism was not just a movement, it was a mood. Its main platform – the street – is not as open as it was. Its message, always complicated, is now much more loaded. Its audience – politicians, the press and the public – are seriously distracted. And its funding base, already tiny, threatens to shrivel as charitable foundations and philanthropists see their fortunes shrink with the stock market.

All these charges have a grain of truth. But if global justice activists were slightly slowed in late 2001, subsequent months and years would see their revitalisation, as the problems they identified only became worse.

One way forward was linkage of the movements fighting militarism with those fighting neoliberalism. Thus in Malawi in late 2001, members of social movements and progressive organisations from across southern Africa, including the Zimbabwe Coalition on Debt and Development, gathered at an important workshop to address 'the universality of human rights which we strongly affirm to include political and civil, economic and social, workers', cultural and environmental rights'. Amongst the declarations were that the organisations present:

- extend our solidarity to other people suffering from war and all forms of terrorism throughout the world;
- are concerned that the current global 'war against terrorism' carries serious implications for the human rights, democracy and security of peoples throughout the world; and therefore
- express our support to the international movement mobilising against the war, and above all, condemn the bombing of the people of Afghanistan.

Linking elite geopolitics and neoliberalism

Other resolutions addressed strategies on related issues:

War and human rights:
- developing active campaigns of popular solidarity to contribute to an immediate end to the wars and conflicts in Angola, the DRC and the Great Lakes region and elsewhere in Africa;
- campaigning for a radical reduction in governmental military expenditure and the elimination of the influence of arms manufacturers, traders and the illegal activities of mercenaries, and arms and drug traffickers, diamond and other resource smugglers;
- calling for the implementation of the Pelindaba Agreement on a nuclear free Africa;
- calling for the closure of USA and other foreign military bases/ forces in Africa and the Indian Ocean especially on the islands of Diego Garcia.

Human rights and democracy:
- promoting the adherence and full application by African governments of the terms of the United Nations Declaration of Human Rights;
- developing effective popular organisations for the effective monitoring, defence and promotion of all human rights in all countries of SADC; and
- promoting the immediate democratisation and respect for human rights in Swaziland and the unconditional release and amnesty for all political detainees including the release of Mario Masuka in Swaziland.

Globalisation and human rights:

- disseminating information and creating deeper understanding of the character and purposes of international institutions promoting neoliberal policies for globalisation, above all the IMF, World Bank and the World Trade Organisation and in this context call for their dismantling;
- creating linkages and close co-operation between people's organisations and networks focused on IMF, World Bank and Structural Adjustment Policies, now recast as Poverty Reduction Strategy Papers, which are contrary to the human rights and needs of our people;
- expanding the knowledge of the WTO as the key global institution usurping our democratic rights and especially those agreements which have the most serious negative implications for human rights, above all, Trade Related Intellectual Property Rights and the General Agreement in Trade in Services; and
- linking these to people's campaigns for social services and the recognition and respect of all social, economic and cultural rights.[4]

Fixing the elite institutions?

One way forward would be to attempt to reform the tortuous, self-contradictory projects of international and African elites, such as Highly Indebted Poor Country Initiatives (1997), Comprehensive Development Frameworks (1999), Poverty Reduction Strategy Programmes (1999) and *Nepad* (2000–2001). These top-down initiatives followed at least two decades' worth of other failed or inconsequential reforms, in areas such as environment, gender, transparency, participation and post-Washington Consensus economics. Together, the long string of reform failures suggest quite conclusively that making the Bretton Woods Institutions and World Trade Organisation work for humanity and nature is utopian, given the prevailing balance of forces.[5] The justice movements in Africa were yet to tackle *Nepad* forcefully, but as Appendix Four demonstrates, the May 2001 Jubilee South 'Pan-African Declaration on Poverty Reduction Strategy Programmes' confirmed the leading African activist groups' commitment to progressive work at both global and local levels in coming months and years.[6]

Still, what is continually acknowledged by global-justice activists is that while enormous progress has been made in identifying the world's most substantial social, environmental and economic problems since the movements began building several years ago, subsequently *mass consciousness-raising and protest have not yet translated into substantive change*. Cognisant of the hostile power relations, most activists are humble about the extent to which they imagine the establishment really wants help from those marginalised by their system. In short, it is now clear, the elite-reformist gambit is doomed to fail *because nothing is really on offer*.

The most dynamic forces within the movements have arrived at that simple realisation – not only because of high-profile battles in London, Cologne and Seattle (1999); Washington, Melbourne, Prague and Nice (2000); Gothenburg, Quebec City, Genoa and Brussels (2001) – but because of the conditions that gave rise to 'IMF Riots' and massive anti-neoliberal protests across virtually the entire Third World over the past two decades. For many Southern social and labour movements, Seattle was a catalyst to transcend the IMF Riot as knee-jerk protest against neoliberalism. Instead, mass-democratic activist responses have characterised the subsequent protests, which have featured anti-neoliberal programmatic demands. In some instances, particularly in Latin America (Bolivia, Argentina and Ecuador), the activism reached a near-insurgent stage; in other sites (South Africa, Nigeria and India), many millions of workers became involved in mass strikes against neoliberalism; in yet other protests (South Korea, Brazil, Turkey), tens of thousands of protesters took to the streets in waves of militancy.[7]

Most of these activists reckoned that most attempts underway in the early twenty-first century to construct global-state processes to deal with durable social, environmental and economic problems were *part of the problem*. The global-scale institutions, systems and processes would merely reflect, and in the process amplify, existing geopolitical, military and financial power relations. Applied to the World Bank, IMF and WTO, the answer they gave to 'Fix-it or Nix-it?' seemed increasingly straightforward: do not trust the establishment, and instead *disempower* their institutions.

Rebuttals emerged, however, that if French and German leaders got their act together as they threatened in late 2001, a serious global-policy discussion was imminent about the merits of a 'Tobin Tax' on international financial transactions to halt or slow speculation (which would be a very good thing). But the US/UK regimes, acting for New York/London bankers, were widely expected to continue nixing the idea of a Tobin Tax.

Another rebuttal was that the August–September 2002 United Nations' 'Rio+10' Earth Summit conference in Johannesburg would provide a site for global deals to be done in the interests of humanity and ecology. But activist debates continued over the query 'Can the UN be salvaged?', which notably went unanswered at a large conference called by the International Forum on Globalization – the progressive internationalists' main organised think-tank – during the UN Millennial Summit in September 2000.

The September 2001 World Conference Against Racism in Durban confirmed that the mass-based social movements were losing patience for conciliatory chatter from what they considered to be money-eating UN parasites.[8] The southern African equivalents of an anti-neoliberal 'Social Forum' movement, parallelling the 2001 and 2002 Porto Alegre meetings and Genoa anti-G-8 community mobilisations, began to consider how to best protest some of the most malevolent delegations to Rio+10.

The most destructive UN-facilitated processes, such as the globalisers' attempt to commodify freshwater through the World Water Forum, or the World Health Organisation's disappointingly conciliatory position on HIV/Aids drug patents, would surely be targets. The headquarter location for Rio+10 – the hedonistic Johannesburg suburb of Sandton – would host as many as 193 heads of state and their first-class entourages and would easily inspire grassroots loathing. But could anything coherent emerge amidst the cacophony of this sort of protest?

Anti-(global)apartheid strategies
Whether or not the advice came from the *Financial Times*, it cannot be denied that a cogent approach to replacing monolithic Washington-centred neoliberalism with a far different philosophical and practical arrangements was certainly required. We are not the ones to propose such an approach, but we can point out some of the debates over embryonic principles, analysis, strategies, tactics, and alliance-formation that emerged in the global justice movements during 1999–2001.[9]

To begin, it may be useful to recognise a series of strategic principles of social justice, which are beginning – it appears – to take the following forms in southern Africa:

- 'deglobalisation of capital' and decommissioning of the multilateral agencies that work most aggressively on behalf of transnational capital;
- delinking from those circuits of finance, commerce and direct investment that actively *underdevelop* Africa;
- denuding South Africa of its explicitly subimperialist role in the region and denying (denaai-ing?) Pretoria the pretention that by joining the neoliberal project, on terms largely dictated by Washington and the world's financial markets, Africa as a continent will progress; and

- 'decommodifying' – i.e. making free at a basic lifeline consumption level – access to the basic goods and services that we all need to survive, and in the process defining a generous social wage to which all people have a human right.

More consistently, and with much more democratic input than Thabo Mbeki's African state elites discussed in Chapter Four, various movements for global justice across the globe were carrying out the first task, by:

- firstly, conscientising the world that corporate globalisation was harmful and must be rolled back;
- secondly, putting human bodies in the way of the elites so the latter encountered difficulty both getting into their meetings and retaining their legitimacy; and
- thirdly, by working hard to deny the main front-line institution of underdevelopment the money it needed to keep its project going, via a World Bank Bonds Boycott.[10]

But more work was needed. Especially in the wake of the terrorist attacks, momentum had to be quickly and decisively regained by the mass, non-violent civil disobedience movements that work in the spirit of Gandhi and King. Those who engage in symbolic property destruction – e.g. of three-metre high fences – had to be far more careful, and less prone to provocateurs, adventurism and infiltration, than occurred, say, in Genoa.

The second task encompassed the interlocking and overlapping strategy of diverse southern African debt, development and human rights groups which – alongside crucial international allies – campaign for their governments:

- to repudiate Third World debt and to take on no new foreign debt for basic-needs development;
- to reject intellectual patents and property rights on HIV/Aids drugs so as to save millions of lives; and
- to renounce both imports and exports of arms.

The third task was still outstanding, but as noted above, a movement appeared to be taking seed in Zimbabwe and neighbouring countries via the anti-neoliberal network of eco-social movements and visionary trade unionists: the Southern African Peoples Solidarity Network. A variety of other environmental, social and labour networks were also growing and interlocking at the regional scale: a process to promote an 'African People's Consensus' began amongst progressive church and development groups in Lusaka; the Accra-based Africa Trade Network continued working against the WTO's Doha round; and the large 'Dakar 2000' meeting held out promise that resistance would emerge to the top-down, neoliberal *Map/Nai/Nepad*, across the continent's most advanced civil society groups.

Concrete financial strategies

The principles and core strategies noted above may inspire noble ambitions, but in what ways could they be actualised? Since most of this book has relied upon our reading of intertwined political and financial problems, it is to the latter terrain we again proceed in search of feasible 'non-reformist reforms', which would allow a genuinely democratic nation-state to contend with the financial mess that engulfs so much of the world. Four basic findings emerge from our investigations throughout this book:

- the international financial system's problems are not accidental, but are structural, and in this context capital account liberalisation and foreign borrowing have *harmed not helped Zimbabwe's and other developing country prospects*;
- in any case, *hard-currency* financing for most sustainable development requirements associated with infrastructure *is inappropriate*;
- *domestic financing* can be raised for sustainable infrastructure development projects that do not require foreign inputs; and
- financing of hard-currency inputs can be carried out largely through (transformed and democratised) *international trade financing mechanisms*.

What are the concrete implications of these findings? We can begin by considering the dangers of foreign financial dependence. During an earlier period of dramatic financial volatility, when banking crashes, sovereign Third World debt defaults and stock market collapses were common, John Maynard Keynes responded:

> I sympathise with those who would minimise, rather than with those who would maximise, economic entanglement among nations. Ideas, knowledge, science, hospitality, travel – these are the things which should of their nature be international. But let goods be

homespun whenever it is reasonably and conveniently possible and, above all, let finance be primarily national.[11]

Keynes, the leading economist of the twentieth century, was not merely advocating nation-state control of finance because of concerns over volatility. In addition, at stake was nothing less than economic policy sovereignty: 'In my view the whole management of the domestic economy depends upon being free to have the appropriate interest rate without reference to the rates prevailing in the rest of the world. Capital controls is a corollary to this.'[12]

These insights apply equally as well to low- and middle-income countries today, as to Britain during the 1930s. By the late 1990s, the leading practitioner of international finance, George Soros, confirmed that cross-border financial flows were out of control:

The private sector is ill-suited to allocate international credit. It provides either too little or too much. It does not have the information with which to form a balanced judgment. Moreover, it is not concerned with maintaining macro-economic balance in the borrowing countries. Its goals are to maximise profit and minimise risk. This makes it move in a herd-like fashion in both directions. The excess always begins with overexpansion, and the correction is always associated with pain.[13]

Deglobilisation of finance therefore represents a serious and laudable objective. In the spirit of Keynes, therefore, we can return to the idea of *national-scale* finance, instead of chaotic, destructive and self-contradictory international financial flows, in part by restoring national sovereignty via capital controls. But to realistically envisage a dramatic change in how domestic finances are raised, lent and spent, also requires envisaging how international financial power relations can be radically (but feasibly) overhauled – simply so as to open the space for the reclamation of national financial sovereignty.

Domestic financial self-reliance
Keynes' most important dictum may well have been, 'above all, let finance be primarily national'. The problem of financing development occurs not only in those middle-income countries which have periodically been attacked by currency speculators, but also in the lowest-income countries – including now Zimbabwe – where basic-need development inputs are still denied the vast majority of citizens.

Typically, badly distributed political power and weak technical understandings of financial markets prevented state bureaucracies from both establishing safeguards against foreign financial raiding, and redirecting local financial resources towards areas of basic needs.

The following are the potential ingredients of a programme to democratise finance and re-establish economic sovereignty, appropriate to low- and middle-income countries:

- *local basic-developmental needs with no foreign inputs should be paid for with local currency*, not with hard currency (like dollars, yen or euros);
- the re-establishment of *capital/exchange controls* is necessary to allow states to adopt pro-poor policies without fear of a financial run by the rich;
- a great deal *more public information and transparency* must be achieved in relation to financial resource flows, through disclosures of, for example, large transfers and cash transactions;
- *state-owned banks should be central* to redirecting financial flows, since the 'public good' and public-utility functions of financial markets are so important;
- *directed credit and credit-related subsidies* have, in the past, helped many countries to assure that finance flows into areas of greatest need and potential, and should be resurrected as industrial and social policy tools;
- for private-sector financial institutions that are reluctant to participate in meaningful development finance, one option is '*community reinvestment legislation*', including requirements for cross-subsidisation of financial services (e.g. through lifeline accounts);
- *prescribed assets* have also been used effectively by developmental states, so as to assure that privately-raised finance is used more productively (while earning a market-related rate of return);
- another vital component of domestic financial resource mobilisation is a return to *progressive taxation* (income taxes to support both development and redistribution) and tariff resurrection (to raise resources, to promote important infant-industries, and to guard against transfer pricing);
- a feature of macro-economic management consistent with financial resource mobilisation is *fiscal and monetary expansion* (i.e. printing money to finance deficits, so long as the deficits are justifiable, so long as hyperinflation is not threatened, and so long as protections against inflation are in place for low-income people);

- in the area of domestic financial regulation, a return to '*financial repression*' is important, including techniques such as interest rate capping, dual interest rates, re-regulation, deposit-insurance for socially-important depository institutions, and state development finance guarantees that are demand-side not supply-side; and
- in all these respects, *central bank democratisation* – not formal independence (hence excess influence by the banking fraternity) – is vital;
- *social/labour movement leadership* is essential, so as to sustain the deeper political basis for change; and
- organic experiences in controlling finance for development are, in this process, crucial to build upon, including *existing community/labour-controlled savings/credit systems.*

A complementary international-scale agenda

It is only, of course, in each particular *national* setting that alliances between popular organisations and movements can be achieved, so as to realise whatever parts of the above agenda are prioritised. Nevertheless, given the upsurge in protest against the existing international financial architecture, and given the role of the United Nations in promoting a 'Financing For Development' discussion process, the international terrain deserves consideration.[14]

Consistent with gaining space to accomplish the above agenda, a menu for international action on development finance would logically include the following components:

- *Third World debt is cancelled once and for all*, without conditions associated with the 'Washington Consensus' philosophy, and with attention to demands for *reparations for past 'odious debts'* made to undemocratic regimes or for failed projects, which were already repaid;
- *international tax havens are closed*, by means of wealthier countries' prohibitions on their banks operating in, or transferring funds from/to such centres;[15]
- *foreign direct investment in banking is restricted;*[16]
- *the Bretton Woods Institutions are abolished;*[17]
- *redistributive North–South funding flows occur on a (no-strings-attached) grant basis;*[18] and
- *trade finance becomes freely available from export credit agencies for progressive input-requirements.*[19]

By restructuring international financial architecture in the interests of the world's majority, there would be no need for Bank/IMF loans (which even for impoverished countries when provided at a 'soft' rate of less than 1% – for which a post-Mugabe Zimbabwe would potentially qualify – are extremely expensive when currencies crash, and when hard currency is required to repay the lender). Instead of hard-currency loans (for soft-currency purchases such as rural schools and teacher salaries, or microcredit programmes), an ideal-type, alternative development finance strategy is needed at global and national scales. Such a strategy is discussed in the next section.

2. Zimbabwe's options

Our understanding of Zimbabwe's intertwined political and financial problems leads us again to respond to this reasonable query: but what kinds of solutions are feasible? Here we limit ourselves to considering what sorts of debt-related options exist for a genuinely democratic Zimbabwean government, in the event one is elected that truly desires an end to tyrannies associated with not only malgovernance, but also neoliberal economics.

Of course, what is ultimately needed in Zimbabwe is a universal, 'rights-based' philosophy built into a new and improved, popularly-designed constitution, which gives strong mandates for extremely innovative, progressive development strategies, and harsh penalties to those public servants who fail to properly serve the society. But to get to that point, Zimbabwe requires a blank public-debt slate. Only then can a popular government address the multiple failures associated with two decades of rule by Zanu, whether in terms of political governance, economic management, military adventurism, socio-environmental concerns or abuse of Zimbabwe's cultures and traditions for narrow party-political ends. The lenders who allowed Mugabe to make so many of these mistakes, must and will share the blame and their costs.

To ensure that the slate is truly clean for a new and democratic way of governing the country, a democratic finance ministry would have to embark upon a combination of technical – though highly political – economic interventions:

- repudiation of the foreign debt;
- deflation of the domestic debt;
- regulation of the foreign exchange system; and
- verification that resulting distortions – overvalued property and share markets, inadequate pension payouts, and the consequences

of inflation for poor people – are mitigated through a strong but slim, efficient and benevolent state.

The argument is laid out below, but it is worth insisting at this stage that the apparently radical positions we propose *are not particularly controversial* for countries – other than Zimbabwe – which reach the debt-trap stage. As we noted earlier, on several occasions in history countries had to default on their debt. During the late 1990s, even the South African government contemplated default as one potential policy course in the midst of the emerging markets crisis. Pretoria's most austere finance ministry official, Maria Ramos, was heard to remark, during a conference discussion on Brazil's economic problems, 'In an extreme crisis situation, default will have to be part of the equation. In that case, the only way in which you are going to prevent a short-term outflow of capital is through some pretty tough exchange control measures.'[20]

By December 2001, *Washington Post* editorialists – notoriously pro-neoliberal – had begun to recognise the obvious when it came to Argentina:

> Here is a country that has received two rescue packages in the past year from the IMF, yet still finds itself in a desperate state. The government has already forced domestic creditors to accept lower interest payments and placed a semi-freeze on bank deposits. For Argentina's people, an explicit default on the country's debts would be better than further efforts to stave off the inevitable with tax hikes, which is what the government now suggests.[21]

And, as in Zimbabwe, the debt was only one symptom. As the founder of 'World Systems' analysis, Immanuel Wallerstein, commented,

> As 'collateral damage' of the world economic downturn Argentine workers are hungry and unemployed, and the Argentine middle class is justifiably terrified that all its savings are disintegrating (a bit like the pensions of the employees of Enron). It is this combination of despairs that has created the volatile and almost anarchic situation in Argentina today.
>
> If it were just a matter of Argentina, the US would shrug its shoulders, and so would the world. (Actually that's what seems to be happening at the moment.) But this sort of upheaval is contagious amidst an economic deflation. Indonesia might be a good next location for such a development in terms of its economic situation.

And the political consequences are most unpredictable, not least in Indonesia.

Everywhere that such breakdowns occur we shall probably have a populist upheaval whose character (left or right) may be unclear, at least at first. We may get military coups, of uncalculable stability. We may get governments clinging to power by dictatorial means that are ugly.[22]

From Argentina to Zimbabwe, Brazil to South Africa, people were asking: at what price do we repay the debt, at what price do we suffer social breakdowns?

Repaying foreign debt?

At the time of writing, Zimbabwe's foreign debt was not being repaid. It was simply too large to justify full repayment, and nor was there any incentive to partially repay, since new loans were not forthcoming. As explained by Eddie Cross in December 2001:

Zimbabwe will come out of the presidential elections with a new government burdened by over US$10 billion (*sic*) of debt. We will have arrears of up to US$1.5 billion in unpaid debt servicing charges. We will face critical food shortages for at least two years whilst we try to restore our agricultural production, we will have no reserves of fuel and no international credibility. We will face a huge crisis in our health and education system – both of which are going to have to be rebuilt from the ground up. Up to two thirds of our population will be out of work and up to 80% living below the poverty datum line. Inflation will be running at well over 100%.[23]

Under these circumstances, Zimbabwe cannot afford to repay the foreign debt. But in any event, as argued in Chapter Two, *Zimbabwe should not be compelled to repay*, since it has already paid excessively for loans taken out by Zanu leaders. There are moral and legal reasons to consider the foreign debt invalid, and instead, we promote the idea of *a public, participatory debt tribunal to examine all the foreign loans inherited and contracted by the Zanu government, to consider whether there exist grounds for repayment.*

We believe the starting position in any negotiation should be repudiation, for the five reasons outlined above. To recap, the first issue is whether debt stock that mounted during the 1980s–1990s is formally 'legitimate', given the hundreds of millions of (US) dollars in Odious Debt associated with the illegal UDI regime and inherited by Zimbabwe, plus hundreds of millions of more dollars considered to be 'apartheid-caused debt' during the 1980s. Secondly, the foreign debt has already been repaid in large part via the squeeze on Zimbabwe's trading and debt repayment capacity.[24] Thirdly, conditions associated with the new IMF and World Bank credits that would be necessary to service old debt, are unreasonable, in part because they are excessively painful to the most vulnerable Zimbabweans and in part because they reflect an unreconstructed Washington's distorted priorities.[25] Fourthly, likely punishment for ongoing non-repayment can be partially discounted.[26] Fifthly, since so much has already been repaid, since legal provisions for taking on reasonable debt were violated, and since the structural adjustment programme – responsible for such a large amount of the debt – was a failure, lenders must share the blame for the failed loans.[27]

Repaying domestic debt?

Like the foreign debt, the domestic debt is unrepayable as it stands. The interest bill on local and foreign loans was projected by the finance minister in late 2000 to reach 48% (about Z$94 billion) of the annual state budget in 2001. The vast majority was for domestic debt servicing, on a domestic debt then estimated at $170 billion. That debt had to be 'deflated', and there are only a few ways to carefully whittle down debt.

What becomes clear, at first blush, is that the domestic debt can only be repaid under conditions of very relaxed monetary policy. The technique is to keep interest rates very low – negative after inflation is subtracted – so that savers receive a minimal return on their government investments. The two other options – privatisation so as to raise revenues, and 'externalising' the debt (a foreign lender taking over from local borrowers) such that foreign debt rises dramatically – are advocated by the MDC economics desk, but are untenable.

Privatisation, or 'selling the family silver', is not an appropriate debt-management strategy. Selling potentially profitable state-owned enterprises allows a once-off decline in the public debt. The 48% debt servicing burden announced in the 2001 Budget would have been even higher were it not for a misguided promise to privatise state assets worth Z$22 billion. In reality, during 2001, apparently only Z$5 billion in privatisation revenues were raised. The Zanu government was determined to hang on to patronage opportunities until the last possible minute, and then to privatise (to cronies). Such behaviour is not uncommon amongst governments that have reached the desperation stage that Zimbabwe is now experiencing.

But the most important reason not to privatise is the potential to realise benefits that take the form of corrections for market failures, which can only be resolved through state enterprises. Only state control of electricity distribution can ensure the cross-subsidisation of household energy supplies for low-income people, for example, so as to mitigate against burning of firewood and coal inside homes (with resulting health impact), or to prevent deforestation, or to abate fires caused by paraffin, or to promote gender equity, as noted in the above discussion on Kariba hydro-electricity. None of these social and environmental objectives merit the interest of private-sector suppliers, whose sole interest is to make profit, thereby ignoring social externalities. Hence privatisation should not be considered without taking into account the full range of positive social and environmental externalities associated with state production of goods and services.

There also emerges a question as to which companies would want to privatise Zimbabwean state assets given the extreme difficulties the economy faces and the shortage of foreign exchange for profit repatriation. One British water company, BiWater, decided to forego a municipal water privatisation deal on offer in 1999 because of limited profitability associated with the vast needs for subsidised Harare water.[28]

That aside, bureaucracy has been a formidable obstacle. Not-withstanding Jonathan Moyo's claim – reviewed in Chapter Three – that Zanu's objective was to sell state assets in order to improve 'efficiency and effectiveness of service delivery', Zimbabwe's recent record meant that the phrase privatisation 'has become just another derided institution in Zimbabwe, mainly because it is seen as an excuse for Zanu to steal money', as business commentator Martin Rushmere put it, using a contemporary parastatal's example:

> An agro-industrial company, one of the biggest of its kind, is the subject of a tussle over ownership. A management buyout seemed assured when the Privatisation Agency gave its full backing to the proposal. But along comes a rival bidder in the form of a well-connected individual who has often been in the news for wheeling and dealing. He has the backing of senior politicians who are trotting out the computer-generated accusation of Zanu, when its greed comes to the fore, that the management offer is 'a front for whites'.
>
> The Privatisation Agency has been overruled and the well-connected individual is about to become the biggest single investor in a business that employs 1 200 people. The term 'asset stripping' is being bandied about as the reason for the take-over, which means that the jobs of 1 200 people are in jeopardy.[29]

Rushmere had commented, in early 2000, that 'selling the grossly inefficient and corrupt parastatals is the best way to get the country out of the economic dung pile that it has sunk into. The government has trumpeted that sales of the first few bloated corporations will rake in Z$5 billion.' But on second thought, he conceded, the three agencies on the sales block in early 2000 – Affretair, Cold Storage Commission and the Forestry Commission – were themselves indebted by Z$5 billion at the time:

> It is ludicrous to assume that this bankrupt government could look after them and so the hapless taxpayer will be shouldering the burden. And this is before the main meal comes – what's left of the National Railways of Zimbabwe after the Beitbridge–Bulawayo Railway company has picked up its most profitable operations, and the debt-crippled power authority, Zesa . . . and the rest.[30]

Likewise as noted in Chapter Three, the MDC's *Esarp* also conceded 'limited net returns for the fiscus' due to the existing debts.

It *is*, however, possible to whittle the domestic debt down through a rigorous, careful but very loose monetary policy. The monetary policy adopted in January 2001 set the interest rate very low, both to make domestic debt repayment easier and to make it possible for productive investors to borrow more cheaply, so as to induce more investment. It was thus estimated in mid-2001 that only half the debt service previously estimated would be required, as a result of the new policy. However, prescribed assets and other methods of persuading institutional investors to buy low-interest government Treasury Bills are needed, so as to redirect monies that are now being externalised (on the parallel market) or transferred into real estate and the Zimbabwe Stock Exchange.

Some people lose and some win from a loose monetary policy. Essentially, the Zanu government spread the pain of debt payback to relatively wealthier savers, who received a negative rate of return on their interest-earning assets, after discounting high (and rising) inflation. By year-end 2001, the negative rate of return on savings – with a 15% interest rate and 100% inflation – was −85%. One estimate (in the MDC *Esarp*) is that Z$26 billion per year was being drawn from savers through the negative interest rates.

What would justify this unprecedented attack on savers? Financiers and those with extensive financial assets were the main beneficiaries of structural adjustment during the 1990s, given that interest rates were extremely high (after inflation), thus rewarding those who simply left their money in financial institutions to accumulate, rather than taking risks. Those excessive financial profits are now being taxed by the loose monetary policy. As noted below, however, the poor will be hurt unless protected through a rights-based strategy based upon subsidisation of basic needs. A side benefit of the negative real interest rate was that productive investment could be financed more cheaply than at any time in the last decade, for those very rare businesses interested in expanding during the midst of depression.

As a result, regulation of financial flows became more vital than ever before. Because institutional investors were not getting the return on interest-earning assets that they demanded, they pushed unprecedented funding into property and shares. The Zimbabwe Stock Exchange was the fastest rising in the world during 2000–2001, at a time most stockmarkets were experiencing dramatic negative corrections. Moreover, the stocks that Zimbabwean investors bought became absurdly overvalued, so investors will lose again when normalcy returns, and when the very small profits and dividends per share are announced.

Currency-pegging?

Another distortion that arose from 1999 onwards was the pegging of the Zimbabwe dollar to the US dollar, typically at an overvalued rate. There are two considerations when determining what rate the Zimbabwe dollar should trade at. Firstly, government rationalises maintaining an official exchange rate that is a small fraction of what is available on the black market. The justification is that the state cannot afford to pay for vital imports at the market rate. The private sector reverts to the higher rate for its own imports, while government insists on charging 40% of all hard currency revenues from exporters, at the lower rate, so as to pay at least US$12 million each month on fuel and electricity imports.

Secondly, some people will lose more than others from ongoing overvaluation of the currency. Ruling party opposition to devaluation reflects the desperation of the state, and the need to spread the burden of failed policies to another group which systematically benefitted during the 1990s liberalisation era: exporters who are not given the full forex value of their receipts. However, at some point it is obvious that vast currency distortions are being taken advantage of by both the notorious Zanu-linked 'briefcase businessmen' to whom state financial managers provide forex, and to other companies which, in the words of the MDC *Esarp*, simply 'borrow Zimbabwe dollars and purchase foreign currency' thus driving the currency's parallel-market value down further. Much tighter regulation, along the lines of the 1962 and 1965 exchange control systems, will be needed, along with the political will to prosecute forex chisellers no matter what party they belong to.

Reducing other distortions?

To deal with fallout from price distortions, additional steps would also be needed: redirecting financial capital towards productive investments; protecting the pensions of ordinary workers; and shielding the poor from inflation.

The Zimbabwe government's contradictory economic policies are not tenable over the medium-term. But they are the kinds of desperation measures that may prevent – indeed have prevented since 1997 – a full-fledged meltdown. Expanding capital controls and tightening on 'transfer pricing' of profits out of the country are essential aspects, given the incentive for financial institutions and exporters to cheat the system.

Secondly, controls on domestic financial flows must be tightened. Financial capital is now flooding away from interest-bearing assets in record amounts. The beneficiaries are the stock market and real estate market, where extreme price inflation is being recorded. Since so many assets held by pension and insurance companies are invested in (low-paying) government assets thanks to the prescribed assets requirement, it is disturbing that the discretionary investment funds are moving into two unsustainable outlets.

The overvaluation of property and stock markets mean not only the greater likelihood of those markets crashing, as they have done repeatedly in recent decades. In addition, pension and insurance funds are buying overvalued assets which will not provide a reasonable rate of return on the basis of profit and dividend flows. The earnings/share ratio will come under increasing stress, as the price/earnings ratio rises higher.

Institutional investors were neglectful during the 1980s and 1990s when they could and should have been establishing primary and secondary markets in venture capital and other productive sector outlets. Because such markets were not established, the major institutional investors deserve very little sympathy if their current investment course is self-destructive. However, for society's sake, the redirection of financial resources into more productive outlets should be undertaken, even if that requires compulsion and higher prescribed asset rates.

Thirdly, pensions must be protected so low-income workers do not suffer. Where there are clear cases that pension managers are spreading the pain of loose monetary policy overwhelmingly to current and future pensioners, protection of the real value of those pensions will be crucial. In some cases, pension surpluses increased during the era of structural adjustment (1993–1997) due to overvalued share market investments. More recent upward Zimbabwe Stock Exchange (ZSE) movements confirm this in many cases. But additionally, the tragic onslaught of HIV/Aids has had a devastating impact on worker longevity, with many who contributed to pension funds now dying before they mature. The responsibility of government is not only to have a National Social Security System as a safety net, but to more rigorously ensure that pension funds are maintaining the value of retirement incomes, which otherwise diminish extremely rapidly due to inflation.

Fourthly, shielding poor people from inflation is likewise a task for a strong state. There are many means of ensuring that high inflation does not continue to ravage the living standards of impoverished Zimbabweans, especially those from vulnerable groups.

Ideally, something like a 'People's Development Charter' would be established by civil society organisations to give detailed guidance as to budgetary and policy priorities. In the meantime, free 'lifeline' supplies of food, water and sanitation, other municipal services, energy, shelter, healthcare and education are vital. A system of price-control, subsidisation and cross-subsidisation exists for some vital goods and services. But too often, because of a charity mentality and large holes in the safety net, these have not worked.

A holistic debt strategy

In sum, to deal with the debt (local and foreign), there are four logical ways forward:

(1)   The foreign debt – approaching US$5 billion in early 2002 thanks to the huge arrears which are typically 'capitalised' on the end of the loan – is unpayable, and should not be repaid, because so much has already been spent by president Robert Mugabe's government in servicing foreign debt and because foreign lenders – especially in Washington – have to share in the blame for failed loans.

(2)   The domestic debt – approaching Z$200 billion – can only be repaid to domestic institutional investors under conditions of very relaxed monetary policy (i.e. interest rates of 15–20% that in early 2002 were at least 85% below the inflation rate).

(3)   Dealing with the forex crisis by pegging the currency at Z$55 to one US$ from mid-2000 through early 2002 (when the parallel market rate had reached a level at least six times that rate) is

extremely distortionary and difficult to maintain, but some form of controlled overvaluation and forex-allocation system might be justified under circumstances not so beset by official patronage and corruption.

(4) Because of systematic distortions of a variety of prices, three additional steps must be taken by this government and the next government to deal with the fallout:

- redirecting financial capital that flooded away from interest-bearing assets into the stock market, towards productive investments;
- protecting the pensions of ordinary workers; and
- shielding the poor from inflation, for instance through well-conceived subsidies on basic needs.

Local government debt and underdevelopment

The latter point leads us to a comment on the most basic of needs: water. Local authorities are the primary suppliers, but they are fed by a water-supply system that includes a national utility and catchment-based agencies which are themselves coming under extreme neoliberal pressure from Washington, as noted below.

Perhaps most importantly, because local authorities took on enormous amounts of debt, they too will require a holistic strategy for escaping the debt trap. The World Bank has begun preparing plans for a bond market for Zimbabwe's largest municipalities, which we believe could be avoided if central government better utilised its borrowing capacity in future. In the meantime, our sense is that, ideally, local government debt should be cancelled and central government should take over the guarantee function provided for in law, so that negotiations with creditors can be conducted from a position of strength. What we fear, however, is that two factors will make this impossible, and instead, municipalities will be the coming site of enormous class struggle over debt repayment.

The first factor is the apparent capacity of the MDC to win any and all urban elections in coming years, which on the one hand will mean an opportunity for cleaner and more democratic local government than under Zanu's corrupt and repressive reign. On the other hand, if Zanu wins the 2002 presidential election, such a political misfit ensures a drastic cut in central-local funding flows. In late 2001, to illustrate, Zanu's minister of local government already erased Bulawayo from one major donor scheme, in the wake of the MDC's mayoral victory.

The second factor, whether Zanu wins the 2002 election or not, is an opportunity that the neoliberal faction in the MDC might try to exploit: municipal-services privatisation. The sale or outsourcing or management-contracting of water, sanitation, waste removal and various other municipal services was already underway by the mid-1990s thanks to a national neoliberal policy for local authorities that the World Bank encouraged Zanu to adopt. In some cities, like Harare and Gweru, municipal managers were being aggressively recruited by the full assembly of neoliberal agencies – the World Bank, African Development Bank, European Investment Bank, French Development Agency, US Agency for International Development, British Department for International Development, the German aid agency GTZ, the South African Municipal Infrastructure Investment Unit, international water companies and Harare merchant banks – to promote 'PPPs': public-private partnerships.

Simultaneously, the World Bank also began to work closely with African water utilities – including the Zimbabwe National Water Authority – and municipalities, with the aim of water commodification. The 'Kampala Statement' – drafted by the Bank in association with the African Water Utilities Partnership at a February 2001 meeting – is the most important aspirational vision of water-neoliberalism yet produced.[31] The Statement is misleading, for it makes the case that poor people, and women in particular, deserve primary consideration in water policy. However, the actual content of the Statement – and all the follow-up work planned – is very much towards market-oriented reforms and privatisation. Typical is the Statement's unfounded allegation that 'the poor are willing and have the capacity to pay for services that are adapted to their needs.'

Not surprisingly, omitted from the Kampala Statement is any substantive information that would assist African policy-makers to understand and address – even via state regulation – four crucial draw-backs to such private partnerships:

- the high profit rate extractions, in hard currency, typically demanded by the transnational corporations which dominate water privatis- ation;[32]
- the issue of whether hard-currency World Bank loans are required to promote water privatisation;[33]
- the change in the incentive structure of water supply once private suppliers begin operating (especially in relation to pricing);[34] and
- the difficulty of a private supplier recognising and internalising positive socio-environmental externalities.[35]

Aside from private sector involvement, another feature of the Kampala Statement is its promotion of water-system cost recovery. As a result, the Statement denies the most fundamental reality faced by water services providers:

> The objectives of addressing the needs of the poor and ensuring cost recovery for utility companies are not in contradiction; well thought-out mechanisms for cross-subsidies, alternative service provision, and easing the cash-flow demands upon the poor can allow the utility to survive whilst attending to their needs.

There is an enormous contradiction, in reality, between the drive to cost-recovery and the needs of the poor – as well as other vulnerable groups, and the environment – for the *decommodification* of water. The Bank's insistence that water-system 'reform' occur in neoliberal mode, relies upon the universally-acknowledged fact that African water systems do not work well, especially when associated with public utilities that enjoy a relaxed budget constraint (i.e. ongoing subsidies from general revenues). But progressive critics of the African state – dating at least as far back as Fanon in *The Wretched of the Earth* – have typically pointed out this problem, as characteristic of neo-colonialism, *compradorism*, neoliberal economic pressures, petit-bourgeois bureaucratic class formation, and patriarchal power relations, whereby elites garner far more resources from local states than do the masses.

In contrast, the Kampala Statement derives water problems from one fundamental cause, namely, Africans get the prices 'wrong': 'The poor performance of a number of public utilities is rooted in a policy of repressed tariffs which leads to lack of investment, poor maintenance lagging coverage, and subsidised services reserved for the privileged who are connected to the network.' The mandate for full cost-recovery and an end to cross-subsidies – with meagre subsidies allegedly to be available for poor people at some future date – follow logically. As a result, one of the most important issues associated with water resource management, namely the abuse of water by large-scale agro-corporate irrigation and wealthy consumers, is barely remarked upon. The word 'conservation' is only used once, in passing.

Politically, the Kampala Statement is extremely naive – or disingenuous: 'Labour can also be a powerful ally in explaining the benefits of the reform to the general public. It is essential therefore that the utility workers themselves understand and appreciate the need for the reform.' In reality, the more advanced trade unions of Africa, including Zimbabwe, are rejecting 'the benefits of reform', because those benefits are mainly captured by for-profit companies and wealthy households, as has been documented in many settings.[36]

What is the importance of the debate over water commodification for Zimbabwean politics? The spectre of municipal water privatisation reflects a struggle for the country's soul and spirit, that we believe will soon transcend Zanu-MDC conflicts and rural-urban splits which currently represent the superficial state of class and electoral struggle in Zimbabwe. In the event that Mugabe wins an unfree, unfair election in 2002 and maintains Zanu's repressive rule for another six years, urban constituencies will be even more harshly punished for their universal opposition. But that punishment may be exacerbated by trends we have identified towards municipal neoliberalism. In 2002, the MDC will either/both win a national electoral victory – and if the MDC *Esarp* is implemented, consequently *privatise all parastatal activity, and outsource most health/education services* – and/or win control over municipal services, for which enormous pressure to privatise has also emerged.

That pressure, as noted above, had roots in Harare and Gweru, but by early 2002 appeared ready to intensify. The catalyst was a 1995 directive by the senior secretary of the Ministry of Local Government, Rural and Urban Development, 'encouraging urban local authorities to consider options for commercialisation, privatisation and contracting in and out some or all of their services'.[37] In 1996, the Task Force for Commercialisation of Municipal Services was established, with three Gweru representatives.

But the subsequent municipal privatisation of refuse collection in Harare was widely considered to be a disaster. Likewise, in 1996 the disgraced Harare mayor Solomon Tawengwa signed a letter of intent to BiWater to repair water infrastructure worth billions of rands, but BiWater backed out when objections arose and profitability was too low.[38] A few years later, as Harare water was beset by quality, shortage and leakage problems, more multi-dollar public-private-partnership proposals were mooted by international agencies. The main sites for a set of international privatisers aiming to 'cherry-pick' the most profitable municipal services are the wealthiest councils – Victoria Falls, Ruwa and Gweru – whose per capita urban council revenue has been about double that of the main MDC stronghold, Bulawayo.[39]

In 1999, the British subsidiary of French water privatiser Saur was selected by Gweru officials to prepare a plan. They demanded a 100% increase in water tariffs which was initially rejected. As one pro-privatisation consultancy reported in 2001, 'However, since the negotiation stage the council has introduced a programme of massive tariff increase and thus removed one of the primary hurdles in the negotiations.'[40] Moreover, consistent with the international evidence of privatisation, lower-income residents would be forced to accept much lower service levels, including communal toilets and pit latrines.

Cutting off the supplies of water to those unable to afford payment was also on the cards. Not merely theoretical, this problem had emerged by early 2002, after the minister of local government told urban and rural councils not to increase rates and tariff bills to residents by more than 10% over 2001. (The populist electioneering request was ignored, but offered a telling indication of future struggles between central and local tiers of government.) After suffering consumer debts approaching Z$600 million, the Bulawayo city council approved disconnection of water supplies to residents, as punishment for failure to pay for a variety of municipal services: rates and supplementary charges, water, sewage, refuse removal, ambulance and interest on overdue accounts. As city treasurer Middleton Nyoni put it, 'Although we appreciate that our residents are facing economic difficulties, it is important for them to realise that council can only continue to provide the services if they pay.'[41]

At the same time, while debate raged over the ongoing management of Harare by a non-elected commission, city councillors asked officials to cut off the bulk water supplies that they provided to neighbouring municipalities Norton, Ruwa and even Chitungwiza, on grounds of non-payment.[42] And simultaneously, rumours emerged that Mugabe would introduce legislation to replace elected mayors with carefully selected, unaccountable chief executive officers – which would probably lead to yet more rapid municipal privatisation, even if the officials were appointed by the allegedly socialist Zanu.

Will this, then, become the most durable site of political conflict in Zimbabwe, long after the passing of the Zanu/MDC phase of electoral contestation? At that future stage, will the struggle for social justice which we point to now, mature into a struggle for political power, particularly state power? Will the nationalist/post-nationalist divergence evolve into a debate over neoliberalism/post-neoliberalism? At some point in the very near future, we are certain, a more focused fight to establish a progressive alternative to neoliberalism will become explicit.

A broader development strategy

As noted at the outset of this section, space constraints prevent us from doing more than unpacking technical aspects of the debt crisis and of its political-economic implications, which worry us so much from national to municipal scales, and offering technical solutions. But obviously any debt defaults or decommodification strategies – associated, for example, with water – would have to be applied within a broader, deeper strategy for inward-oriented, equitable development.

One set of proposals has been supplied by the *Zimbabwe Human Development Report* published in February 2000. Sponsored by the United Nations Development Programme's Carlos Lopes, the study was conducted by progressive civil-society intellectuals associated with the Poverty Reduction Forum (PRF) and Zimbabwe Institute of Development Studies (IDS).[43] They came to similar conclusions about the financial and fiscal difficulties Zimbabwe faces in coming months and years, after detailed investigations of the background to and course of structural adjustment. The report makes six recommendations for government economic development policy – the last two of which are worth citing in full – with which it is appropriate to contrast the export-led decline, high-debt strategy pursued during most of the post-independence period:

(1) Overall objective: restore confidence by creating conditions of fulfillment of basic human material and social needs, and by opening up democratic space for dialogue in all sectors of life . . .

(2) The hitherto neglected responsibility of ensuring conditions for the reproduction of labour and ensuring a life of dignity must form the core of the new strategy . . .

(3) Better integration of gender concerns . . .

(4) A well-focused land reform and agricultural regulation policy framework are necessary . . .

(5) Restore production and safeguard the domestic market from external competition in respect of essential commodities and services, as a basic complement to fiscal and monetary tools. Probably considered subsidies and tariff protection might be necessary.

(6) Carry out an audit of imports and introduce measures to cut down all inessential imports and luxury products. Carry out a similar audit of debt, retire illegitimate debts, and negotiate with the creditors for the payment of the legitimately incurred debts on the *principle of joint responsibility*. Put in place capital controls, regulate the banking sector, and review financial liberalisation measures to develop an indigenously led banking sector.

The UNDP/PRF/IDS report concludes by noting that such recommendations hark back to earlier periods of state intervention:

> Zimbabwe has a way out as it moves into the third decade of its Independence. It has a rich dual heritage. One, ironically, is the heritage left by the UDI regime that built itself up on a largely internally-oriented economy with minimal dependence on the outside world. Its illegitimacy was the cause of its demise. The second legacy is that of *chimurenga* (liberation war). That spirit is still present and often not properly channelled. The people of Zimbabwe can, once again, assert their primacy and with sober and deliberate intervention in national matters bring back the state and economy to serving first and foremost the interests of the people based on people's efforts and resources, and not one based on foreign dependence.[44]

These recent programmatic and strategic suggestions are interesting not because they were formed in a democratic, thorough-going manner. But they do hint at a scenario by which alternatives to exhausted neoliberalism and looming neoliberalism can and must emerge.

3. Conclusion: Scenarios for social change

The overarching aim of our concluding chapter thus far, has been to restore some hope in the idea that the nation-state – if democratically constituted and rid of the kind of corruption so long associated with Zanu – can indeed withstand the pressures associated with Washington's version of corporate globalisation. Is there any hint of activist initiatives that correspond with this way of approaching politics and finance in a more democratic future Zimbabwe?

Unfortunately, in the wake of Zanu's long-standing attack on independent civil society organisations, the idea that donor-dependent, ideologically-diverse NGOs can stand in for a mass democratic movement is ludicrous.[45] Nevertheless, a variety of civil society groups – church agencies, a resurgent movement of residents' associations, community health workers, and the more progressive currents within the ZCTU itself – have established a broadly anti-neoliberal perspective. They make regular demands on the state to provide not simply good governance, but also the goods and services that Washington financiers – or the MDC's Eddie Cross – insist should rather be offered by for-profit suppliers. The 1999 National Working People's Convention resolutions were illustrative of these sentiments (Appendix Three).[46]

A subsequent example was a joint budget statement – 'Civil Society Position on Minimum Standards of a Democratic Budget Process' – issued in November 2000 by the Combined Harare Residents Association, Community Working Group on Health, National Association of Non-Government Organisations, National Council for Disabled Persons of Zimbabwe, Public Services Association, Zimbabwe Coalition on Debt and Development, Zimbabwe Council of Churches, Zimbabwe Congress of Trade Unions, Zimbabwe National Chamber of Commerce, Zimbabwe Teachers Association, Zimbabwe United Residents Association, and Women's Action Group. The groups' statement began:

> The current budget process is deeply flawed. This is a major reason for the mounting public dissatisfaction over the way public priorities are reflected in the national budget and over the manner in which expenditures are managed. Persistent economic decline, weak re-distribution of economic opportunity, *ad hoc* expenditure decisions, inadequate funding of social sector obligations and weak parliamentary control over spending have all combined to undermine the critical role of the budget as an instrument of public policy.

While by no means radical, this perspective does at least shy firmly away from promoting fiscal contraction, which is a core goal of the MDC's business supporters. Efforts intensified during 2001 to build a Civic Alliance for Social and Economic Progress, drawing on both national-level advocacy projects and the grassroots struggles of residents' associations, community healthworkers, and others. We might conclude with the observation that in Zimbabwe, like so many other sites of struggle on the semi-periphery and periphery of the world economy today, the challenge for mass-based organisations is to resist distractions, such as 1990s-style corporatism,[47] and instead, pull together both social and political movements that forthrightly contest neoliberalism.

Barriers to social justice
But we are by no means sanguine about how quickly this process can lead to a mass-based progressive consciousness in such a difficult terrain as early twenty-first century Zimbabwe. The confused, radical rhetoric associated with Zanu's dying nationalism may well poison the kind of critique we make of Washington and the MDC Economics Desk, if Mugabe continues to prosecute his brutal war on political opponents.

To return to Fanon, recall his warning that under conditions of atrophying nationalism, the party 'militant is turned into an informer. He is entrusted with punitive expeditions against the villages. The embryo opposition parties are liquidated by beatings and stonings. The opposition candidates see their houses set on fire. The police increase their provocations. In these conditions, you may be sure, the party is unchallenged and 99.99% of the votes are cast for the government candidate.'[48]

Hopes that Zanu's repressive streak would fade after the June 2000 parliamentary elections proved unfounded, as witnessed in a July soccer match stampede caused by police arrogance and in the army's use of force to quell October urban protests over price increases. Matters deteriorated further in 2001. According to a report by Amani Trust, a reputable monitoring group, '27 633 people have fallen victim to human rights violations in Zimbabwe and 20 853 have been forcibly displaced by violence' between January and October 2001.[49] State harassment continued: one day absurd (arresting Tsvangirai for not having a walkie-talkie license), the next comic (labelling any anti-government provocation as 'terrorist' apparently in synch with George W. Bush's rhetoric), the next brutal (periodic murders of opposition party activists, frame-ups and intensifying paramilitary activity), the next counterproductive (having the Malawian secret police arrest civil society visitors to a SADC meeting on Zimbabwe's crisis), the next ominous (the January 2002 announcement of a potential military coup if Tsvangirai is elected president).

That threat came in a January 2002 Joint Operation Command press conference, from Zimbabwe Defence Forces commander Vitalis Zvinavashe, police commissioner Augustine Chihuri, prisons commissioner Paradzai Zimondi, Zimbabwe National Army commander Constantine Chiwenga, Central Intelligence Organisation director-general Elisha Muzonzini, and air marshal Perence Shiri (a key figure in the 1980s *Gukurahundi* massacres). As Zvinavashe put it,

We wish to make it very clear to all Zimbabwean citizens that the security organisations will only stand in support of those political leaders that will pursue Zimbabwean values, traditions and beliefs for which thousands of lives were lost, in pursuit of Zimbabwe's hard-won independence, sovereignty, territorial integrity and national interests. To this end, let it be known that the highest office in the land is a straitjacket whose occupant is expected to observe the objectives of the liberation struggle. We will, therefore, not accept, let alone support or salute, anyone with a different agenda that threatens the very existence of our sovereignty, our country and our people.[50]

Tsvangirai interpreted:

> If one takes into account the recent spate of repressive laws and the general negative public sentiment towards the ruling party, it would seem Zanu is running out of legitimate ways to perpetuate its misrule. The party itself acknowledged this when it sent the top brass of the military to give some bizarre advance notice of a coup d'etat when they lose.[51]

Panic was indeed in the air at Zanu's 'Shake-Shake House' headquarters in Harare. According to a reliable press account, a 'confidential Zanu central committee report' of December 2001 had included 'a submission by the party's security department' which warned: 'Corrupt leaders within the party are seriously endangering and eroding the party's fortunes in the forthcoming presidential election.' In Masvingo, the potential loss of the 'Zvobgo faction's' support for Mugabe would potentially 'cost the party the presidential election'.[52]

A variety of overlapping strategies, combining carrots and sticks, suddenly came in to play to prevent what seemed a sure Mugabe loss in a free, fair poll. To prevent the vote itself being free and fair, registration was limited to those current Zimbabwe residents who could show proof of residence such as credit accounts, or verifiable letters from their landlords – anything to dissuade urban residents from registering (while Zanu-aligned rural chiefs and headmen were permitted to vouch for 'their' constituents).

Just as important as vote rigging, vote-buying began in earnest. Populist measures such as price controls were applied. State patronage was stepped up, from the capital city across the countryside. Urgent work orders were given so as to show the electorate some progress by March.

From the Harare satellite township of Chitungwiza, the so-called 'Freedom Train' was a highly-subsidised rail link whose introduction in mid-2001 provided competition to commuter taxis, which had just imposed huge fare increases due to a 70% petrol price hike. Mugabe announced in his December 2001 'State of the Nation' address that 'construction of shelters, platforms and lighting of stations has already commenced and should be completed within the first six months of 2002.'[53]

A few weeks earlier, the Supreme Court had reversed its earlier rulings, so as to support fast-track land acquisition. Mugabe's main ally, chief justice Godfrey Chidyausiku, replaced Anthony Gubbay, who had resigned under threats of violence from war vets. By early 2002, the government made claims of dramatic land reform successes – 201 942 households resettled under the A1 scheme and 51 464 under A2 – but although any improvement in land access for the masses was to be applauded, independent media investigations found these to be wildly inflated.

And while land minister Joseph Made, aided by the war vets, had certainly expanded the pool of available land for resettlement by millions of hectares, he maintained a two-decade old practice by allocating the best farms to top government and Zanu officials, including ministers, the police commissioner, high-ranking police and army officers, members of parliament, senior civil servants, war vet leaders and ruling party officials. In theory, beneficiaries had to show proof of experience, access to resources, and entrepreneurship, but these did not serve as barriers to the well-connected. Privatisation proceeds of Z$2.7 billion and another Z$2 billion in state funds were allocated to paying for farm inputs such as seed, tillage services and fertiliser (when it was available).

Likewise, to curry favour with his special constituents, Mugabe offered security personnel a 100% raise in early 2002. As law and order spiralled out of control and internationally-publicised reports of violence increased in January, Mugabe and the minister of youth, gender and employment Elliot Manyika reportedly tried to calm down the more violent wing of the party after interventions by other African leaders – especially Olusegun Obasanjo (himself in the midst of repressing labour protest). On the other hand, though, the likes of Joseph Chinotimba – Harare's main war vet, and leader of a bogus trade union federation opposing the ZCTU – continued to whip up antagonism, and the police conducted increasingly hostile roadblocks alongside Zanu youth, demanding party cards.

In addition, as one example of the ruling party's divide/conquer strategy, the *Bulawayo Chronicle*'s efforts to split the opposition vote in Matabeleland was sabotaged in December 2001 when Zapu's leader Agrippa Madlela agreed to withdraw from the presidential poll. But that did not slow the barrage of misinformation by the official media as 2002 campaigning began – such as an alleged anthrax postal attack on Jonathan Moyo (with Rhodesian fingerprints), the MDC's alleged involvement in a massive Johannesburg airport robbery and Thomas Mapfumo's alleged endorsement of Mugabe's land policies.[54]

Repression was also threatened through the January 2002 introduction of four laws in parliament, aiming to tilt the electoral playing field by barring monitors and banning distribution of leaflets and posters; to impose absurd new security restrictions, including making it an offence to criticise the president; to shackle the media by imposing licensing requirements, barring foreign journalists and making it illegal to publish news that would 'cause alarm and despondency'; and to repress labour by denying rights of assembly and the right to strike.[55] Some of these were passed prior to the mid-January SADC meeting, which won some slight concessions from Mugabe, including a rollback of Moyo's media gags. But it was already clear that under these conditions, there was no way that any observer could legitimately call Zimbabwe's presidential election 'free and fair,' as virtually all the minimum conditions had been sabotaged by the ruling party months prior to the poll.[56]

Very rarely, reports surfaced of documented violence against the ruling party, such as murders in late 2001 of a war vet in Chipinge, and of Zanu's relatively moderate Matabeleland South war-vet leader, Cain Nkala. But the latter incident remained a mystery, with confessions by MDC youth allegedly forthcoming, thanks to police torture. Instead, virtually all the election-oriented unrest was catalysed by informal Zanu militias, with MDC members (including MPs) as victims, some fatal: at Bikita, Bindura, Chinoyi, Chitungwiza, Gokwe, Gweru, Kuwadzana, Kwekwe, Lupane, Mabvuku, Magunje, Mutorashanga, Ruwa, Shamva, Wedza, Zaka and Zvimba.[57] The government's 'Border Gezi Youth Training Centre' in Mount Darwin was one rehearsal site for an emerging paramilitary, with many of the first batch of 1 000 graduates in December 2001 immediately proceeding to Harare's urban townships to foment trouble. Zanu youths in the opposition stronghold of Bulwayo even successfully disrupted a mass MDC rally, hand-in-hand with tear-gas wielding cops, in one well-publicised January incident.

Not only was the threat by Mugabe to make 'real war' – uttered at the December 2001 Vic Falls Zanu party congress – being taken seriously by his loyal cadres. The *povo*'s political misery was amplified by a rash of pre-election shortages: maize, cooking oil, sugar, fertiliser and even milk in some sites. Were these the result of hoarding by mainly white wholesalers, as Jonathan Moyo regularly alleged? Or did scarcity logically follow the widespread imposition of excessively-strict price controls – by early 2002 applied to bread, maize meal, beef, margarine, cooking oil, soap and washing powder, sugar, chicken, pork, fresh milk, salt, fertiliser, seed, stock-feed and cement? To justify their interpretation that price controls were not unreasonable, officials pointed to the consistent availability of cheap bread (whose price had been lowered from Z$60 to Z$48 by state fiat a few months earlier). But private-sector suppliers of many other essentials could not keep up with demand, given the shrunken and in some cases negative profit margins.

The economy continued to decay, and to pay for vital imports, Mugabe was reduced in late 2001 to emergency band-aid measures, such as barter-oriented trade deals with Malaysia, Nigeria, Thailand and Vietnam, and import finance from the Arab Bank for Economic Development in Africa, the Libyan Arab Foreign Bank, Afreximbank, the African Preferential Trade Area Bank and the People's Republic of China. Still, he announced in his December 2001 State of the Nation address, 'US$150 million of privatisation proceeds will go towards repayment of the external debt,' and in relation to the electricity company Zesa, Zimbabwe was making external payments to cover 'supply arrears and service debt, equivalent to US$259.9 million, as well as paying for current power imports'.

A time for sanctions?

These boasts provided hints about how the ruling party would bust sanctions, were they to become more serious than already existed due to non-payment of debt and the aid boycott. After the SADC special summit in Malawi failed to generate sufficient pro-democracy rhetoric, Tsvangirai angrily told the BBC that he expected far more from Big Brother to the South: 'The threat to undermine the elections by the military, by President Mugabe himself, should actually send shock waves to South Africa and say, under those circumstances, we are going to cut fuel, we are going to cut transport links. Those kind of measures, even if they are implemented at a low level, send the right signals.'[58]

South African deputy foreign affairs minister Aziz Pahad quickly dismissed the request to turn his failing 'quietly-quietly' strategy into more concrete solidarity: 'We've been working at this for a long time, trying to convince (people), that what is called (for is) quiet diplomacy. Calls for sanctions are misplaced. Effectively sanctions have been applied in Zimbabwe. All foreign aid has been terminated. There is effectively no new development aid. Investment has been frozen and exports from Zimbabwe have been stopped, I think. Sanctions are not the way to go.'[59]

The condescending 'I know better' tone and content were, together, reminiscent of capitalist-class rhetoric against the ANC during the 1980s, when Pahad was a vociferous international proponent of anti-apartheid sanctions. The ANC began its active sanctions-campaigning during the 1960s, and Pahad and his comrades always argued that even if black South Africans were hurt in the process, the short-term pain was justified by the long-term gain: removing the illegitimate regime. Was Pahad now merely self-interestedly hypocritical – or could a case be made that Tsvangirai's call for a more serious targeted-sanctions threat from Pretoria would backfire? The main reasons Zimbabwean democrats debated this very point were, firstly, Mugabe would use tightened sanctions as a whitewash excuse for his own economic mismanagement; and secondly, while Zanu could retain power in a military-backed *laager*, sanctions would mainly disrupt the white-owned business sector, which supported the MDC financially, and employed most of its core working-class loyalists.

These points are valid. Yet at some stage in a struggle for political justice, a people have to decide what kinds of pressure points they are willing to ask others, acting in solidarity, to impose upon their enemy, even if the side-effects affect them. Did Morgan Tsvangirai's call for a serious South African sanctions threat reflect a full-fledged debate amongst Zimbabwean democrats (or even amongst MDC leaders)? Was the decision arrived at through as much reflection and consensus as is probably required? Apparently not, yet the need for the MDC to ratchet up the pressure was obvious, especially in the event Mugabe clung to power, or Zvinavashe prepared to speed his 'slow-motion coup' in March 2002.[60]

The MDC and the mass of Zimbabwe's people would need all the help that they could get under such circumstances, including sanctions once popular organisations called for them following mass consultations. If the ANC had forgotten the meaning of the term solidarity – by not registering Tsvangirai's desires in its debates[61] – then at least there were others in London and Washington power centres ready and willing to help unseat Mugabe. But at what cost? Could the Brits and Yanks be counted amongst genuine allies of the Zimbabwean masses?

Jonathan Steele of the London *Guardian* has pointed out a few unpleasant home truths about Zimbabwe's international friends and enemies, comparing the punishment that Zambia received after its unfree, unfair December 2001 election:

> It was a disgraceful election which European Union observers and local monitors severely censured. The media were controlled. Criticising the president risked criminal charges. The police regularly

moved in to prevent opposition candidates campaigning and the vote-count was marked by irregularities.[62]

But, as Steele explained, the Blair government turned the other cheek:

Zambia is no longer run by the quasi-socialist elite which took the colony to independence, so that Britain's post-imperial resentment has dissipated and the neo-liberal enforcers in the big international financial institutions find the new rulers acceptably pliant ... Frederick Chiluba has gone along with World Bank demands to privatise the copper mines which used to be the main source of budget revenue and foreign exchange.

So the Movement for Multiparty Democracy was allowed to stay on in power, illegitimately, notwithstanding mass civil-society protests in the main urban centres. The contrast to Britain's treatment of Zimbabwe was explicit, Steele continued:

The issue is racism. Zimbabwe's best land is still in white hands, and this provokes inordinate interest in Britain. Mugabe's approach to land reform has been inconsistent and volatile. His methods have often been violent and unlawful. But for largely racist reasons he had very little support from successive British governments. They put a 10-year block on changes in the land tenure system in the constitution drawn up at independence, and have failed to provide much cash for the international fund which they promised to set up to buy the settlers out.

Racism pervades other aspects of Whitehall's approach. The government condemns Mugabe's increasing reliance on political repression but has done its utmost to reject black Zimbabweans who seek asylum here – so much so that even the Tories have challenged this policy from the left. The Home Office took a welcome decision this week to suspend deportations until after Zimbabwe's election but the assessment of Zimbabwe's problems which it gives to immigration adjudicators is flawed. Terence Ranger, Britain's leading academic on Zimbabwe, has pointed out that Home Office reports condemn the so-called war veterans for invading white-owned businesses while omitting the invasions of African- and Asian-owned businesses. They say Mugabe's legislation against dual citizenship is aimed at whites when the main victims will be black farm-workers in Zimbabwe who have connections with Malawi and Mozambique.

Robert Mugabe made much the same point about double standards, in his December 2001 State of the Nation address to parliament:

> Senator Jesse Helms, the prime mover of the [US congressional] sanctions bill, was an actor here in defence of Ian Smith's UDI. He defended white Rhodesian supremacist policies. He supported the 1978 racist constitution that yielded the Internal Settlement and subsequently the ensuing bogus elections of 1979. Then there is also the fact that the United States sought to continue trade in chrome with UDI Rhodesia by falsely arguing that chrome was a strategic mineral. Senator Helms also brazenly championed the view that the United States should recognise the UDI Government of Rhodesia.

Fair points, these. And indeed the logical solution to the problem was a pox on both houses, for principled reasons. Thus in a pamphlet – 'No to dictatorship! No to neoliberalism!' – the International Socialist Organisation of Zimbabwe appealed for a more insurrectionary mood:

> The only way to smash this two headed snake that Mugabe is creating is to attack it on all fronts at the same time, uniting all forces under attack in a democratic and transparent united front without domination of any one group.
>
> The demands must be broad: firstly resisting the attacks on democracy by Zanu(PF), and secondly resisting its IMF, World Bank, i.e. US and EU sponsored neo-liberal agenda which has brought massive poverty to workers, students unemployed and ordinary people.
>
> The movement must be based on action, i.e. general strikes, class boycotts and demonstrations – the tradition of 1997–1999 – in dealing with this arrogance. It is obvious that parliament is a toothless dog and going to the courts will not achieve much as Chidyausiku will be waiting for us there. None but ourselves will liberate ourselves.

Indeed, might enough Zimbabweans align with progressive civil-society challenges to *both* Zanu's repression and to the MDC's orthodox economic policies, to make a real difference to their own country's future? Or are radical rhetoric and ideological confusion associated with the exhaustion of both African nationalism and Zimbabwe's capital accumulation cycle going to close the current window of opportunity for social change?

A programme for social justice?

We have posited in this book that the country's ongoing political conflict can only be turned to advantage by progressives if surface-level confrontations with the Mugabe regime are also understood as *manifestations of an impossible task: managing semi-peripheral neoliberalism more generally.* At some stage soon, a more profound programmatic vision must emerge, breaking decisively with neoliberalism, and embracing rights-based, eco-feminist, humanist, and socialist development strategies. Organic struggles for social justice will intensify across a variety of sectors. In harmony, a programme will have to emerge and be robustly debated, and then be firmly taken up by progressive, mass democratic movements. It must then attempt to *convince* society in general – perhaps, in the period after the 2002 election, the middle-class leadership of the MDC in particular.

A precedent was the *Reconstruction and Development Programme* which South African trade unionists and community leaders compelled the ANC to adopt in March 1994 as its campaign platform. We raise this not because the RDP was actually implemented in the years since – only the most conservative and corporatist mandates can be said to have been genuinely adopted by ANC ministers.[63] But we think the South African experience of drawing together a programmatic strategy from the demands generated in social struggles is terribly important, in the same way that Fanon talked of

> the experiments carried out by the Argentinians or the Burmese in their efforts to overcome illiteracy or the dictatorial tendencies of their leaders. It is these things which strengthen us, teach us, and increase our efficiency ten times over.
>
> As we see it, a programme is necessary for a government which really wants to free the people politically and socially. There must be an economic programme; there must also be a doctrine concerning the division of wealth and social relations. In fact, there must be an idea of man and of the future of humanity; that is to say that no collision with the former occupying power can take the place of a programme. The new peoples, unawakened at first but soon becoming more and more clearminded, will make strong demands for this programme. The African people and indeed all underdeveloped peoples, contrary to common belief, very quickly build up a social and political consciousness.[64]

What will a programme aiming to codify the struggle for social justice contain? Who can predict? But we suggest that the key sites of contemporary confusion, flagged above, cannot be avoided. The main one that will beggar Zimbabwe for years to come is the inherited Mugabe-era foreign debt, which has to be repudiated. Others are the debate over price controls (a short-term palliative to be sure, but a popular bandaid to some of the inflationary problems); foreign exchange controls; massive expansion and redirection of basic-needs state subsidies (e.g. to provide free lifeline water, electricity, food, healthcare and education) to low-income households; growing state ownership and worker control of important – and potentially viable – bankrupt private firms (and mines and farms); redirection of investment capital (including pension funds); and a re-orientation of budgetary spending and imports towards working-class and poor people's needs.

On the one hand, such a programmatic challenge risks yet more confusion ahead. Whether in or out of power, Zanu would try even harder to turn its skills in populist rhetoric into mass support. However, popular disgust with the Mugabe government amongst urban and more sophisticated rural Zimbabweans is not likely to wane. On the other hand, by returning to more robust confrontations over programmatic demands – in parliament, in various other venues of advocacy, in street protests – the progressive forces in and around the MDC will also find themselves pulling Left all future electoral discourses, including the local government campaigns that will follow the March 2002 elections.

That, in turn, could potentially clarify to Zimbabwe which politicians – from Zanu, the MDC or possibly even a genuine workers'/peasants' party in the not-so-distant future – are best placed to address Zimbabwe's ongoing economic plunge. Moreover, forceful advocacy of a progressive programme by civil society will more rapidly weaken not only the power of the neoliberal elements within the MDC, but within Zimbabwean society more generally – as well as in relation to the financial-technical hold that Washington aims to re-acquire over Harare.

What would happen if the left-leaning forces within the MDC took this kind of political turn – away from a post-nationalist neoliberalism, to post-neoliberalism? It would appear too late in the day for the MDC Economics Desk to undergo a change of heart or personnel. Still, the idea of an MDC rooted in the February 1999 Working People's Convention, not the August 2001 *Esarp*, is worth contemplating even if merely for hypothetical purposes: if progressives won sufficient hearts and minds of society and leading politicians, and in doing so overwhelmed the residual elites of Zanu and the bourgeois alliance between Harare big business and Washington, what options might then emerge? If power were decisively transferred in 2002, could Zimbabwe indeed embark upon a more inward-oriented, basic-needs strategy?

The (global) neoliberal cul-de-sac

No, argues Eddie Cross and his Economics Desk allies: There Is No Alternative to *Esap* and its structural adjustment successor *Esarp* (Appendix Two). In early 2000, in order to get roughly US$2 million worth of campaign resources from wealthy donors (in Zimbabwe and abroad) via Cross' friends and colleagues in the white business, donor and farming communities, Morgan Tsvangirai seemed to agree. But this is by no means his permanent perspective: witness Tsvangirai during the late 1980s–early 1990s.

Robert Mugabe, meanwhile, contests the moral and political acceptability of such power relations, but still offers nothing to change either the crisis-trajectory or even the technical management of the economy. The reign of Simba Makoni as finance minister – which gave bourgeois Zimbabwe a modicum of hope when the appointment was announced in July 2000 – did not change matters, notwithstanding his ongoing pro-privatisation and debt-repayment ambitions (Appendix One). Social movements will observe such disarray, once their programme is popularised, and understand better the hopelessness of proceeding along any of the routes suggested by the orthodox political and economic leaders.

Neoliberal orthodoxy is, we insist, in question everywhere. John Bellamy Foster of the *Monthly Review* school summed up the international situation provocatively at the end of 2001:

> The period of capitalism's historic ascendance has now ended. Capitalism has expanded throughout the globe, but in most of the world it has produced only enclaves of capital. There is no longer any promise of the underdeveloped world as a whole 'catching-up' economically with the advanced capitalist countries – or even of sustained economic and social advance in most of the periphery. Living conditions of the vast majority of workers are declining globally. The long structural crisis of the system, since the 1970s, prevents capital from effectively coping with its contradictions, even temporarily. The extraneous help offered by the state is no longer sufficient to boost the system. Hence, capital's 'destructive uncontrollability' – its destruction of previous social relations and

its inability to put anything sustainable in their place – is coming more and more to the fore.[65]

Many southern Africans recognised this problem, to be sure. As just one example, the Johannesburg Institute for Global Dialogue often provided the balance lacking in mainstream think-tanks, and its associate Rok Ajulu issued an analysis in October 2001 that pinpointed neoliberalism's false claims:

> Authoritarian governance has, over the last decade, been exacerbated by the impact of globalisation and attendant market fundamentalism, namely, the idea that economic justice must be reduced to equality of opportunity and expressed through the market. The contemporary march of capital all over the world in search of consumers and markets has visited devastation in many countries. While on the one hand, economic globalisation has unleashed productive forces throughout the world, on the other it has engendered fragmentation and marginalisation. This has inevitably led to a declining resource base, triggering unmitigated contestation and conflicts over control of resources. Not surprisingly, the contemporary era of globalisation has been marked by fratricideal wars all over the continent.
>
> Zimbabwe has been no exception, and it is against this background that the current crisis must be understood. At a broader level, the Zimbabwe crisis raises a much more fundamental and critical question and that is: how do countries at the marginal pole of the global economy engage the forces of globalisation, and what implications do such strategies suggest for democratic governance? . . .
>
> The so-called 'Zimbabwe Crisis' is essentially the failure of a kleptocratic elite to respond constructively to generalised economic crisis.[66]

Beyond crisis-management

At the outset of this book, we argued that Zimbabwe's 'crisis' could not be resolved because of the lack of effective socio-economic equilibrating mechanisms. At such a stage, a force whose logic is external to the prevailing systematic logic must be invoked to establish the conditions required for the system's restoration. The logic of capitalism – even on the semi-periphery – is based on accumulation, growth and expansion of markets. During a typical capitalist crisis, the external counterforce is some variant of recession, depression and 'devaluation', i.e. a process in which there is a write-off of economic 'deadwood' – overcapacity in plant and equipment, excess unemployed labour power, crashes in the value of financial assets (including via inflation) and the like. The corresponding resistance by poor and working people, environmentalists and women, indigenous movements and other oppressed people, slows down or moves the devaluation around. But truly resolving the crisis for a new round of capital accumulation occurs only with sustained restructuring of economic and social relations.

Such devaluation and resistance characterised Zimbabwe's history during several crucial periods: the 1890s, late 1920s–1930s, and late 1950s–1960s. In contemporary Zimbabwe, the 1970s also witnessed 'overaccumulation crisis'. The devaluation process – and necessary shift in racial/class relations – began in earnest during the late 1970s, continued through the 1980s notwithstanding a minor stabilisation of the social wage, resumed again in the early 1990s, and accelerated with a vengeance from late 1997 through the present.

But there has been something extremely unusual about Zimbabwe's recent experience. The more the devaluation has hurt prospects for social development, the more that a desperate Robert Mugabe conjured up radical rhetoric to outflank the alienated working class on its Left. Zimbabwean nationalism's 1990s exhaustion had the unintended consequence, perhaps, of reradicalising official discourses. Yet by the time Mugabe realised how disastrous his Washington-designed policies were for the masses, in late 1997, it was too late.

From this ideologically-muddled situation, we simply learn, yet again, that economic conflict generates political and social strife, in the course of any period of crisis management and displacement – and that as a result, class configurations and alliances potentially shift very rapidly. The outcome can never be certain, for no matter how much left-wing rhetoric is invoked, the real practical activity of the state can just as easily bolster the interests of capital, as happened through much of the past decade under the banner of *Esap*.

But this should not be a disempowering analysis. Zimbabwe's social movements can also take confidence from previous episodes of tough macro-economic management throughout the country's history. As noted in Chapters One and Two above, concrete strategies included imposition of watertight exchange controls; careful reflation of the economy through strategic state spending; prescribed assets on financial institutions; increasing nationalisation of strategic sites of the economy; directed investment requirements; creative juggling of import/export requirements; default on outstanding foreign debt; and a more general commitment to 'get the prices *wrong*', if need be, to assure maximum local backward/forward linkages. The last two times such policies were adopted, during the 1930s and just after UDI was declared in 1965, *the Zimbabwean (then Rhodesian) economy grew at nearly double-digit rates each year for a decade.*

On those occasions, however, growth-through-deglobalisation occurred in a way that amplified racial, gender and class divisions. Assuming the political balance of forces can be changed in coming years, it should be even more feasible, technically, to impose the same mechanisms but this time, to re-orient production to meet basic needs: particularly of rural women, and particularly in areas that should be easy to expand – rural water/sanitation and small-scale irrigation systems, electricity, public works – without debilitating import requirements.

These are probably the minimal policy arrangements in the sphere of national political-economy required for Zimbabwe to prosper as a society. At the international scale, reduced pressure from neoliberal actors and markets will also be vital (as demonstrated repeatedly by visiting IMF missions and World Bank resident representatives). Fortunately, this is being achieved through initiatives ranging from mass protests to more surgical activist campaigns, such as the World Bank Bonds Boycott and the successful October 2000 campaign against IMF- and World Bank-imposed user-fees in health and education programmes.

And finally, what lessons does this confusing period in Zimbabwe's post-independence experience provide to other Third World progressive social forces? We are certain, for example, that the appropriate normative formula is *not* the dismissal of strengthened state-sovereignty as a short-medium-term objective, as is fashionable in some left-wing quarters.[67] Instead, aligned simultaneously with international popular struggle against Washington and various other transnational corporate headquarters, the goal must be the rekindling of nation-state sovereignty: *but under fundamentally different assumptions about power relations and development objectives* than during the nationalist epoch. Such power relations can probably only be changed sufficiently if the masses of oppressed people contest those *comprador* forces who run virtually all their nation-states. To do so will require the articulation of a multifaceted post-nationalist political programme, grounded in post-neoliberal economic formulations.

Zimbabwe is not the only such site of economic and political strife. For example, in the wake of tossing out several unsavoury presidents in late 2001, Argentina's mass movements have begun building on the preliminary work of their Jubilee South affiliate chapter, to demand not just debt cancellation, but a redistributive, inward-oriented economic reconstruction strategy. But the struggle in Zimbabwe holds crucial lessons for the African continent. If it is possible to generalise, the most exciting social struggles in contemporary Africa tend to be between advocates of progressive politics and basic-needs development within formal and informal organisations – based in workforces, communities, women's and youth groups, environmental clubs and churches – on the one hand, and on the other, nationalist political parties that still rule most states, often pursuing neoliberal policies yet still capable of deploying radical rhetoric.

We have enough confidence in the struggle for social justice, and enough skepticism about both exhausted nationalism and looming neoliberalism, to know who will win in the end.

Notes

1. The most impressive analysis of the global justice movements to date is Starr, A. (2000), *Naming the Enemy*, London, Zed Press.

2. The personality list in Table 7 is merely indicative, given the lack of hierarchy in the best segments of the movements, but includes names of internationally-renowned activists, scholars, commentators and politicians like Samir Amin (based in Senegal), Maude Barlow (Canada), Walden Bello (Thailand), Alejandro Bendana (Nicaragua), Pierre Bordieu (France), Jose Bove (France), Dennis Brutus (South Africa), Alex Callinicos (Britain), Camille Chalmers (Haiti), Noam Chomsky (US), Kevin Danaher (US), Eduardo Galeano (Uruguay), Susan George (France), Boris Kagarlitsky (Russia), Marin Khor (Malaysia), Naomi Klein (Canada), Lula Ignacio da Silva (Brazil), Wangari Maathai (Kenya), Subcommandante Marcos (Mexico), George Monbiot (Britain) Ralph Nader (US), Antonio Negri (Italy), Archbishop Njongonkulu Ndungane (South Africa), Trevor Ngwane (South Africa), Njoki Njehu (Kenya), Medha Patkar (India), John Pilger (Britain), and Vandana Shiva (India). Zimbabwean public figures who are highly regarded in the same circuits include Jonah Gokova and Davie Malungisa of the Zimbabwe Coalition on Debt and Development, International Socialist of Zimbabwe activist (and MDC MP) Munyaradzi Gwisai, University of Zimbabwe intellectual Brian Raftopoulos and Yash Tandon of the Southern and Eastern African Trade Information and Negotiations Initiative.

3. *Financial Times*, 10 October 2001. For a more paternalist and uncomprehending version, see the open letter by Belgian prime minister and European Union president Guy Verhofstadt (2001), 'Protesters ask right questions, yet they lack the right answers', *Financial Times*, 26 September.

4. Southern African People's Solidarity Network (2001), 'Peace and Human Rights, Democracy and Development in Southern Africa in the context of Globalisation', http://www.aidc.org.za/sapsn, Mangoche, Malawi, 29 November. To

give a flavour of the kinds of southern African justice movements that make these appeals, this particular gathering – hosted by the Malawi Economic Justice Network – was attended and endorsed by the Inter-African Network for Human Rights and Development; the Alternative Information and Development Centre; the Synod of Livingstonia Church and Society Programme; the Malawi Centre for Social Concern; the Malawi Civil Society Coalition for Quality Basic Education; Coalition Jubilee 2000 Angola; the South African Ecumenical Services for Socio-Economic Transformation; Jubilee South Africa; the Mauritian group Ledikasyon pu Travayer; the Malawi Economic Justice Network; Malawi News; the Mineworkers Development Agency in Lesotho; the National Community Services Programme; the Nkhomano Centre for Development; Mozambique's main trade union federation, the OTM; the Southern African Institute for Economic Research; the Tanzania Association of NGOs and Tanzania Coalition on Debt and Development; Transparency South Africa; the Wits University Municipal Services Project; the Zimbabwe Coalition on Debt and Development; and the Zimbabwe National Students Union.

5. For critiques, see Bond, *Against Global Apartheid*, Chapter Ten.
6. Jubilee South (2001), 'Pan-African Declaration on PRSPs', Kampala, 12 May.
7. See documentation by the World Development Movement: http://www.wdm.org.uk/cambriefs/DEBT/unrest.htm
8. http://southafrica.indymedia.org
9. These are taken up in much more detail in Bond, *Against Global Apartheid*, Part Four.
10. http://www.worldbankboycott.org
11. Keynes, J.M. (1933), 'National Self-Sufficiency', *Yale Review*, 22, 4, p. 769.
12. Moggeridge, D. (ed) (1967), *The Collected Works of J.M. Keynes*, Vol 25, London, Macmillan, p. 149.
13. Soros, G. (1997), 'Avoiding a Global Breakdown', *Financial Times*, 31 December.
14. The process derailed early on, when the repressive, neoliberal Mexican ex-president Ernesto Zedillo was named chair of Kofi Annan's commission on development finance. Worse, Zedillo appointed as his main advisor and author John Williamson of the bank-funded Institute for International Finance, one of the most vigorous of Washington Consensus ideologues. Zedillo persuaded the UN to hold the Financing for Development conference in Monterrey, Mexico, in March 2002. Findings and proposals were to be tabled at the World Summit on Sustainable Development in Johannesburg, in September 2002.
15. An important proviso is that closure should be consistent with alternative development strategies for low-income people in those tax havens.
16. The rationales for opposing foreign financial FDI include the outflow of (hard-currency) profits, questionable nature of banking practices, and the tendency of foreign banks to 'cream' local markets by providing services only to wealthy and corporate customers (in the process diminishing scope for cross-subsidisation for small business and consumer financing).
17. The grounds here include inappropriate financing mechanisms, failure to reform, and need to run down capital so as to cancel debt.
18. These could be drawn, for example, from Tobin-type financial-speculation taxes – but preferably should not operate through existing ineffectual, overly-ideological and corrupt Official Development Assistance channels.

19. The movement to reform export credit agencies is focusing on halting inappropriate megaprojects, but could easily expand to opposition to luxury goods imports and to maintaining a progressive Third World country's financing options under conditions of debt default.
20. See Bond, *Against Global Apartheid*, pp. 280–281.
21. *Washington Post*, 11 December 2001.
22. Wallerstein, I. (2002), 'The 21st Century – The Next Five Years', Commentary 81, 15 January, http://fbc.binghamton.edu/commentr.htm
23. Cross, E. (2001), 'Economic Implications of the Adoption of the Zimbabwe Democracy and Economic Recovery Act by the Congress of the United States of America', MDC Secretary for Economic Affairs, Harare, 7 December. The US$10 billion figure apparently assumed that the exchange rate would remain at Z$55/US$1.
24. Recall that in 1998, the last full year Mugabe authorised repayment of the foreign debt, there were only two other countries in the world (Brazil and Burundi) paying higher debt-servicing charges in relation to their ability to earn exports. Since that time, Zimbabwe's terms of trade worsened dramatically.
25. Recall the conditions associated with IMF pressure in 1999, including removing the luxury goods imports tax, abolishing price controls aimed at helping poor people survive, and permitting further mercenary-adventurism in the DRC only if other budgetary allocations were reduced to make up for military spending.
26. Trade finance remains the most important single factor to sustain, although as noted below serious problems arose in the management of foreign currency more generally.
27. Recall that over the period 1990–1995, gross domestic product fell by a fifth, from US$8.50 billion to US$6.80 billion, as foreign debt soared 55%, from US$3.25 billion to US$5.05 billion, according to the World Bank's own accounts.
28. *Zimbabwe Independent*, December 1999.
29. *Zimbabwe Standard*, 25 November 2001.
30. *Zimbabwe Standard*, 13 February 2000.
31. The Kampala Statement was drafted at the World Bank and issued in mid-March. It attempted to speak for 'a total of 270 participants drawn from government, the utilities (including the private sector), financial institutions, external support agencies, and civil society . . . All quotations below are from the final e-mail version sent from the Bank on 14 March 2001.
32. These have often been cited in the 30% range, payable in hard-currency (i.e. if the local currency falls, then the profit rate is even higher). See for example, African Development Bank (1997), 'Investment Proposal: South Africa Infrastructure Investment Fund', ADB Private Sector Unit, Abidjan, p. 13, Annex 6.
33. The Statement argues, on the contrary, that multilateral and bilateral agencies 'are keen to support' privatisation, and that 'in view of the limited budgetary resources in most African countries, external financing should be available to cover the operational deficit resulting from the lag between improved service and increased revenue during the initial years of PPP.' No mention is made of the lack of hard-currency revenue that comes from selling water services to low-income people, yet the need to repay the multilateral and bilateral financiers in hard-currency revenues.
34. The Statement's only concession along these lines is that 'where price increases to cover costs and improve service are planned, these should be gradual and should follow service improvements to maintain public support.'

35. It is well known that there are public and merit good effects from provision of water and sanitation to the homes of low-income people, including (measurable) improvements in public health (e.g. abatement of diarrhoea, cholera and opportunistic AIDS infections) and income-generating possibilities (especially for women), as well as many unquantifiable but substantial benefits, including gender equity, environmental protection, class desegregation and other aspects of economic productivity. Logically, these should be factored in to any water provision strategy, so as to justify the case for greater lifeline subsidisation. Instead, tellingly, the Kampala Statement offers only extremely shallow rhetoric on this point:

> While the role of the private sector should increase in most cases, the public aspects of water and sanitation services should not be compromised. The creation of an independent regulator and corresponding legislation before any major transfer of operational activity to the private sector can help to ensure the priority of the public interest through increased fairness, transparency, accountability and better monitoring of contract performance.

36. See http://www.psiru.org and http://www.queensu.ca/msp
37. Speech, cited in Plummer, J. and G. Nhemachena (2001), 'Preparing a Concession', GHK Working Paper 442 04, Birmingham, p. 7.
38. *Zimbabwe Independent*, 20 August 1999.
39. Phelps, P. (1997), 'Expanding Municipal Finance in Zimbabwe', US Agency for International Development, Washington, p. 14.
40. Plummer and Nhemachena, 'Preparing a Concession', p. 1. The water increases from 1998–2000 were 140% across the board for water services and 198% for sewage. Important water privatisation, pilot projects in Manila and Buenos Aires share this feature: let the city officials take the flack for higher tariffs and then the international water privatiser will not look so bad. See evidence at http://www.queensu.ca/msp
41. *Herald*, 8 January 2002.
42. *Herald*, 4 January 2002.
43. As noted earlier, the 1998 budget alternative that these organisations endorsed did not break from neoliberalism, but by February 2000 a far different sentiment was dominant.
44. UNDP/PRF/IDS, *Zimbabwe: Human Development Report 1999*, pp. 82–83.
45. For Zanu's attack on independent movements, see Moyo, J. (1993), 'Civil Society', *Zambezia* 20, 1; and Loewenson, R., N. Jazdowska and R. Saunders (1995), 'Civic Organisations in Zimbabwe', Harare, Cuso. For an update on the problems faced by the NGO sector, see Moyo, S., J. Makumbe and Brian Raftopoulos (2000), *NGOs, the State and Politics in Zimbabwe*, Harare, Southern African Political and Economic Series Books; and forthcoming doctoral theses by Sara Rich Dorman, Erin McCandless and Raj Patel. For an extremely sharp critique of NGOism during the epoch of neoliberalism, see Petras, J. and H. Veltmayer (2001), *Globalization Unmasked: Imperialism in the 21st Century*, Halifax, Fernwood and London, Zed Press, Chapter Eight: 'NGOs in the Service of Imperialism'.
46. The main far-Left political group in Zimbabwe – the International Socialist Organisation – plays a crucial (if often zealous) watchdogging role.

47. One such ploy was the revived Tripartite Negotiating Forum, whose redistributive tax-related provisions were ignored by Simba Makoni in the 2002 budget, according to an angry Wellington Chibhebhe, ZCTU secretary-general (*Daily News*, 5 November 2001). Like Tsvangirai in 1999, Chibhebhe threatened to walk out of the Forum at the end of 2001, on grounds that Zanu could not be trusted.

48. Fanon, *The Wretched of the Earth*, p. 182.

49. Confirming that this violence was sharply unbalanced, a third of those victims asked their political preferences in mid-2001 said they were members of the MDC, 5% belonged to Zanu, and 62% did not reveal a political affiliation. Amani alleged that nearly three-quarters of perpetrators were Zanu supporters and war veterans, 16% were police officers, 1% were members of the Central Intelligence Organisation, 2.5% were MDC supporters, and 3.2% were unknown (*Financial Gazette*, 1 November 2001).

50. *Daily News*, 10 January 2002. A *Financial Gazette* report (12 December 2001) speculated – on allegedly good authority – that the same group had, prior to the Vic Falls Zanu congress, suggested Mugabe be replaced by a team of Zanu leaders, which Mugabe rejected. Although that speculation was rejected, the failure of the command to explicitly endorse Mugabe at the press conference has been interpreted, e.g. by Rocky Williams, as a sign that Mugabe could indeed by replaced by another Zanu leader.

51. *Business Day*, 21 January 2002.

52. *Daily News*, 5 January 2002.

53. Mugabe, R. (2001), 'State of the Nation Address', Parliament, Harare, 18 December.

54. On the other side, justifying the coming clampdown on the media, Zvinavashe's January 2002 statement of intended treason included criticism of several articles in the independent press since 1999: 'Ray Choto and Mark Chavhunduka's coup story; the alleged burial of a headless soldier by Grace Kwinjeh; alleged looting of DRC resources by the Zimbabwean military and political leadership; and attacks on the person and office of the President. He also cited the Geoff Nyarota-Masara assassination case; allegations of political victimisation of prison officers and a *Financial Gazette* report by David Masunda alleging that security chiefs had advised President Mugabe to go' (*Herald*, 10 January 2002).

55. When Zanu could not muster enough members to pass the General Laws Amendment Bill on its third reading in early January, Zanu's Patrick Chinamasa unconstitutionally suspended parliament's standing rules so as to return to the law and finally find sufficient Zanu MPs to outvote the MDC.

56. The minimum conditions set out by the non-governmental Zimbabwe Election Support Network in October 2001 were:

(1) Establishment of an independent and impartial electoral commission that conducts and manages elections;

(2) Impartial, intensive, and broad voter education which imparts information about the voting process, procedures and regulations;

(3) Sufficient publicity and dissemination of information about voters' registration, constituency boundaries, nomination court(s), location of polling stations, dates and procedures of voting;

(4) Voter registration taking place for a long period with proof of registration in the form of registration slips being given to all;

(5) An accurate and updated voters' roll which must be available on request to all stakeholders and interested parties at least three months before an election, copies of the voters' roll to be given to all party agents and monitors during polling;

(6) All stakeholders (monitors, observers, media, candidates and political parties) to be involved in the development and signing of codes of conduct for electoral actors, and strict application of sanctions and penalties to those breaching the code of conduct;

(7) All stakeholders to have equal access to all public media, with fair and transparent guidelines regarding media coverage and advertising during the campaigning period;

(8) A transparent and well publicised postal voting system which is accessible to all eligible Zimbabwean voters living outside Zimbabwe, and if voting is done by constituency then an internal postal voting system should be used to cater for those who cannot be in their constituencies on voting day, including officials involved in conducting the poll such as police officers, polling officers, monitors and drivers;

(9) Tolerance of divergent political views and the rejection of all forms of election related violence and intimidation;

(10) Timeous accreditation of domestic monitors and open access to international observers for pre-polling, polling days and post election period;

(11) Impartial treatment of candidates and their supporters by law-enforcement agencies including the police, army, state security agencies and the courts of law;

(12) Impartial treatment of any election complaints, impartial reports on election results and acceptance of the election results by all involved;

(13) Professional and competent electoral authorities whose work does not compromise the voters' right to vote, including the provision of all voting materials and adequate human resources and ensuring that all procedures of voting and counting are adhered to;

(14) All voters to have the opportunity to cast their votes in complete and absolute secrecy; and

(15) Provisions should be made for those who do not appear in the voters' roll or who do not have sufficient identification to vote by oath and these votes to be considered as tendered votes. (http://www.zesn.org.zw)

Later, a 14 January 2002 SADC Summit gained a commitment that Mugabe would undertake the following:

- full respect for human rights, including the right to freedom of opinion, association and peaceful assembly for all individuals;
- the commitment to investigate fully and impartially all cases of alleged political violence in 2001 and action to do so;
- a Zimbabwean Electoral Supervisory Commission which is adequately resourced and able to operate independently;

- the accreditation and registration of national independent monitors in good time for the elections;
- a timely invitation to, and accreditation of a wide range of international election observers;
- commitment to freedom of expression as guaranteed by the constitution of Zimbabwe;
- re-affirmation by Zimbabwe of its practice of allowing national and international journalists to cover important national events, including elections, on the basis of its laws and regulations;
- commitment by the government of Zimbabwe to the independence of the judiciary and to the rule of law; and
- the transfer by the government of Zimbabwe of occupiers of non-designated farms to legally acquired land.

The same list had only been partially agreed to by foreign minister Stan Mudenge and information minister Jonathan Moyo at the European Union meeting in Brussels on 11 January.

57. For documentation, see for example Amnesty International (2002), 'Memorandum to the Heads of State or Government of the Southern African Development Community on the Deteriorating Human Rights Situation in Zimbabwe', London, 11 January.
58. *Herald*, 15 January 2002.
59. *Herald*, 15 January 2002.
60. Myopic and confused excuses for the Zimbabwe generals ('loyalty to Zanu clearly does not mean loyalty to Mugabe'), along with a call for SADC defence forces to continue 'quiet diplomacy in which professional and personal links are maintained', were made by Rocky Williams in his article, 'There are no Standing Orders to Support Zanu at Poll', *Sunday Independent*, 20 January 2002. This reflected the state of paralysis and the degeneration of principles (e.g. that standing armies should not be treasonous) not only in the South African National Defence Force, but in Pretoria more generally.
61. The same was true for South Africa's most important liberal commentator, Ken Owens, in a January 2002 column advocating Mbeki's status quo policies, so as to 'do everything possible to insulate ourselves from the coming turmoil' (*Business Day*, 21 January 2002).
62. Steele, J. (2002), 'Zimbabwe Moves us Mainly Because Whites are Suffering', *Guardian*, 18 January.
63. Bond, *Elite Transition*, Chapter Three; Bond, P. and M. Khosa (eds) (1999), *An RDP Policy Audit*, Pretoria, Human Sciences Research Council.
64. Fanon, *The Wretched of the Earth*, pp. 203–204.
65. Foster, J.B. (2001), 'Imperialism and Empire,' *Monthly Review*, 53, 7; <http://www.monthlyreview.org/1201jbf.htm>. The review is of Istvan Meszaros' *Socialism or Barbarism*.
66. Ajulu, R. (2001), 'Zimbabwe at the Cross Roads – What Next?', *Global Insight*, 12, p. 1.
67. See for example, Hardt, M. and A. Negri (2000), *Empire*, Cambridge, Harvard University Press; Boswell, T. and C. Chase-Dunn (2000), *The Spiral of Capitalism and Socialism*, Boulder, Lynn Reiner. For skepticism about local applications and

critiques, see Moore, D. (2000) 'Zimbabwe's Crisis: Reflections on the Aftermath of Empire', *Arena Magazine*, 49; and Bond, *Against Global Apartheid*, Part Four, and Bond (2001), 'Radical Rhetoric and the Working Class during Zimbabwean Nationalism's Dying Days' in the *Journal of World-Systems Research*, 7, 2.

Zanu's *Esap/Merp* debate[1]

Jonathan Moyo: 'The chief weakness of *Esap* was to ignore land reform'[2]

Q: *Critics say the decision to dump* Esap *has to do with the coming presidential elections? That you are trying to win back urban voters?*

A: We are flattered that people and the opposition think that by dumping *Esap* we are enhancing our chances in next year's elections. In a democracy parties must come up with policies and manifestos and surely no one should accuse us of coming up with the scrapping of *Esap* as a policy. Elections are about policies and programmes and it's too bad that the opposition is unashamedly peddling the discredited market-centred reform policy.

They should carry their own cross and not expect us to carry their cross. *Esap* was born dead and it has taken a lot of good to make a bad thing better. Maybe it could have worked if those who wanted it were honest people who had used it to benefit business. But it turned out that it was a weapon against the people and part of the criticism has not started today.

The people who sold us *Esap* have run away from their responsibilities. We wanted oranges and they left us with lemons.

Q: *Was government ever sincere about* Esap *or was it something that was forced down your throats by the Bretton Woods institutions?*

A: We have had *Esap* for ten years and would have thrown it away after two years. It has been an albatross around our necks for ten years. Government was sincere, but has the World Bank (WB) been sincere? Has the middle class been sincere?

Q: *There are those who say* Esap *failed because the government did not follow the programme to its letter and spirit?*

A: What letters and of what alphabet? *Esap* has been an injection to a slow death and each dose weakens the strength of government. When you get antibiotics you don't get worse but better. *Esap* has proved that it weakens the capacity of government to provide services for its people. The Zimbabwean currency has been devalued 300 times but exports have not increased. People are now asking what is government doing to us? There is no economic growth and anyone who thinks market-centred policies work is mad.

The British Labour Party came into power by attracting voters with a claim of the Third Way, more leaning towards socialism.

By removing the state we created artificial actors and manufactured a civil society, which has existed for only ten years during the period of *Esap*. Civil society must be as old as the state. This civil society is opposed to independence and its sovereignty. They criticise the liberation war as wrong and having violated human rights. We need the restoration of genuine civil societies and the revival of the state to intervene on behalf of everyone.

Q: *Is there any precedent in Africa or the Third World, where countries have dumped programmes similar to ours?*

A: Yes, it has been everywhere. South Africa has refused it, Kenya has done it many times, so has Tanzania. The World Bank has been known by its history of having been dumped everywhere. Their programme is known as TINA (There Is No Alternative), TINA was a ghost that has terrorised for no reason. There are always alternatives. We should be grateful that Zanu has remained steadfast and very critical of *Esap*. The vision and articulation of the party is something that has something to fall back on and we have an alternative to *Esap* as a party.

The policies must be implemented through the party and it is important to crystallise these policies through the party that people select. We have to take our programme to the electorate to curb the extortionate prices, closure of factories and reduction of employment.

Q: *Does the end of* Esap *mean also the end of the* Millennium Economic Recovery Programme *and if so how can you go into an election without an economic programme?*

A: The Millennium programme is a sub-programme with certain objectives consistent with *Esap*. It has its own macro-economic fundamentals and as a party we need to stabilise the macro-economic situation by bringing down inflation which is now at 80%. We should have interest in those objects that make economic sense by generating employment and stimulating growth of our export earnings.

There has to be a radical change. And the most fundamental change is land reform. The Millennium programme was very weak on land reform and failed to acknowledge that progress did hinge on land. They assumed that tourism, mining and manufacturing are answers. But we should get the land reform right first and use it as a base for a new recovery.

The chief weakness of *Esap* was to ignore land reform. There was what we called *idle* capacity because of the underutilisation of land, non-utilisation and racial use of land. Most of the major programmes are agro linked with mining, tourism and manufacturing.

Land has been regarded as a secondary issue but it is a pivotal issue and the Abuja meeting realised this as the core of the problems. Every other issue is consequential, like politics and economics.

The fast track land programme has seen 130 000 people being resettled and people will now focus on empowering themselves economically in a manner in which we get maximum benefit.

Q: *By talking about socialism, is it not a case of going where others are coming from?*

A: Everyone is going that way, especially for the enlightened. The French have elected Mr Jospin as prime minister who is a socialist to be part of their government. What does this mean?

It is no longer the simplistic argument of socialism against capitalism. We never had socialism in Zimbabwe. We tried to have it but enemies of the people fought against it. We had a vision but we were not given the chance to implement it. A person who says that socialism does not work is an ignoramus. In Africa we have tried to spread socialism but faced formidable opposition. But now government has the chance to implement it. We need such social programmes like building public houses, public transport and people's stores. Imagine what the situation would have been like had bread been sold at people's stores during the days when bakeries were withholding bread supplies.

It's not about socialism being a sloganeering tool but a powerful fundamental economic weapon to address our problems.

The kind of socialism we are talking about is meant to empower the people economically. For twenty years we only resettled 70 000 people and yet in less than two years we have resettled 190 000 households. After *Esap* chances of resettling people were very low, when the engine was run by foreigners and racists who don't believe in the independence of a country. Our socialism is land driven. The *Third Chimurenga* is part of socialism.

Q: *Does the dumping of* Esap *mean that the government will no longer engage the IMF in discussions or does it simply mean things will be done according to your terms?*

A: It means that the IMF/WB engaged us under lopsided and unacceptable terms. What we are looking at is people first and does the WB offer this? We will be seeking alternatives to the IMF/WB and new partners.

Q: *Are we then likely to see a reversal of some of the privatisation and commercialisation of state institutions, e.g. hospitals, universities that are causing untold suffering to Zimbabweans?*

A: The objective of our policy is that people must not suffer. And these policies must be reviewed to ensure that people do not suffer. We have to adjust and review. We should not mortgage our assets to policies that do not benefit our people.

We should have a viable education system, and effective health delivery and good economy, all which should be reviewed.

Zimbabwe is proud to have an elite skilled human resource base. Some of the people are here and others in Malawi, South Africa, Zambia, Australia, Canada and Britain.

Just look at the farmworkers who are being deported and think of how many skilled Zimbabweans are employed in South Africa. Some of them are making inquiries to come back home. One day they will come back home.

Q: *Is the current land and agrarian reform programme an economic programme or just a political programme?*

A: Land reform is political and fundamental in a sense. We have rights to use land as our natural resource and for economic and political use. Land is the final demonstration of our freedom, the emancipation, dislocation and disenfranchisement can be corrected through land reform. It is the final statement. It's political but it also means economic and political freedom.

Nathan Shamuyarira: 'I'm glad it failed . . . it was a capitalist project'[3]

Nathan Shamuyarira, Zanu's secretary for information and publicity, says he has always opposed the International Monetary Fund-sponsored *Economic Structural Adjustment Programme (Esap)*, since its introduction in 1990.

Asked to qualify his statement, Shamuyarira on Monday said he had expressed serious reservations against *Esap* during cabinet meetings. He said: 'When the cabinet accepted the *Esap* programme, I predicted it would fail and retard our economy. Today I am glad that it has failed because it was a capitalist project. I was totally against it.'

He said he had, however, been bound by the decision of the majority and the ill-fated programme was subsequently implemented.

Shamuyarira, a former minister of industry and commerce at the height of *Esap*, said he 'fought hard' to ensure the failure of the IMF/World Bank-backed economic reform measures as the panacea to the country's crumbling economy after a ten-year experimentation with Marxism-Leninism.

In September, the IMF withdrew continued aid to the country, citing Zimbabwe's failure to service outstanding arrears worth at least US$53 million (Z$2 915 billion) as of August this year.

Shamuyarira and Tendai Biti, the MP for Harare East, jointly addressed a meeting dubbed 'From *Esap* Back to Socialism: Assessing the Implications of Price Controls', at a local Harare hotel last Thursday. The meeting, which attracted economists, journalists and politicians, was organised by the Zimbabwe Coalition on Debt and Development to discuss the government's move to re-introduce price controls.

Early this month, the government re-introduced price controls on basic commodities, a move opposed by most businessmen. Shamuyarira's remarks last week drew sharp criticism from some economists who labelled him a hypocrite.

The economists said a few years after *Esap* was introduced, Shamuyarira was appointed minister of industry and commerce, a ministry which was key to the successful implementation of the programme, yet he never publicly voiced his concerns against it. One economist, who declined to be named said: 'Shamuyarira should shut up and not pretend to be sympathising with the suffering Zimbabweans when he helped to implement *Esap*. He is now playing cheap politics because he spoke glowingly about the failed programme.'

Asked why he did not resign, Shamuyarira said it was not proper for him to do so because he and his colleagues worked as a team when he was in cabinet.

Shamuyarira said: 'I had serious misgivings and told a friend that this economic reform policy would fail and it surely failed. When President Mugabe announced the end of *Esap*, I telephoned my friend and told him that my position had been vindicated.'

Addressing the same gathering, Biti said the government should come up with economic policies that can attract the sympathy and understanding of the international community. He said: 'Zanu supporters should be made to understand that the only effective way to turn around Zimbabwe's economic fortunes is to vote their party out of power.'

Biti said the high unemployment rate and increasing poverty, was being exacerbated by Zanu's skewed economic policies. Shamuyarira said: 'Price controls are an important step forward and the government's decision to re-introduce a ceiling on price increases of basic commodities should be commended.'

Simba Makoni: 'Prioritise arrears . . . using privatisation proceeds'[4]
Economic review

Mr Speaker Sir, Hon. Members will recall that, in the August 3 statement, I said that our country is in crisis. The current state of our economy is characterised by:

- persistently high interest rates and inflation, fuelled by high budget deficits;
- deteriorating terms of trade, leading to acute balance of payments problems;
- electricity and fuel shortages; and,

- loss of confidence within the business community and our international development partners.

The national crisis manifests itself through deepening poverty, growing unemployment, shorter working hours in business and company closures, a rising cost of living, and a general decline in the quality of social service delivery. Some of the symptoms of this crisis are:

- many families can no longer afford more than one meal a day;
- many workers can no longer pay transport fares, and now walk or cycle to work;
- fewer people are able to visit their loved ones in the rural areas, regularly; and
- individuals, families and society as a whole, are increasingly failing to care for the needy.

This situation invokes images of Dambudzo Marechera's *House of Hunger*, the caricature of the lot of our people during the colonial era of our country . . .

The 2001 budget

Mr Speaker, the budget proposals I will shortly present to our nation, is the product of the collective efforts of many contributors. His Excellency President Mugabe and Vice Presidents Msika and Muzenda gave me clear guidance. My colleague Ministers and their Permanent Secretaries, Honourable Members of this House, the Public Service Commission, my MDC counterpart, Hon. Mashakada, national leaders in the business community, labour movements and civil society, all made invaluable inputs. The budget consultations which started in June, ended this Monday evening.

Budget objectives

Through this budget, we aim to achieve the following strategic objectives:

- establish confidence in, and credibility of government among citizens of our country, citizens as individuals, organisations and businesses. We wish citizens to believe in government, that government means what it says, government will do what it says, and government will share the hardships the people are enduring;
- demonstrate our commitment to live within our means;
- provide the basis for arresting the decline in the economy;
- stimulate economic activity in the short term, and sustainable growth and development in the long term;
- establish conditions for restructuring expenditures in favour of capital formation and social services delivery; and
- provide a platform for restoring positive co-operative relations with the international donor and business communities.

The 2001 budget will be guided by, based on, and targeted at realising the provisions of the *Millennium Economic Recovery Programme (Merp)*, whose core objectives are to:

- instil fiscal discipline;
- reduce government expenditures and lower inflation and interest rates;
- raise more revenues;
- regenerate business confidence, and stimulate activity in the productive sectors, particularly in the generation of exports;
- establish a credible and predictable exchange rate system; and
- restore normal relations with the international community.

Budget framework
We propose to implement a the three-year rolling budget with the following targets:

- revenues of $140 billion in 2001, $195 billion in 2002 and $232 billion in 2003;
- total expenditure and net lending of $224 billion in 2001, $254 billion in 2002 and $258 billion in 2003; and
- a budget deficit of $83.6 billion or 15.5% of GDP in 2001, 8% in 2002 and about 3% in 2003 . . .

Salaries and wages
In line with the *Millennium Economic Recovery Programme*, a ceiling will be placed on the public service salary and wage bill, at not more than 12% of GDP, against the anticipated outturn of 16.7%, this financial year. Ministries and the Public Service Commission have undertaken to live within this limit, and to allocate the resources in a manner, and to those staff members that enable government to deliver on its priority core business . . .

Defence
The operational budget of the Ministry of Defence amounts to $2.2 billion, compared to this year's allocation of $3.3 billion. This allocation has taken into account the anticipated positive outcome of the initiatives to bring peace to the DRC, and therefore, enable us to disengage from that country . . .

Capital expenditure
The main focus of the Public Sector Investment Programme is the provision of economic and social infrastructure required to facilitate and support national development. In affirming government commitment to re-directing more resources towards capital investment, I regret that the realisation of this objective in FY 2001, is constrained by the inescapable commitments to non-discretionary expenditures. In the proposed budget for 2001, a modest $10 billion has been allocated for capital development.

This represents only 4.6% of total government expenditure, and 1.9% of GDP. This is grossly inadequate, against a total requirement of $75 billion. Ideally, the capital budget should constitute at least 20% of total expenditure, in order to fully address the development requirements of the country . . .

I need to affirm that we expect the private sector to play an increasing role in the provision of economic infrastructure, as government re-defines its core business. The policy framework for private sector participation in infrastructure development was approved in 1998, and we will strive to put in place the necessary legal and regulatory framework during 2001. This will facilitate implementation of various projects, especially toll roads and the concessioning of major infrastructure facilities, such as airports, grain silos, abattoirs and fuel tankage and distribution facilities.

Again in the capital budget, $500 million has been provided to meet obligations arising out of called-up guarantees. The called-up guarantees are in respect of public enterprises whose operations were not sufficiently viable to service debts secured by government. In order to safeguard the fiscus from such exposure, government has now adopted a policy whereby guarantees are provided only for projects or enterprises that conform to strict criteria of viability or strategic national interest.

Debt management and budget financing

Mr Speaker, we acknowledge that government debt has become a heavy albatross round the neck of the country. A disproportionately large amount of the domestic debt of some $125 billion, is held in Treasury Bills, with maturities of not more than 91 days.

We shall, therefore, seek to restructure the domestic debt so that at least 30% becomes medium to long term, while not more than 70% will be Treasury Bills of 91 days, six months and one year maturities. Government is already engaged in consultations with leaders of financial institutions, who have intimated their willingness to assist government restructure its debt. This would reduce the interest bill, and dampen inflationary pressures.

In order to restore the country's credit worthiness and credibility, as well as unlock critical international assistance and commercial credit lines, we shall prioritise the clearance of external arrears, by using part of the privatisation proceeds. In addition, it will be necessary to promote exports and attract foreign direct investment in order to generate more foreign currency.

The flow of resources required to finance the debt, is also dependent on our ability to restore donor and market confidence. We shall, therefore, seek to fully re-engage the international community in the country's development efforts.

Government also owes local authorities and national businesses huge sums. We hereby affirm our commitment to pay off those debts, in order to restore the viability of our creditors, and provide resources for renewed business activities and service delivery. To that end, we shall engage in discussions with our creditors, to work out payment plans. In the meantime, we have provided in the 2001 estimates, a sum of $500 million, to initiate repayment. We also intend to limit the accumulation of further debt.

Conversely, government is owed handsome amounts by beneficiaries of programmes such as the War Victims Compensation Fund, the Government Housing Scheme, the Grain Loan Scheme, Commodity Import Programmes and the early Indigenisation Funds. Efforts will, therefore, be made to recover these monies.

Privatisation

The disposal and/or privatisation of state assets are key elements of the *Millennium Economic Recovery Programme (Merp)*. In this regard, government has recently approved an initial list of assets for disposal and privatisation. The successful implementation of this programme should raise a minimum of $28 billion during the framework period. Proceeds from the disposal of these assets will be used largely to clear external arrears, retire domestic debt and capitalise the revolving fund for SMEs, indigenisation and the informal sector.

Government has also decided to restructure loss making public enterprises, through debt-equity swaps.

Through the Privatisation Agency of Zimbabwe, government will invite key stakeholders to participate in the disposal and privatisation process . . .

Value Added Tax

Mr Speaker Sir, government took the decision to introduce Value Added Tax (VAT) in Zimbabwe. Following wide consultations with relevant economic partners, we are now drafting appropriate legislation, which we shall table in this House early next year.

In order to ensure the successful introduction of VAT, the Departments of Customs and Excise and Taxes are already undertaking intensive training programmes for their staff. Together with other stakeholders, Government will launch a national educational and promotion campaign on VAT. We intend to implement VAT not later than 1 January 2002 . . .

Conclusion

Mr Speaker, the budget I have presented to this House is not for the government alone. It should belong to all Zimbabweans. We should, therefore, make our individual and collective contributions to ensure that the budget becomes an effective instrument of development.

I must pay tribute to the resilience of our people, who continue to persevere under difficult conditions. This resilience is an asset, which will be instrumental in reversing the current economic crisis. In order to expedite economic recovery and enjoy the fruits of a growing economy, we need to pull together as a nation.

Mr Speaker Sir, the success of this budget depends, among other factors, on what I term contextual issues. These are:

- consistency between policy and action on the part of government;
- clarity on the way forward with land reform; and
- positive developments to end the DRC war.

Prosperity and progress come on the back of difficult choices, and sharing the pain with others. The expenditure measures I have presented will be painful in the interim, but they pave the way for our recovery and growth in the near future. The success of this budget demands our collective commitment to live within our means.

The tripartite partners are engaged in serious discussions towards a national Social Contract. The conclusion of such a Social Contract would provide an appropriate basis for equitable burden sharing by citizens, as we strive to work our way out of crisis. We urge the negotiators to put national interest first, and work resolutely to conclude negotiations speedily.

We in government are implored to respect the national budget in the same way that households and the corporate sectors respect their budgets. I trust that honourable members, and the Portfolio Committees of this august House will assist in ensuring that we keep our part of the bargain.

Notes

1. The *Millennium Economic Recovery Programme (Merp)* was never formally published. The following, from late 2001, are three conflicting statements about neoliberal policy from Zanu's three main economic spokespeople.
2. *Sunday Mail* interview of minister of state for information and publicity in the president and cabinet, Professor Jonathan Moyo, published 21 October 2001.
3. *Daily News* report, 'Shamuyarira accused of Cheap Politicking over *Esap*', published 31 October 2001.
4. Finance minister Simba Makoni's Budget speech, Zimbabwe Parliament, 1 November 2001 (main excerpts, below, are those that deal with economic policy).

The MDC's Economic Stabilisation and Recovery Programme[1]

Immediate restoration of confidence under the MDC government

The presidential elections are scheduled to take place in March 2002. Unless there is massive electoral fraud and voter intimidation, the Movement for Democratic Change's candidate, Morgan Tsvangirai, is expected to win the election. Under the current constitution, the president of the country is empowered to appoint the cabinet to govern the country, choosing as ministers sitting members of parliament or nominating ministers, who then take up the 'reserved' seats in the parliament. Morgan Tsvangirai will thus be forming a new government as soon as he is elected.

The MDC Economic Stabilisation and Recovery Programme has been formulated so that the new government is able to take action to stabilise the macro-economy and initiate an economic recovery as soon as it comes to power. This document constitutes the Executive Summary of the full programme, which will be progressively made public during the presidential election campaign. Given the dramatic worsening in the macro-economy as the present government continues its destructive political antics, the MDC's technical team will revise the numerical aspects of the programme as appropriate close to the March 2002 deadline (or sooner if an early presidential election is called).

The MDC programme is not just a technocratic exercise, but one in which the MDC's political objectives and aspirations have been fully incorporated, while at the same time being tailored to fit into a consistent budgetary and macro-economic framework. There is full political commitment within the party to the programme, giving assurance that it will be implemented with vigour and determination once the MDC is in power. The final programme which will be implemented from April 2002 will also be enriched by interactions with local stakeholders (trade unions, business organisations, etc.) during the election campaign, as well as on-going discussions with multilateral and bilateral donors (particularly the IMF, the World Bank and the European Union).

No in-coming government would choose to take on the severe, inter-related economic problems that Zanu will leave behind it. The new government will inherit an economy, which has experienced three years of stagnation followed by three successive years of negative growth associated with high levels of government spending and inflation. It will inherit a social services sector that is run down, badly in need of rehabilitation and an economy plagued by shortages of every kind due to the foreign exchange crisis in the past two years. The government will also take on huge national debts.

The incoming administration will have to contend with a civil service that has had to operate in a highly politicised environment, leading to low staff morale exacerbated by low salaries and high inflation. There will also be need to depoliticise the armed forces and the police, elements of which have been extensively used by Zanu in its campaign for survival. Furthermore, the new government will have to deal with widespread corruption in every aspect of government activity and the challenge of recovering funds looted from the public sector in the past few years.

Looked at from every perspective the task of rebuilding Zimbabwe is going to be a daunting one. The Movement for Democratic Change offers new social and political leadership intent on making Zimbabwe a democratic state with a fast growing economy, which reduces income and wealth inequalities. The in-coming MDC government will immediately move to rebuild confidence through:

- *Restoring the rule of law* in all its dimensions. That is the principle that everyone is equally subject to the law, with no one being above the law, that law enforcement agencies (especially the police) and the courts enforce and apply the law impartially and that everyone is equally protected by the law against illegal action causing harm.
- *Putting land reform onto a national, non-partisan basis.* This will be achieved by establishing an autonomous, professional Land Commission to acquire land legally and allocate it on a non-partisan basis within a sound policy framework. New settlers will be provided with adequate inputs and technical assistance to make a success of their farming ventures and, once they have proved themselves, are to have secure tenure. The programme is to be linked to, and integrated with, the wider MDC agenda of agrarian reform.
- *Implementing the MDC Economic Stabilisation and Recovery Programme.* By the time the MDC comes to power, this will be widely understood within the country and by the donor community and will be endorsed as a comprehensive, consistent and achievable programme to address the underlying economic problems (not just the symptoms) in a rapid yet sustainable fashion.

The MDC's economic agenda

As laid out in the MDC manifesto, sustainable, human-centred development is the basis of the party's economic strategy. Putting people at the centre of future policy initiatives and activities underlies the economic agenda of a future MDC government. This means addressing the underlying structural problems in the economy in order to create an equitable basis for development. The MDC is intent on breaking the cycle of the entrenched poverty of the majority of Zimbabweans through a genuine land redistribution programme, coupled with agrarian reform that results in higher productivity and incomes throughout the agricultural sector, but particularly in the resettlement and communal areas. In the urban areas, the emphasis will be on the creation of employment, the broadening of ownership of productive enterprises and access to housing.

To achieve these goals of structural reform, which are the only way of making possible sustained poverty reduction, the party's immediate economic priorities, which are to be addressed in parallel during the period when macro-economic stabilisation measures are being implemented, are as follows:

- *Agrarian reform*: The MDC government will go beyond the narrow concept of land reform to a comprehensive programme of agrarian reform, designed to raise the productivity and income generation potential of all small-scale farmers, whether located in the communal areas or on new resettlement schemes. To reduce poverty, land resettlement is a crucial starting point, but even the most successful resettlement programme would still leave the bulk of the rural population living in the communal areas in a state of abject poverty. It is only through a comprehensive agrarian reform programme that it will be possible for farmers in communal areas to become more productive and to thereby generate higher levels of income. Only then will it be possible to ensure significant and sustainable poverty reduction in Zimbabwe.

  The MDC's detailed agrarian reform programme is nearing completion and will be available for implementation from April 2002. Adequate financial provisions for this exercise are included in a budget to be announced within one month of the MDC coming to power. The MDC programme will address the problems of the historical imbalances in land ownership. At the same time, the productive base of the industry will be protected and re-established to ensure food security and a resumption of export orientated production in all sectors. The MDC will take measures to ensure that all productive farmers will have security of tenure and that land use is intensified.

- *The creation of jobs and the provision of resources for income generation*: There will be rapid growth in formal employment arising from the greater confidence and stability generated by the MDC's macro-economic strategies. These will be complemented by employment-oriented investment and trade policies. Support will be given to small enterprise development via financial sector policies, direct assistance to microfinance institutions and the provision of appropriate workspaces for small enterprises. To kick-start the process of employment growth, short-term employment programmes will be introduced in mass housing schemes and rural infrastructure projects, involving labour-intensive construction techniques. The informal sector will be recognised and given full support.

- *Education, health and social services*: The main MDC objective will be to make these services accessible to all, equipping people (particularly women) for employment and entrepreneurial opportunities in a twenty-first century economy. The objectives will be to ensure the primary health of the population, the provision of curative services at affordable cost and to provide educational opportunities to all children to a level that will enable them to compete. The necessary budgetary provisions are being planned to ensure that significant improvements will be achieved in the first two years of the MDC government. Detailed programmes of action in the health and education sectors will be made public during the election campaign.

- *Infrastructure*: The MDC intention is to restore and expand the country's basic infrastructure, at the same time increasing access of the majority of the population to modern infrastructural services. In the rural areas, particular attention will be given to infrastructure which will accelerate the pace of agrarian reform (water, roads, communications, marketing channels, agro-industry, etc.) while in the urban areas, workspace provision (such as factory shells), housing and mass transit systems will be emphasised.

- *Housing*: The country's current social problems are being exacerbated by the extreme shortage and high cost of housing. It is estimated that up to 40% of the urban population has no permanent housing. Addressing the housing shortage will be important economically because of the backward linkages to the building materials supply industries, which will have significant employment effects over and above the construction of the houses themselves. Equally important, provision of sufficient housing is part of the MDC's 'whole family' settlement concept, where families will be able to live together in urban and rural areas, an important consideration in combating AIDS.

It is recognised that the ability of the MDC government to immediately pursue the above economic agenda will be severely compromised by the economy-in-crisis that it will inherit. The first priority of the MDC will necessarily be to get the economy back on its feet, requiring budgetary and macro-economic measures to take a degree of precedence initially. However, as described in more detail below, the economic strategies have been designed to address the above MDC agenda items to the maximum extent possible at the same time as macro-economic stabilisation is being achieved.

Economic policy-making and management involves making choices, some of which are difficult and unpopular. The MDC government will not shrink from making the tough decisions that are needed and sticking by them, but it will also seek to involve major economic actors in a continuous national consultative process. Through being open about the options the nation faces and transparent in the national budget process, the MDC will strive to build a consensus around the policies which will ensure that they can be implemented smoothly.

Democratic and representative consultative structures will be established. The unwieldy and ineffective National Economic Consultative Forum will be dissolved and replaced by a body established through a Social Contract involving government, organised business and the Zimbabwe Congress of Trade Unions. This body will establish workable structures for an effective consultative process on decision-making for the economy. Consensual decisions in this forum will be binding on the parties and will be used to guide the actions of the three social partners . . .

The MDC economic policies: The first 100 days

The immediate objective of the MDC government on taking power will be to ensure the resumption of economic growth within a environment in which the rule of law is secure and there is a sound and predictable economic framework. As the main cause of current economic problems has been poor management of the macro-economy, it is essential to start by getting the fiscal and monetary policy framework right. This must involve a complex series of actions, which will together provide an enabling environment for the economy.

The MDC's main economic agenda (agrarian reform, the creation of jobs, self-employment, education, health, housing, etc.) will receive the maximum attention possible within the resource constraints of the stabilisation programme. However, it must be accepted that the immediate solution to the economic crisis lies in a comprehensive re-assertion of control over the fiscal and monetary policy domains.

In respect of fiscal policy, the MDC's budget strategy embraces seven main action areas:

- restoration of confidence in the budget process;
- increasing revenues and improving the tax environment;
- reducing recurrent expenditures;
- increasing social spending and investment;
- increasing flows of privatisation proceeds where appropriate;
- attracting external budgetary support; and
- supporting the budget with complementary monetary, exchange rate and trade policies.

Various aspects of these budgetary action areas will be emphasised over different time horizons. In the first 100 days after assuming power, the MDC will:

- Reduce the number of ministries to a maximum of fifteen, eliminating unnecessary and duplicative expenditures, including deputy ministers and governors. Ministries will be required to identify further posts for abolition and functions to be privatised and outsourced.
- Eliminate expenditure on all government activities that are not concerned with the immediate domestic priorities. This will involve reviewing the number of external missions abroad, the orderly withdrawal of troops from the Congo and any other areas where they may be operating at present and the re-negotiation of contracts for military hardware.
- Assert new priorities – expenditure priorities will be immediately shifted towards providing the resources needed for the Land Commission to be effective, for re-settled farmers to be given adequate fixed and working capital to make their farms productive and to restore the health and education systems. More resources will be needed for housing and for social safety nets, including public works schemes to create employment.
- Use the political changes to win support from the multilateral financial institutions and donors to restructure the national debt. This will involve using grants and concessionary loans to reduce the budgetary debt sufficiently for a 'breathing space' to make it possible for the economy to grow out of the debt trap. The foreign exchange inflows will help restore stability to the foreign exchange markets. Complementary policies will (over time) restore growth in export revenues to rebuild foreign currency reserves and reduce the burden of debt servicing to sustainable levels.
- Review the composition of the board of the National Revenue Authority (NRA) to ensure that it has people of appropriate skills, stature and independence, including private sector experts on tax issues. The NRA will be given the mandate and the resources to do the job of tax collection efficiently and fairly. The MDC approach is to increase revenues through improved tax collection, not increased tax rates.
- Appoint new boards to all parastatals and give the new boards instructions that they move to privatise within an agreed period of time, the object being to achieve the privatisation of all parastatal activity within two years. Special attention is to be given to the largest privatisations (PTC, Zesa and NRZ). This will be done in such a way that the resulting arrangements are competitive in character and provide consumers with real choices. The method of privatisation will ensure that the exercise leaves the assets of the parastatal in competent hands.
- In most cases, the Zanu legacy is one of high indebtedness, so that even if the parastatal can be sold for a high price, there may be limited net returns for the fiscus. In any event, the MDC approach will be to give

primary weight to the social and broader economic objectives of privatisation, as these will lock in the longer-term gains, rather than giving excessive attention to short-run revenue maximisation.

- During the privatisation process, employee ownership schemes and the strategies to bring more Zimbabweans into the mainstream economy will be actively pursued. Where insufficient conditions for market competition exist after privatisation, independent, professional regulatory authorities will be created. These will be appointed by and formally accountable to parliament.

- Contract a competent fund manager to dispose of to best advantage, the government-owned ZSE shareholdings that have not been sold before the MDC takes power.

- Review the budgets of all ministries and present a mini-budget to parliament within a one-month time-frame to restore stability to the civil service, enhance resource flows to critical areas of social distress, ensure important investment projects can be completed and generally start re-orienting public expenditure to MDC priorities. The necessary measures to promote a secondary housing mortgage market will be included in the mini-budget.

- Introduce new management systems for the control of government expenditure as well as strict reporting and control systems to limit overruns in expenditure by ministries.

- Review all outstanding government debt and other payment commitments, clearing as many as possible during the first 100 days and establishing a clear timetable to bring the remainder up to date; similarly, begin negotiating the settlement of outstanding parastatal debt.

In the monetary policy domain, there will be an immediate need to tackle the nexus of inflation, interest and exchange rates. Given the unprecedented size of the mis-alignments that are anticipated by March 2002 and their severe negative consequences throughout the economy, particular care has been exercised in designing this aspect of the MDC programme. Although rates of inflation will by then be over 100%, Zimbabwe may not yet be experiencing true hyperinflation, in which the rate of inflation itself is continually accelerating and monthly inflation levels move into the three digit range. Such chaotic episodes tend to be short-lived and are, to a large extent, fairly easy to grapple with. This is not true of the other common inflation variant, which is inflation that is persistently high but relatively stable. This phenomenon, usually referred to as 'chronic' inflation, is closer to the state that the MDC government will inherit.

Chronic inflation can be tackled in two main ways. The first is the 'orthodox' approach of sharp monetary contraction without accompanying policies (such as wage and price controls). This approach has severe immediate costs in terms of foregone output and growth and hence rising unemployment (a 'hard landing'). The alternative 'heterodox' approach, which is now widely endorsed, is to lock in expectations through adopting a nominal anchor (usually the nominal exchange rate), together with some equitable form of wage and price controls or restraints agreed by consensus. Such a package requires complementary fiscal and monetary policies to be in place, but then it should be possible to sharply reduce inflation while at the same time expanding (or at least not contracting) the economy (a 'soft landing').

The MDC strategy is based on this second approach, which has come to be referred to as 'exchange rate based stabilisation'. This takes into account the specific circumstances anticipated for Zimbabwe *circa* March 2002, as well as lessons from other countries on what can go wrong over time with such programmes. All other things being equal, the massive distortions in interest and exchange rates should be removed very rapidly as soon as MDC comes to power. However immediate dramatic changes to unify exchange rates and re-establish positive real interest rates risk having undesirable effects in provoking a new bout of inflation and threatening the viability of productive enterprises and banks.

In some respects, removing the particular distortions anticipated in March 2002 will have counter-inflationary effects, in particular unifying exchange rates will remove the artificial premium in the parallel market rate, bringing down general import prices quite sharply. At the same time the import costs of fuel and electricity (previously covered by the retention of an artificial exchange rate) will rise. The MDC will adopt bold measures to restructure the liquid fuels sector, doing away with Noczim and its corrupt and expensive procurement procedures, and thereby mitigating the impact of rising import costs on consumer prices of energy.

The installation of a new government of vision, commitment and ability to formulate and execute coherent economic policies will mark the clear break with the past that is needed to change perceptions and expectations. This way of achieving the break will allow a degree of fine-tuning of the stabilisation package. After an initial corrective devaluation, a crawling peg, with pre-announced rate of crawl to remove uncertainty and add to confidence, will be instituted. When the parallel market has gone, and export performance has been restored, a crawling band system can be considered.

Against the background of a credible commitment to fiscal probity, monetary policy will be tightened with the assurance that inflation will decline. The use of the overdraft facilities at the Reserve Bank will be halted, requiring financing to be sought in the domestic market progressively driving up interest rates to real levels. There may be a need for the process to be accelerated by Reserve Bank open market operations.

To give integrity and credibility to the programme, the Reserve Bank will be restructured and given a proper level of autonomy. An independent board of directors will be appointed to the Reserve Bank with responsibility for managing the monetary aspects of the transition to stability and thereafter for maintaining interest rates and the exchange rate on a market-related basis and providing tough, independent regulation of the financial sector.

The economic crisis is of such severity, that scant pay-off can be expected within the first 100 days of the MDC government, but before the end of 2002 some positive benefits will become evident. Having a government which restores the rule of law, clearly understands the requirements of managing a modern economy and takes bold steps to put the economy on a path to recovery will immediately boost confidence, and this will grow as the macro-economic measures start producing predicted improvements. This will result in export activity picking up and the start of flows of investment. Increased export revenues and inflows from the donor budget support programmes will stabilise the foreign currency market. Increased levels of essential imports, at lower prices, will allow economic activity to gather pace and investment programmes to be restored.

The MDC's land reform programme will have started, with orderly and non-partisan resettlement being supported with inputs and other forms of assistance to ensure enhanced agricultural output and improved incomes for the settlers. Progress will be evident in restoring target levels of per capita expenditure in education, health and social security, preparatory to making major improvements in these sectors.

The creation of a secondary mortgage market will enable institutional savings (pension and life insurance funds) to be channelled into mortgage financing, resulting in an immediate dramatic increase in the resources available to people to borrow for home building. This considerable increase in building activity will encourage the recovery in the construction industry. Site and service housing schemes will also be developed in all urban centres with homeowners undertaking the subsequent building themselves or doing their own contracting as and when they have the means to do so.

The first year of the MDC government

During the first year of an MDC government, additional macro-economic measures and strategies will be in the following areas:

* *Government restructuring*: In conformity with international 'best practice', a comprehensive programme to restructure government through privatisation and outsourcing of a wide range of activities previously carried out by civil service structures will be established. Obvious areas for immediate action will be implemented at the same time as more comprehensive planning is being finalised. The programme will be given high priority and implemented with vigour. Over a five-year period, the objective will be to create a small, highly professional civil service, with many services being efficiently supplied by private sector companies competing for contracts. This will create new opportunities for local

businesses, many being owned by, or employing, former civil servants or other local entrepreneurs.

It should be noted that a major part of this restructuring will involve the armed forces and both the teaching and the health ministries. In respect to the former, Zimbabwe currently has 89 000 men and women in the armed forces, which is large for a country with no enemies or external threats. In respect of the teaching and health sectors, it is anticipated that these will be restructured so that the majority of the personnel currently employed in these areas will become the responsibility of the private sector supported by a per capita grant scheme funded by government.

- *Gender*: The MDC government will *not* have a gender ministry, nor a gender portfolio in the president's office. Experience in Zimbabwe and elsewhere is that compartmentalising gender issues through such institutional structures in fact diverts attention from the real issues, particularly those which affect women's access to resources and equal status in society. Instead, the MDC will ensure that gender perspectives inform policy-making and implementation in each and every ministry, thereby giving prominence to the party's commitment to gender equality in every sphere of public life. Programmes will also be initiated to ensure that the private sector emulates the new approach in government to gender.

- *Expenditure prioritising*: Part of the savings in expenditure and the expected resources to be made available by donors will be used to initiate the agrarian reform programme, to restore education, health and social security programmes and to provide seed financing for public housing. A proper balance will be restored between capital and recurrent expenditure in the national budget, as the direct public sector contribution to restoring high levels of GDP growth. Projects of social significance and those which will 'crowd in' investments from the private sector will be emphasised.

- *Agrarian reform*: Particular stress will also be placed in all budgets on providing adequate resources for speedy implementation of the MDC's land and agrarian reform programmes. The objectives of both programmes are to support equitable access to productive assets, growth in agricultural production, and sound management of land and water. Included in the MDC's agrarian reform is the planned reform of the tenure system in the communal areas so as to provide all farmers with security of tenure within an acceptable social framework.

- *Environment*: The agrarian reform programme will be designed and executed with due regard to environmental requirements for sustainable development. The MDC government will go well beyond this in the environmental field to ensure that the essential linkages between environment, poverty and economic growth will be fully incorporated into the country's overall development strategy. Institutional and legal changes will be needed to make this effective.

The MDC will ensure that there is a proper balance in environmental responsibilities between central and local government, with links and structures also being established outside government to ensure consistent and meaningful stakeholder participation in environmental policy formulation and implementation. Zimbabwe has a potentially important role to play in the attempts by the international community to come to grips with global warming. The MDC will ensure that Zimbabwe positions itself to pilot many of the innovative ideas arising in the global debate, aiming to be the first country to demonstrate the viability of 'carbon neutral growth'. In so doing, Zimbabwe would be able to tap 'green' funding sources and obtain technical support for developing new ideas, all of this adding to the momentum of the country's growth.

- *Tax reform*: The objectives of this will be to widen the tax net and create an equitable and competitive tax system, while minimising the tax burden, particularly on low income households. Tax thresholds will be put onto a formula basis to ensure that income tax is paid only by those above a professionally established and nationally agreed poverty datum line. Other fiscal incentive objectives will be employee ownership and export promotion. Value Added Tax will be introduced by the end of 2002, with basic foodstuffs zero-rated. (VAT discussions at the local level will be needed. The National Revenue Authority will work thereafter with local tax committees in all centres to ensure full local compliance with all tax regulations.) Income and corporate tax levels will be reviewed for regional competitiveness, border tariffs and duties reduced, except for petroleum products where duties will be raised to international levels.
- *Trade integration*: The MDC government will ensure that Zimbabwe derives maximum benefit from bilateral and multilateral trade agreements with various partner groupings, particularly the SADC Trade Protocol, COMESA Free Trade Area and Cotonou Agreement with the European Union. Currently Zimbabwe is not accepted for the potentially important US Africa Growth and Opportunity Act, which gives access to the USA market for over 1 800 products. The new government will attach a high priority to securing access to AGOA. This will stimulate key sectors such as textiles and clothing and assist with the recovery of the manufacturing sector.

The second and third years of the MDC government

In the second and third years of the MDC government, the measures already outlined will be continued and indeed, in areas such as the civil service reform programme, will gather momentum. In addition, as macro-economy stability becomes a reality and investor confidence is restored, broader MDC economic objectives and policies will be initiated:

- *Education and Health*: Modernising and re-inforcing the education and health delivery systems in such a way that they are capable of delivering a good quality of service to all, including the poorest and most vulnerable communities.
- *Tertiary education*: Upgrading and strengthening tertiary education at both university and technical college level to ensure the availability of a pool of skilled personnel in all areas, so Zimbabwe can take full advantage of the challenges which being a player in the global economy presents.
- *Housing*: Establishing private sector driven housing policies, which will eliminate the backlog in urban housing (750 000 units) within five years and provide good basic family housing on farms and mines.
- *Infrastructure provision*: Involving domestic and foreign private investors not just in buying existing infrastructural assets, but in bringing significant new investment into all areas of the provision of infrastructure. This is to be managed to ensure competitive conditions prevail, efficient and cost effective services are provided and access in the more remote areas steadily improved.
- *Trade*: Making a firm commitment to creating a regional free trade area in the SADC while at the same time supporting the creation of a rules-based global trading system facilitated by the WTO which aims to give developing countries a place at the table in terms of global trade.
- *Removing duality in the economy*: Taking steps to integrate the marginalised informal sector economy into the formal economy, partly through the agrarian reform programme, linked to programmes of support for micro and small-scale enterprises in urban areas. Particular attention will be given to assisting emergent enterprises in all sectors to gain access to domestic and export markets.
- *Foreign exchange control*: When the economy has been stabilised and economic growth has resumed, all remaining restrictions on foreign exchange will be reviewed with a view to moving towards fully liberalised conditions in money and capital markets.

The main economic role the MDC government will seek to fulfil is that of facilitator, with the dynamism required for high levels of growth of income and employment coming from the private sector. Past studies of investment have made clear that high levels of investment by domestic economic agents is an important factor in encouraging international investment. Building on local investment, it will be the intention of the MDC government to attract investment into a number of sectors and projects, which will be attractive to foreign players when the political and policy environment in Zimbabwe has been restored. Investor confidence is regarded as being essential to the restoration of economic growth and the achievement of all other objectives including job creation and the provision of social services . . .

Internal and external support to accelerate the recovery

In its recovery phase, Zimbabwe will be greatly assisted by a number of factors. Internally, the main factor is the legendary resilience of the economy and the people of Zimbabwe: the same skills that have enabled us to survive the extremes of bad government will enable us to use the new environment to best advantage.

Externally, there is a strong international desire to see the land issue resolved amicably and in a way that will enhance stability in the region and contribute to economic growth and poverty reduction. There will be considerable international goodwill towards a democratically elected leadership in Zimbabwe that accepts its responsibility to govern in the interests of its people and its neighbours. In addition it is to be noted that the Zimbabwean economy is minuscule by world standards and its problems are equally small in global terms. It will not take very large injections of foreign exchange to stabilise the economy and once it is released from the debt trap, the natural vigour and enterprise of its people will re-assert itself.

That said, the economic models indicate that it is vital that the international goodwill translate into substantial and timely external support for the MDC government. A total of US$2 500 million of official development assistance has been incorporated into the calculations over the three-year stabilisation period (2002–2004). Sensitivity tests show that if the level of external support is significantly less than this or is not made available according to the timetable assumed (e.g. $500 million in 2002), the projected stabilisation will falter. Under such circumstances growth will not resume as rapidly as planned and the projected employment and social benefits will be very much slower to materialise.

Much of the external support is expected to come from the large multilateral development agencies, but with substantial and complementary resources from bilateral sources. Whether grants or soft loans are allocated purely for budgetary support or are earmarked for the key priority sectors, the impact will be the same because the external resources will essentially allow the domestic debt to be bought back. The Zimbabwe dollar resources, liberated by this process, will be used for the priority sectors for poverty reduction: agrarian reform, health, education and social safety nets. The foreign exchange element of the external support will help to stabilise the foreign exchange market, allowing the arrears accumulated over the 2000–2002 period to be paid off and normal levels of imports to resume.

It has to be stressed that the strategy for addressing the immediate macro-economic crisis when the MDC first comes to power depends on economic actors understanding the intent and logic of the programme and giving it their active support. It is not just a question of public acknowledgement of a new approach to economic management, but a requirement for the expectations of economic actors about inflation and other macro-economic variables to be changed. The carefully co-ordinated technical details of the programme are not sufficient in themselves, but success can be assured if a properly formulated programme is accompanied by a shift in expectations. Indeed, once the MDC programme is understood and is being forcefully implemented, growing confidence will lead to changes in behaviour which could well deliver more rapid macro-economic convergence and faster GDP and employment growth than has been envisaged . . .

An MDC government implementing the programme laid out in this paper is the last chance that Zimbabwe has for recovery within a timeframe that is in any way acceptable. If the models are run with a continuation of a Zanu government, an unmitigated disaster for Zimbabwe emerges. Even if such a government were to improve its fiscal policy to the extent of running a primary surplus, the legacy of past profligacy, coupled with this year's irresponsible short-term policies would lead to unstoppable accumulation of domestic debt. This would lead to spiralling interest burden and borrowing requirements, which would drive the economy into real hyperinflation. Even on the most optimistic economic assumptions but no change of government, Zimbabwe would be saddled with debts several times the current levels by 2004.

Conclusion

It is often said that Zimbabwe has the best prospects for growth of any country in Africa. We have natural resources in abundance, a reasonable infrastructure by world standards. We also have a well educated population with literacy at first world levels. Our people are hard working and innovative. World development history tells us that none of these factors are enough in themselves. They are useful, but can be totally negated by bad governance and corruption. If anyone doubted this, the recent history of Zimbabwe confirms this conclusion.

Against this background, it is clear that the MDC, once given the mandate by the people to form a government, can make an immediate and a long-lasting difference to Zimbabwe's well-being and its future prospects. What the MDC brings to the table is the fact that the party is a mass movement of ordinary people whose commitment to democracy, transparency and accountability is strong. The MDC is also deeply committed to constitutional reform and the rule of law. Its leadership has a long history of competent and honest administration in the trade union movement over the past twenty years, or longer. They are a new generation of leaders who offer a new spirit and style of leadership on a multi-ethnic and cultural basis.

The old leadership of Zanu, established in the late 40's and dominant for all of the following half century, has now completely discredited itself. They succeeded in 1980 in bringing independence and dignity to the country and began well when they first came to power, but have progressively abandoned their early espoused principles in favour of corruption and the naked pursuit of power at the expense of the people. They no longer have the confidence of the people, the regional community or the world at large and must step aside and allow new leadership to take over.

The policy position of the MDC is well developed and clearly enunciated. It will pursue a bold, well thought through strategy that seeks to address once and for all the fundamental structural weaknesses, which serve to perpetuate poverty. Instead, it will create conditions for equitable increases in prosperity and a wide range of opportunity for all the people of the country. With appropriate external support and a firm commitment to implementing these strategies vigorously after gaining power, the rapid stabilisation and recovery of the Zimbabwe economy will be achieved in the shortest time possible. The economy will then be on course to deliver significant improvements to the standards of living of all Zimbabweans. In this framework it is confidently expected that, within a decade, poverty can be eliminated altogether from Zimbabwe.

Notes

1. Presented by Tapiwa Mashakada and Eddie Cross, Harare, 22 August 2001. The excerpts below do not include the background material or details of the MDC macro-economic model and anticipated 'outputs'; these can be accessed at the MDC website: http://www.mdc.co.zw

The National Working People's Convention[1]

The National Working Peoples Convention held in Harare on 26–28 February 1999, gathered working people from all corners of Zimbabwe, rural and urban, and from all economic sectors for the following reasons:

- to identify and state the concerns, aspirations and priorities of the nation;
- to identify the strategies to address these national priorities; and
- to unify working people around an agenda for action based on these strategies.

The Convention noted:

- the disempowerment of the people and breach of rule of law through state sponsored violence and abuse of human rights;
- the inability of the economy to address the basic needs of the majority of Zimbabweans;
- the severe decline in incomes, employment, health, food security and well being of people;
- the unfair burden borne by working women and persistence of gender discrimination in practice;
- the decline, and in some cases collapse of public services;
- the lack of progress in resolving land hunger and rural investment needs;
- the weak growth in industry and marginalisation of the vast majority of the nations entrepreneurs;
- the absence of a national constitution framed by and for the people;
- the persistence of regionalism, racism, and other divisions undermining national integration; and
- widespread corruption and lack of public accountability in political and economic institutions.

The Convention noted that the inability to implement any meaningful steps to redress these basic economic and social problems emanates from a crisis of governance within the nation. This crisis expresses itself as a failure of government to observe the separation of powers between executive, legislature and judiciary; to obey basic rules of accountability and transparency; to respect human rights and to decentralise power in ways that enable meaningful participation of people in public institutions.

Accordingly, the Convention debated and adopted specific strategies to address these problems and to meet the aspirations of working people in Zimbabwe. These strategies are outlined in detail in the Agenda for Action of the National Working Peoples Convention.

More generally, the Convention resolved that a path to positive and sustainable economic and political development be restored in Zimbabwe, and in this respect:

- The writing of a people's constitution be initiated with immediate effect, through a constitutional commission not based on presidential/partisan appointment, but defined by and accountable to a conference of representatives of elected, civil and other social groups. Such a constitution should provide clearly for basic social, economic and civil rights; for the clear separation of powers between the executive, judiciary and legislature; for the limitation of the powers of the executive; for such powers of parliament and the judiciary that they are not subordinated to the executive and for such powers of the electorate as to make parliament fully accountable to the people. The electoral process should be guaranteed in the constitution, run and supervised by an Independent Electoral Commission.
- A peoples constitution, as a reflection of a national value system, should be accompanied by a Truth and Reconciliation Commission to deal with unresolved aspects of our past that hinder national integration. It should further be supported by a clear, accessible and popularly understood mechanism for arbitration on and enforcement of constitutional rights.
- National policies should prioritise the mobilisation and organisation of resources to meet people's basic needs for food, security, shelter, clean water, health and education; the equitable distribution of resources such as land, skills, capital and technology for production and industrialisation strategies that are based on building and using the capabilities of the people for production.
- Immediate measures should be taken to reduce inflation, including complementary monetary policy and fiscal policy; rationalisation of ministries and reduction of wasteful expenditure; strengthened independence and powers of state audit and action on transgressions found; widening of export incentives and control of non essential imports; vigorous promotion of local products and self reliant approaches to food security.

- These measures be supported by negotiations to reschedule and restructure the debt, including possible debt relief, with strengthened controls on and powers of parliament in respect of any areas of new borrowing. The country should aim to reduce its dependency on foreign loans and the loss of sovereignty that this brings.
- These and other measures be specified and implemented through a mechanism for national consensus that involves all national stakeholders, that has a mandate to negotiate, implement and evaluate economic measures; that is defined by law and that is mandated to negotiate a social contract on immediate pressing issues in an open, transparent manner that builds trust and accountability between the parties and that is carried out in an environment of respect for the rights of the participating parties.
- Zimbabwe position itself more effectively for the next millennium and for global competition through strategic investment in skills, technology, infrastructure, product design and supporting education and labour market systems, to enable the country to develop market niches and value added production.
- The state's role in production systems be redefined towards facilitation rather than interference, with state intervention strategic, targeted, transparent and time bound; aimed at resolving market failures; augmenting the market in a manner that maximises social welfare and overcoming constraints to or providing incentives for development of areas of future growth and economic opportunity. Where market failures severely weaken the ability of people to procure basic rights to food, shelter, health and education, the state shall intervene with targeted, end user directed and time bound subsidies.
- Active, transparent and time bound measures be taken to resolve land hunger in a manner that links the ownership, distribution and use of land to a policy of sustainable agricultural development and rural industrialisation and that balances agricultural employment with wider and new job opportunities in rural areas. That land be redistributed in a manner that is driven by the people through democratic, transparent and gender sensitive processes; with clear criteria and mechanisms for accountability guiding redistribution, backed by the social and economic investments to make that redistribution meaningful and with any land or agricultural taxes plowed back into agricultural development.
- Land should be recognised as a national asset, and that it therefore remain in state ownership, with individual ownership through tradeable long term leases, backed by legal protection of individual rights. The legal provisions for ownership of natural resources (land, water, minerals) be reviewed to ensure that access to these resources can be widened for sustainable production.

The Convention further resolved that measures be taken to restore a people driven process towards social development, that mobilises and organises capacities within communities and that matches them with complementary inputs from the state, according to agreed and legally defined standards. Accordingly the Convention resolved that:

- The right to a minimum standard of health inputs (food, water, shelter) and health care be defined and entrenched in the constitution, guaranteed and funded on an equitable basis by the state through its mobilisation of national resources. Greater priority should be given to prevention of ill health. Community mobilisation of resource inputs for health should be complemented by the equitable allocation of health resources (drugs, staff, etc.) to the district level. Public participation and accountability in health should be entrenched through stakeholder health development structures from village to national level that are adequately supported to plan, mobilise and monitor agreed health standards and interventions.
- Mechanisms should be put in place to equitably and efficiently distribute public, private and household resources for education to enhance the quality of education, and to review the nature of the education curriculum and the support services provided to better prepare children with the skills and orientation needed to tap the economic and employment opportunities in the next millennium. Education and learning should be treated as an ongoing process, with facilities for decentralised vocational training, in service training and incentive systems to encourage and reward such training. The changes in education should be driven by intersectoral planning, to ensure education is oriented towards and supports areas of economic and social development, and by mechanisms for participation of key stakeholders, including parents.
- The right of equality of opportunity and treatment for men and women should be recognised and entrenched in the constitution, with appropriate measures to implement this in law and practice in the domestic, educational, health, economic, employment and political spheres where gender discrimination is still found.
- A housing policy should be developed that integrates housing development across the country; matches community efforts and resources with state, employer and institutional resources; develops new possibilities for building materials and for procurement and distribution of materials; decentralises the organisation of housing delivery and ensures, through joint state/stakeholder mechanisms and public reporting, public accountability in the management of finances for and delivery of land and other inputs to housing.
- Media freedom should be enshrined in the constitution, supported by an Independent Media Commission and by laws providing for public rights of access to information and for curtailment of government control over

and interference in the media. Media and public information should respect the diverse cultures and religious groups.

The National Working Peoples Convention noted that these resolutions, and the more detailed Agenda for Action that arises from them, will not be realised without a strong, democratic, popularly driven and organised movement of the people. Such a movement should recognise and protect the discrete and independent role and mandates of the various organisations of working people, including the labour movement, informal traders organisations and peasant farmers associations. The Convention thus resolved to take these issues to the people across the country, to mobilise them towards the working peoples agenda, and to implement a vigorous and democratic political movement for change.

Notes
1. Document prepared in Harare, 28 February 1999, and published on the Zimbabwe Congress of Trade Unions website: http://www.samara.co.zw/zctu/position.htm

Jubilee South's Pan-African Declaration on Poverty Reduction Strategy Programmes[1]

Poverty Reduction Strategy Papers: Structural Adjustment Programmes in disguise

The World Bank and International Monetary Fund (IMF) have produced their Poverty Reduction Strategy Programmes (PRSPs) within the context of corporate globalisation. This process is being driven by and for the giant transnational corporations (TNCs) and global financial forces. These utilise the economic, political and military powers of their governments, and the World Bank, IMF and World Trade Organisation (WTO) to impose policies on the South and to restructure and run the world to serve their interests.

These forces have led to the enrichment of the corporations and their 'share-holders', as well as small elites in the South – to the heavy cost of the vast majority of people of the world. The World Bank and IMF have found it necessary to impose PRSPs onto the most impoverished countries because the intertwined processes of enrichment and impoverishment have led to growing international resistance to the forces, aims and effects of globalisation.

Social organisations and popular movements across the world have come out against structural adjustment programmes (SAPs) in their various guises, particularly as based on the feminisation of adjustment to the further detriment of women and children. Our campaigns have exposed the use of debt as a deliberate mechanism utilised by the World Bank and IMF to enforce the implementation of ever harsher structural adjustment programmes that are wreaking havoc across the world.

As a result, the World Bank and IMF are facing a deepening crisis of legitimacy. Thus they have introduced PRSPs mainly as a public relations exercise to demonstrate a supposedly new-found concern for the poverty in

the poorest countries of the South, and to prove that they have a genuine
desire to see the people of these countries 'participating' in finding solutions
to their poverty.

But we are not fooled! Our sharing of experiences over the days of this
workshop have strengthened our common understandings. We are clear that
the PRSPs represent nothing other than yet another attempt by the World
Bank and the IMF to continue imposing their structural adjustment
programmes on the people of our countries. In fact, the PRSPs will result in
an even more comprehensive control by the IMF and World Bank – not
only over financial and economic policies but over every aspect and detail of
all our national policies and programmes. This will entrench the continuation
of IMF and World Bank control over our countries, and contribute to the
continuation of the global power relations, in which the rich overwhelmingly
concentrated in the North dominate the South and the whole world.

In this context, and on the basis of the long, deep and painful experiences
of SAPs in our countries, we reject:

- SAPs in any form or with any cosmetic 'adjustments';
- PRSPs as the latest version of structural adjustment;
- HIPC initiative as debt 'relief';
- all SAP–HIPC–PRSP conditionalities in order to be granted debt 'relief';
- 'relief' of only a portion of debt and continued repayment of the
  remaining debt which will simply ensure continued control and
  domination;
- any attempt to use our organisations to legitimise structural adjustment,
  HIPCs, PRSPs or debt 'relief';
- any further role or interference of the World Bank or IMF in our
  countries; and
- any further loans to finance HIV/Aids programmes which only serve to
  further indebt our countries, which increase our dependence on the
  institutional finance institutions, while millions of our people continue
  to suffer and die in the pandemic in our countries.

On the basis of our review in this workshop of a number of experiences of
PRSPs in countries in Africa (and Latin America) and on the basis of
in-depth analysis and wide-ranging discussion, we note:

- PRSPs are located within the IMF and World Bank macro-economic
  framework and this is not open for debate. The poverty programmes are
  expected to be consistent with the neo-liberal paradigm including
  privatisation, deregulation, budgetary constraints and trade and financial
  liberalisation. Yet these have exacerbated economic and social crises in
  our countries.
- They focus only on internal factors and ignore the role of international/

global factors and forces in creating economic crises and poverty in our countries.

- The only aspects of our realities that are open to consultation are those 'outside' the macro-economic realm, and even the realisation of these is actively contradicted by the requirements and constraints of the macro-economic prescriptions.
- The neo-liberal paradigm is also not acceptable because it fails to explicitly locate programmes to tackle poverty and subordination within effective gender equity perspectives and gender frameworks. Mere gender 'mainstreaming' is totally insufficient as a remedy.
- The World Bank and IMF are manoeuvering to regain their legitimacy by offering poverty 'reduction' and debt 'relief' whereas we demand full release from all debt bondage and the total eradication of poverty.
- These so-called poverty programmes have been imposed on countries in a manner which ignores and replaces existing anti-poverty and national development programmes. As such, they are an external intervention with little or no regard for national dynamics, and are an unacceptable intrusion. But they cannot easily be ignored given that countries have to implement these programmes as an additional conditionality even for the much criticised HIPC debt 'relief'.

The experiences of the functioning of PRSPs in our countries raise a number of additional concerns with regard to the involvement of organisations of civil society:

- The PRSPs are not based on real people's participation and ownership, or decision-making. To the contrary, there is no intention of taking civil society perspectives seriously; but to keep participation to mere public relations legitimisation;
- The lack of genuine commitment to participation is further manifested in the failure to provide full and timeous access to all necessary information, limiting the capacity of civil society to make meaningful contributions.
- The PRSPs have been introduced according to pre-set external schedules which in most countries has resulted in an altogether inadequate time period for an effective participatory process.
- In addition to all the constraints placed on governments and civil society organisations in formulating PRSPs, the World Bank and IMF retain the right to veto the final programmes. This reflects the ultimate mockery of the threadbare claim that the PRSPs are based on 'national ownership'.
- An additional serious concern is the way in which PRSPs are being used by the World Bank and IMF, both directly and indirectly, to co-opt NGOs to 'monitor' their own governments on behalf of these institutions.

In some instances, notably in those countries in which governments have not been open to civil society participation or have not had poverty and development on the agenda for discussion, the PRSPs initially appeared to open up a space for civil society organisations to engage their governments. However, this has not achieved the desired effect of challenging structural adjustment. Furthermore, many organisations have invested so much energy in the PRSP processes that they have been distracted from their work in opposing SAPs and HIPCs and campaigning for debt cancellation. The lesson we have learnt is that we need to return to our own agendas and re-invigorate and further strengthen our engagement and work with people at the grassroots. We as African civil society organisations need to:

- intensify our efforts to expose to the people in our countries, and the world, the inter-linked aims and effects of SAPs, HIPCs and PRSPs, and the strategic purposes of the World Bank and the IMF;
- mobilise our people and link up with our allies in the South, and partners in the North, for immediate and total cancellation of our external debts without external conditionalities;
- pro-actively engage with our governments on issues as determined by our agendas and on the basis of genuine participation and popular empowerment within our own societies, communities and cultures;
- mobilise to encourage and push our governments to stand together and repudiate the debt;
- mobilise our people to challenge and change the global economic system through campaigns and actions to shut down the World Bank and IMF and to stand up to other forces, including the WTO, Northern governments such as the EU (through the Cotonou Agreement) and the US (through AGOA), as well as their TNCs; and
- mobilise our peoples to oppose the ruling elites who are implementing structural adjustment programmes and further entrenching neo-liberal policies in our countries.

We call upon our peoples to develop further – and deepen through intensified analysis, discussion and full participation – our own democratic, people-centered, gender equitable and environmentally sustainable national, regional and continental alternatives as the basis for a united African challenge to the current oppressive, exploitative and destructive global system.

Participants
ActionAid (Uganda)
African Organisation on Debt and Development
African Women's Economic Policy Network
Africa Trade Network (Southern Africa)

Alternative Information and Development Center (South Africa)
Associacao para Desenvolvimento Rural de Angola (Angola)
Asapsu (Cote d'Ivoire)
BEACON (Nairobi)
Botswana Council of Churches
Catholic Commission for Justice & Peace (Malawi)
Center for International Studies (Nicaragua)
Civil Society for Poverty Reduction (Zambia)
CMID (Ghana)
CONGAD (Senegal)
Divida (Mozambique Debt Group)
Ecumenical Support Services for Economic Transformation (South Africa)
Gender and Trade Network (Southern Africa)
Peace Humanius (Cameroon)
International South Group Network (Southern Africa)
Jubilee 2000 Angola
Jubilee 2000 Cameroon
Jubilee 2000 Nigeria
Jubilee 2000 Senegal
Jubilee 2000 Zambia
Jubilee South Africa
Jubilee South (Africa)
Karios EUROPA
Kenya Debt Relief Network
Ledikasyon pu Travayer (Mauritius)
Malawi Economic Justice Network
Mwelekeo wa NGO (MWENGO, Southern Africa)
Southern African Peoples Solidarity Network
Southern and Eastern African Trade, Information and Negotiation Initiative
Tanzania Coalition on Debt and Development
Tanzania Gender Networking Programme
T.E.I.A. Mozambique
World Council of Churches
Zimbabwe Coalition on Debt and Development
YWCA Kenya

Notes

1. Jubilee South (2001), 'Pan-African Declaration on PRSPs', Kampala, 12 May.

References

Advisory Committee (J. Phillips, J. Hammond, L.H. Samuels, and R.J.M. Swynnerton) (1962), *Report of the Advisory Committee: The Development of the Economic Resources of Southern Rhodesia with Particular Reference to the Role of African Agriculture*, Salisbury, Southern Rhodesia Ministry of Native Affairs.

Africa Group (2001), 'Proposals on TRIPS for WTO Ministerial', http://www.twnside.org.sg, 19 October.

African Development Bank (1997), 'Investment Proposal: South Africa Infrastructure Investment Fund', ADB Private Sector Unit, Abidjan.

African-American Institute/American Bar Association Conference (1982), 'Investment in Zimbabwe', Conference Proceedings, New York, 26 March.

Ajulu, R. (2001), 'Zimbabwe at the Cross Roads – What Next?', *Global Insight*, 12.

Alexander, J., J. McGregor and T. Ranger (2000), *Violence and Memory: One Hundred Years in the 'Dark Forests' of Matabeleland*, Oxford, James Currey.

Alexander, P. (2000), 'The Zimbabwean Working Class, the MDC and the 2000 Election', *Review of African Political Economy*, 27, 85.

Amnesty International (2002), 'Memorandum to the Heads of State or Government of the Southern African Development Community on the Deteriorating Human Rights Situation in Zimbabwe', London, 11 January.

Arrighi, G. (1973), 'The Political Economy of Rhodesia', in G. Arrighi and J. Saul, *Essays on the Political Economy of Africa*, New York, Monthly Review.

Bakker, I. (ed) (1994), *The Strategic Silence: Gender and Economic Policy*, London, Zed Press.

Barber, W.J. (1961), *The Economy of British Central Africa*, London, Oxford University Press.

Bond, P. (1992), 'Finance and Uneven Development in Zimbabwe', Johns Hopkins University Department of Geography and Environmental Engineering, Baltimore.

—— (1998), *Uneven Zimbabwe: A Study of Finance, Development and Underdevelopment*, Trenton, Africa World Press.

—— (2000), *Elite Transition: From Apartheid to Neoliberalism in South Africa*, London, Pluto Press and Pietermaritzburg, University of Natal Press.

—— (2000), *Cities of Gold, Townships of Coal: Essays on South Africa's New Urban Crisis*, Trenton, Africa World Press.

—— (2001), *Against Global Apartheid: South Africa meets the World Bank, IMF and International Finance*, Cape Town, University of Cape Town Press.

—— (2001), 'Radical Rhetoric and the Working Class during Zimbabwean Nationalism's Dying Days' in the *Journal of World-Systems Research*, 7, 2.

Bond, P. and M. Khosa (eds) (1999), *An RDP Policy Audit*, Pretoria, Human Sciences Research Council.

Boswell, T. and C. Chase-Dunn (2000), *The Spiral of Capitalism and Socialism*, Boulder, Lynn Reiner.

Bowyer-Bower, T. and C. Stoneman (eds) (2000), *Land Reform in Zimbabwe: Constraints and Prospects*, Ashgate, Aldershot.

Cheater, A. (1984), *Idioms of Accumulation*, Gweru, Mambo Press.

Clarke, D. (1980), *Foreign Companies and International Investment in Zimbabwe*, Gweru, Mambo Press.

—— (1980), 'The Monetary, Banking and Financial System in Zimbabwe', in United Nations Conference on Trade and Development, *Zimbabwe: Towards a New Order: An Economic and Social Survey*, Working Papers, Geneva, Vol 1.

Cliffe, L. (1991), 'Were they Pushed or did they Jump: Zimbabwe and the World Bank', *Southern Africa Report*, March.

Comptroller and Auditor General (2000), 'Report on the Management of the Public Debt: Disbursement and Recovery of Loans and Donor Funds', Ministry of Finance, Economic Planning and Development, Government of Zimbabwe, Harare.

Cox, R. (1987), *Power, Production and World Order*, New York, Columbia University Press.

Cross, E. (2001), 'Economic Implications of the Adoption of the Zimbabwe Democracy and Economic Recovery Act by the Congress of the United States of America', MDC Secretary for Economic Affairs, Harare, 7 December.

Cuba, Dominican Republic, Haiti, India, Kenya, Pakistan, Peru, Uganda, Venezuela and Zimbabwe (2001), 'Assessment of Trade in Services', Special Communication to the World Trade Organisation, 9 October.

Dashwood, H. (1996), 'The Relevance of Class to the Evolution of Zimbabwe's Development Strategy, 1980–1991', *Journal of Southern African Studies*, 22, 1.

Deloitte and Touche (1990), 'Doing Business in Zimbabwe', Harare, Deloitte Haskins and Sells.

Drinkwater, M.J. (1991), *The State and Agrarian Change in Zimbabwe*, London, Macmillan.

Fanon, F. (1963)[1961], *The Wretched of the Earth*, New York, Grove Press.

Foster, J.B. (2001), 'Imperialism and Empire', *Monthly Review*, 53, 7.

Frankel, S.H. (1938), *Capital Investment in Africa*, Oxford, Oxford University Press.

Friends of the Development Box (2001), 'Press Statement', Doha, 10 November.

Gann, L. and M. Gelfand (1964), *Huggins of Rhodesia*, London, Allen and Unwin.

George, S. (2000), 'A Short History of Neoliberalism', in W. Bello, K. Malhutra and N. Bullard (eds), *Cooling Down Capital: How to Regulate Financial Markets*, London, Zed Press.

Gibbon, P. (1995), Introduction in P. Gibbon (ed), *Structural Adjustment and the Working Poor in Zimbabwe*, Uppsala, Nordiska Afrikainstitutet.

Gibson-Graham, J. (1996), *The End of Capitalism (as we Know it): A Feminist Critique of Political Economy*, Oxford, Basil Blackwell.

Goldin, I. and A. Gelb (2001), 'Attacks on US Hurt Africa', *Financial Times*, 10 October.

Gondwe, G. and C. Madavo (2001), 'New swipe at fighting poverty', *Financial Times*, 7 October.

Government of Zimbabwe (2001), 'Budget Statement 2002', Presented to Parliament by Minister of Finance and Economic Development Simba Makoni, Harare, 1 November.

Gwisai, M. (2001), 'Revolutionaries, Resistance and Crisis in Zimbabwe', Unpublished manuscript, Harare.

Handford, J. (1976), *Portrait of an Economy Under Sanctions, 1965–1975*, Salisbury, Mercury Press.

Hanlon, J. (1988), 'Destabilisation and the Battle to Reduce Dependence', in C. Stoneman (ed), *Zimbabwe's Prospects*, London, Macmillan.

Hansungule, M. (2000), 'Who owns Land in Zimbabwe? In Africa?', *International Journal on Minority and Group Rights*, 7, 4.

Hardt, M. and A. Negri (2000), *Empire*, Cambridge, Harvard University Press.

Harts-Broekhuis, A. and H. Huisman (2001), 'Resettlement Revisited: Land Reform Results in Resource-Poor Regions in Zimbabwe', *Geoforum*, 32, 3.

Hinds, M. (1990), *Outwards vs. Inwards Development Strategy*, Washington, World Bank.

Hoogeveen, J. and B. Kinsey (2000), 'Land Reform, Growth and Equity: Emerging Evidence from Zimbabwe's Resettlement Programme – A Sequel', *Journal of Southern African Studies*, 27, 1.

Hughes, J. (1987), *Sovereign Risk*, London, Euromoney Publications.

Izumi, K. (1999), 'Liberalisation, Gender, and the Land Question in Sub-Saharan Africa', *Gender and Development*, 7, 3.

Jackson, F. and R. Pierson (eds) (1998), *Feminist Visions of Development: Gender Analysis and Policy*, London, Routledge.

Jubilee 2000 Zambia (2001), 'No loans for AIDS!', Press statement reproduced in *Watching the World Bank in Southern Africa* 2, Alternative Information and Development Centre.

Jubilee South (2001), 'Pan-African Declaration on PRSPs', Kampala, 12 May.

Keynes, J.M. (1933), 'National Self-Sufficiency', *Yale Review*, 22, 4.

Kinsey, B. (1999), 'Land Reform, Growth and Equity: Emerging Evidence from Zimbabwe's Resettlement Programme', *Journal of Southern African Studies*, 25, 2.

Kriger, N. (1992), *Zimbabwe's Guerrilla War: Peasant Voices*, Cambridge, Cambridge University Press.

—— (2000), 'Zimbabwe Today: Hope against Grim Realities', *Review of African Political Economy*, 27, 85.

Kydd, J.G. (1990), 'Rural Financial Intermediation', Background document for Agriculture Division, Southern Africa Department, Washington, World Bank.

Leys, C. (1959), *European Politics in Southern Rhodesia*, Oxford, Oxford University Press.

Loewenson, R., N. Jazdowska and R. Saunders (1995), 'Civic Organisations in Zimbabwe', Harare, Cuso.

Maliyami, S. (1990), 'The World Bank Trap', *Moto*, 84.

Mandaza, I. (1986), 'The Post-White Settler Colonial Situation', in I. Mandaza (ed), *Zimbabwe: The Political Economy of Transition, 1980–86*, Dakar, Codesria.

Manyanya, M. (2001), *The Politics of the Public Debt*, Harare, Zimcodd.

Marais, H. (2000), *South Africa: Limits to Change* (second edition), London, Zed Press and Cape Town, University of Cape Town Press.

Mbeki, M. (2000), 'Zimbabwe's Troubles', *South African Journal of International Affairs*, 7, 2.

Mbeki, T. (2001), 'Answers to Questions in Parliament', SA Presidential website, speech01/011029946a1002.txt, The Presidency, Cape Town, 24 October.

Mies, M. (1986), *Patriarchy and Accumulation on a World Scale: Women in the International Division of Labour*, London, Zed Press.

Mills, J. and J. Oppenheimer (2001), 'Partnerships only way to break cycle of poverty', *Financial Times*, 1 October.

Mkandawire, T. (1984), '"Home-Made" (?) Austerity Measures: The Case of Zimbabwe', Paper presented at seminar on Austerity Policies in Africa: Under IMF Control, Dakar, Senegal, 19–21 June.

Moggeridge, D. (ed) (1967), *The Collected Works of J.M. Keynes*, Vol 25, London, Macmillan.

Moghadfam, V. (ed) (1996), *Patriarchy and Economic Development: Women's Positions at the End of the Twentieth Century*, Oxford, Clarendon.

Moore, D. (1991), 'The Ideological Formation of the Zimbabwean Ruling Class', *Journal of Southern African Studies*, 17, 3.

—— (2000) 'The Alchemy of Robert Mugabe's Alliances', *Africa Insight*, 30, 1.

—— (2000) 'Zimbabwe's Crisis: Reflections on the Aftermath of Empire', *Arena Magazine*, 49.

—— (2001), 'Democracy is Coming to Zimbabwe', *Australian Journal of Political Science*, 36, 1.

—— (2001), 'Is the Land the Economy and the Economy the Land? Primitive Accumulation in Zimbabwe', *Journal of Contemporary African Studies*, 19, 2.

Movement for Democratic Change (2001), 'MDC Economic Stabilisation and Recovery Programme: Executive Summary Covering the Period April 2002–December 2004', Harare.

Moyo, J. (1993), 'Civil Society', *Zambezia* 20, 1.

Moyo, S. (2000), 'The Political Economy of Land Acquisition and Redistribution in Zimbabwe, 1990–1999', *Journal of Southern African Studies*, 26, 1.

—— (2001), 'The Land Question and Land Reform in Southern Africa', Southern African Regional Institute for Policy Studies, Harare.

Moyo, S., J. Makumbe and Brian Raftopoulos (2000), *NGOs, the State and Politics in Zimbabwe*, Harare, Southern African Political and Economic Series Books.

Mugabe, R. (1979), Preface to 'Zimbabwe: Notes and Reflections on the Rhodesian Question', Mimeo, Maputo, Centre of African Studies, March.

—— (1989), 'The Unity Accord: Its Promise for the Future', in C. Banana (ed), *Turmoil and Tenacity: Zimbabwe 1890–1990*, Harare, College Press.

—— (2001), 'State of the Nation Address', Parliament, Harare, 18 December.

Murapa, R. (1977), 'Geography, Race, Class and Power in Rhodesia', Working Paper, Council for the Development of Economic and Social Research in Africa, presented at the Conference on the Special Problems of Landlocked and Least Developed Countries in Africa, University of Zambia, Lusaka, 27–31 July.

Muzulu, J. (1993), 'Exchange Rate Depreciation and Structural Adjustment: The Case of the Manufacturing Sector in Zimbabwe, 1980–91', Doctoral dissertation, University of Sussex.

Mwale, M. (1992), 'Resettlement Programme: An Economic Policy of a Political Gamble?', *Sunday Times*, 19 January.

Ncube, W. (1989), 'The Post-Unity Period: Developments, Benefits and Problems', in C. Banana (ed), *Turmoil and Tenacity: Zimbabwe 1890–1990*, Harare, College Press.

Nest, M. (2001), 'Ambitions, Profits and Loss: Zimbabwean Economic Involvement in the Democratic Republic of the Congo', *African Affairs*, 100, 4.

Ngwenya, M. (2001), 'A View from the Pan – Farms and Prices', MDC Mailing List, 5 October.

Nixson, F. (1982), 'Import-Substitution Industrialization', in M. Fransman (ed), *Industry and Accumulation in Africa*, London, Heinemann.

Nyambara, P. (2001), 'The Politics of Land Acquisition and Struggles over Land in the Communal Areas of Zimbabwe: The Gokwe Region in the 1980s and 1990s', *Africa*, 71, 2.

Palmer, R. (1977), *Land and Racial Domination in Rhodesia*, London, Heinemann.

Payer, C. (1982), *The World Bank*, New York, Monthly Review.

Pearson, D.S. and W.L. Taylor (1963), *Break-Up: Some Economic Consequences for the Rhodesias and Nyasaland*, Salisbury, The Phoenix Group.

Petras, J. and H. Veltmayer (2001), *Globalization Unmasked: Imperialism in the 21st Century*, Halifax, Fernwood and London, Zed Press.

Phelps, P. (1997), 'Expanding Municipal Finance in Zimbabwe', US Agency for International Development, Washington.

Phimister, I. (1988), *An Economic and Social History of Zimbabwe, 1890–1948: Class Struggle and Capital Accumulation*, London, Longman.

Phimister, I. (1992), 'Unscrambling the Scramble: Africa's Partition Reconsidered', Paper presented to the African Studies Institute, University of the Witwatersrand, Johannesburg, 17 August.

Plummer, J. and G. Nhemachena (2001), 'Preparing a Concession', GHK Working Paper 442 04, Birmingham.

Prugl, E. and M.K. Meyer (eds) (1999), *Gender Politics in Global Governance*, New York, Rowman and Littlefield.

Raftopoulos, B. and I. Phimister (eds) (1998), *Keep on Knocking: A History of the Labour Movement in Zimbabwe*, Harare, Baobab.

Raftopoulos, B. and L. Sachinkonye (eds) (2001), *Striking Back: The Labour Moveement and the Post-Colonial State in Zimbabwe, 1980–2000*, Harare, Weaver Press.

Raftopoulos, B. and T. Yoshikuni (eds) (1999), *Sites of Struggle: Essays in Zimbabwe's Urban History*, Harare, Weaver Press.

Ranger, T. (1985), *Peasant Consciousness and Guerrilla War in Zimbabwe*, London, James Currey.

Reynolds, N., H. Masundire, D. Mwinga, R. Offord and B. Siamwiza (1999), 'Kariba Dam Case Study: Scoping Paper: Final Report', Submission to the World Commission on Dams, Johannesburg, August.

Riddell, R. (1983), 'A Critique of "Zimbabwe: Government Policy and the Manufacturing Sector: A Study Prepared for the Ministry of Industry and Energy Development, April 1983, Submitted by Dr. Doris J. Jansen"', Unpublished paper, Confederation of Zimbabwe Industries, Harare, July.

Riddell, R. (1990), 'Zimbabwe', in R. Riddell (ed), *Manufacturing Africa*, London, Overseas Development Institute.

Robinson, W. (1996), *Promoting Polyarchy: Globalisation, US Intervention and Hegemony*, Cambridge, Cambridge University Press.

Sachikonye, L. (1986), 'State, Capital and the Trade Unions', in I. Mandaza (ed), *Zimbabwe: The Political Economy of Transition, 1980–1986*, Dakar, Codesria.

—— (1995), 'From Equity and Participation to Structural Adjustment: State and Social Forces in Zimbabwe', in D. Moore and G. Schmitz (eds), *Debating Development Discourses: Institutional and Popular Perspectives*, London, Macmillan and New York, St Martin's Press.

—— (1998), 'Trade Unions: Economic and Political Development in

Zimbabwe since Independence in 1980', in Raftopoulos and Phimister, *Keep on Knocking*.

Sassen, S. (1998), *Globalisation and its Discontents*, New York, The New Press.

Seidman, A. (1986), *Money, Banking and Public Finance in Africa*, London, Zed Press.

Shamuyarira, N. (1965) *Crisis in Rhodesia*, New York, Transatlantic Arts.

Shiva, V. (1989), *Staying Alive: Women, Ecology and Development*, London, Zed Press.

Sibanda, A. (1985), 'Theoretical Problems in the Development of Capitalism in Zimbabwe: Towards a Critique of Arrighi', *Zimbabwe Journal of Economics*, 1, 2.

Soros, G. (1997), 'Avoiding a Global Breakdown', *Financial Times*, 31 December.

South African Department of Foreign Affairs (2001), 'New Partnership for Africa's Development', Pretoria, 23 October.

South African Institute of International Affairs (2001), *Breaking the Cycle* (video), Johannesburg.

Southern African People's Solidarity Network (2001), 'Peace and Human Rights, Democracy and Development in Southern Africa in the context of Globalisation', http://www.aidc.org.za/sapsn, Mangoche, Malawi, 29 November.

Sowelem, R.A. (1967), *Towards Financial Independence in a Developing Economy*, London, George Allen and Unwin.

Starr, A. (2000), *Naming the Enemy*, London, Zed Press.

Steele, J. (2002), 'Zimbabwe Moves us Mainly Because Whites are Suffering', *Guardian*, 18 January.

Stoneman, C. (1981), 'The Economy', in C. Stoneman (ed), *Zimbabwe's Prospects*, London, Macmillan.

Stoneman, C. (1990), 'The Impending Failure of Structural Adjustment: Lessons from Zimbabwe', Paper presented to the Canadian Association of African Studies, Dalhousie University, 11 May.

Tandon, Y. (1999), 'A Blip or a Turnaround?', *Journal on Social Change and Development*, 49, December.

Taylor, S. (1999), 'Business and Politics in Zimbabwe's Commercial Agriculture Sector', *African Economic History*, 27.

Toussaint, E. (2001), 'Debt in SubSaharan Africa on the Eve of the Third Millennium', Unpublished paper, Committee for the Abolition of Third World Debt, Brussels.

Tsvangirai, M. (1991), 'What We Need is Mass Action!' (Interview), *Southern Africa Report*, July.

United Nations (1975), 'Special Report Concerning the Question of Southern Rhodesia on External participation in the Expansion of the Rhodesian Iron and Steel Commission', United Nations Security Council, New York, Special Supplement Vol 3.

United Nations Development Programme, Poverty Reduction Forum and

Institute for Development Studies (2000), *Zimbabwe: Human Development Report 1999*, Harare.

Van der Walt, L. (1998), 'Trade Unions in Zimbabwe: For Democracy, against Neoliberalism', *Capital and Class*, 66.

Verhofstadt, G. (2001), 'Protesters ask right questions, yet they lack the right answers', *Financial Times*, 26 September.

Wallerstein, I. (2002), 'The 21st Century – The Next Five Years', Commentary 81, 15 January, http://fbc.binghamton.edu/commentr.htm

Wetherell, I. (1993), 'Good Governance: Separating the Reality and the Rhetoric', *Financial Gazette*, 9 June.

Wetherell, H.I. (1975), 'N.H. Wilson: Populism in Southern Rhodesia', *Rhodesian History*, 6.

Whitsun Foundation (1980), 'Peasant Sector Credit Plan for Zimbabwe', Project 3.04(2), Salisbury, Whitsun Foundation.

Wield, D. (1980), 'Technology and Zimbabwean Industry', in United Nations Conference on Trade and Development, *Zimbabwe: Towards a New Order: An Economic and Social Survey*, Working Papers, Geneva.

Williams, R. (2002), 'There are no Standing Orders to Support Zanu at Poll', *Sunday Independent*, 20 January.

Windrich, E. (1978), *Britain and the Politics of Rhodesian Independence*, London, Croom Helm.

World Bank (1982), 'Zimbabwe: Issues and Options in the Energy Sector', Report of the Joint UNDP/World Bank Energy Sector Assessment Program, Washington.

—— (1982), 'Report and Recommendation of the President of the IDA to the Executive Directors on a Proposed Credit in an amount equivalent to US$1.2 million to the Government of Zimbabwe for a Petroleum Fuels Supply Technical Assistance Project', Energy Division, Eastern Africa Regional Office, Washington.

—— (1982), 'Zimbabwe: Power Project', Energy Division, Eastern Africa Regional Office, Washington, Report 3884-ZIM, 16 November.

—— (1982), 'Zimbabwe: Small Farm Credit Project', Staff Appraisal Report, Eastern Africa Projects Department, Washington.

—— (1983), 'Report and Recommendation of the President of the International Bank for Reconstruction and Development to the Executive Directors on a Proposed Loan in an Amount Equivalent to US$70.6 million to the Republic of Zimbabwe for a Proposed Manufacturing Export Promotion Project', Eastern Africa Projects Department, Washington.

—— (1987), 'Zimbabwe: A Strategy for Sustained Growth', Southern Africa Department, Africa Region, Washington.

—— (1987), 'Zimbabwe: Power II Project', Industry and Energy Operations, Southern Africa Department, Washington.

—— (1988), *World Debt Tables: External Debt to Developing Countries*, Vol II, Washington.

—— (1989), 'Zimbabwe: Private Investment and Government Policy', Southern Africa Department, Washington.

—— (1991), 'Zimbabwe: Agriculture Sector Memorandum', Southern Africa Department, Agricultural Operations Division, Washington.

—— (1995), 'Project Completion Report: Zimbabwe: Structural Adjustment Program', Country Operations Division, Southern Africa Department, Washington.

—— (1995), 'Zimbabwe: Performance Audit Report', Southern Africa Department, Washington.

—— (1995), 'Zimbabwe: Achieving Shared Growth', Southern Africa Department, Washington.

—— (2000), *Global Debt Tables, 2000*, Washington.

Yeros, P. (2001), *Labour Struggles for Alternative Economics in Zimbabwe: Trade Union Nationalism and Internationalism in a Global Era*, Harare, Southern African Political Economic Series Monograph Series.

Yudelman, M. (1964), *Africans on the Land*, Cambridge, Harvard University Press.

Zimbabwe African National Union (2000), 'The People's Manifesto', Harare.

Zimbabwe Congress of Trade Unions (1996), *Beyond Esap*, Harare.

Index